The Hidden History of Realism

The Palgrave Macmillan History of International Thought Series seeks to publish the best work in this growing and increasingly important field of academic inquiry. Its scholarly monographs cover three types of work: (i) exploration of the intellectual impact of individual thinkers, from key disciplinary figures to neglected ones; (ii) examination of the origin, evolution, and contemporary relevance of specific schools or traditions of international thought; and (iii) analysis of the evolution of particular ideas and concepts in the field. Both classical (pre-1919) and modern (post-1919) thought are covered. Its books are written to be accessible to audiences in International Relations, International History, Political Theory, and Sociology.

Series Editor
Peter Wilson, London School of Economics and Political Science

Advisory Board
Jack Donnelly, University of Denver
Fred Halliday, London School of Economics and Political Science
David Long, Carleton University
Hidemi Suganami, University of Keele

Also in the Series

Internationalism and Nationalism in European Political Thought
  by Carsten Holbraad

The International Theory of Leonard Woolf: A Study in Twentieth-Century Idealism
  by Peter Wilson

Tocqueville, Lieber, and Bagehot: Liberalism Confronts the World
  by David Clinton

Harold Laski: Problems of Democracy, the Sovereign State, and International Society
  by Peter Lamb

The War over Perpetual Peace: An Exploration into the History of a Foundational International Relations Text
  by Eric S. Easley

Liberal Internationalism and the Decline of the State: The Thought of Richard Cobden, David Mitrany, and Kenichi Ohmae
  by Per Hammarlund

Classical and Modern Thought on International Relations: From Anarchy to Cosmopolis
  by Robert Jackson

The Hidden History of Realism: A Genealogy of Power Politics
  by Seán Molloy

The Hidden History of Realism

A Genealogy of Power Politics

Seán Molloy

First published in 2006 by
PALGRAVE MACMILLAN™
175 Fifth Avenue, New York, N.Y. 10010 and
Houndmills, Basingstoke, Hampshire, England RG21 6XS
Companies and representatives throughout the world.

PALGRAVE MACMILLAN is the global academic imprint of the Palgrave Macmillan division of St. Martin's Press, LLC and of Palgrave Macmillan Ltd. Macmillan® is a registered trademark in the United States, United Kingdom and other countries. Palgrave is a registered trademark in the European Union and other countries.

ISBN 1–4039–7032–7   ISBN 978-1-4039-7032-9

Library of Congress Cataloging-in-Publication Data

Molloy, Seán.
    The hidden history of realism: a genealogy of power
politics / Seán Molloy.
        p. cm.—(The Palgrave Macmillan history of international
thought series)
    Includes bibliographical references and index.
    ISBN 1–4039–7032–7
    1. International relations. 2. Balance of power. I. Title. II. Palgrave
Macmillan series on the history of international thought.

JZ1310.M65 2006
327.1′01—dc22   2005049305

A catalogue record for this book is available from the British Library.

Design by Newgen Imaging Systems (P) Ltd., Chennai, India.

First edition: January 2006

10 9 8 7 6 5 4 3 2 1

Transferred to Digital Printing 2008

To my parents

Contents

Acknowledgments

I would like to thank the Department of Government and Society (now the Department of Politics and Public Administration), University of Limerick for all its wonderful support during the writing of the Ph.D. thesis from which this book is derived. Professor Nicholas Rees, Professor Edward Moxon-Brown, and Dr. John Logan were particularly helpful in promoting my development as a researcher through the provision of funding for my participation in conferences, summer schools, and exchange with UMass, Amherst.

Limerick's vibrant research culture at the turn of the millennium had quite an impact on how this project developed. Luke Ashworth was a thought provoking and idiosyncratic supervisor, while others deserve special mention for their fortitude in listening to me drone on about E.H. Carr and the assorted characters and themes in this book. Stand up John Armstrong, Robbie Downes, Patrick Holden, Rory Keane, Louise Kingston (*muchas sonrisas*), Martin Mullins, John O'Brennan, Bernadette Sexton, Dara Waldron, and my long-suffering students. Similarly, I benefited from a genuinely stimulating encounter with American academia at UMass, where I took a very interesting course with Peter Haas and where Bob Lacey, Paul Adams, and Rebecca Root were both friends and interlocutors.

I would also like to thank the Irish Research Council for the Humanities and Social Sciences and the Plassey Campus Centre for their financial support of my Ph.D. Thanks must also go to the Fulbright Commission and the Watson Institute for International Studies (especially its director, Thomas J. Biersteker) who financed my Visiting Fellowship at Brown University.

I'd also like to thank all those I worked with at the University of Sussex and my current colleagues at the University of Glasgow from whose conversations I have benefited.

A very special word of thanks must go to James Der Derian, whose work first inspired me to begin work on this project, and who has been remarkably helpful ever since I first contacted him.

Finally, I thank Peter Wilson the editor of the History of International Thought Series and Heather Van Dusen of Palgrave for their patience and forbearance.

Permissions

Introduction: A Genealogical Reading of Realism

Granted this too is only interpretation—and you will be eager enough to raise this objection?—Well so much the better.

Friedrich Nietzsche, *Beyond Good and Evil*.[1]

Historia Abscondita: . . . all of history is put on the scale again, and a thousand secrets of the past crawl out of their hiding places . . . . There is no telling what may yet become a part of history: Maybe the past is essentially undiscovered!

Friedrich Nietzsche, *The Gay Science*.[2]

Realism continues to excite controversy and debate in International Relations (IR), generally in the form of Realism versus some other theory. To date, Realism has survived liberal, Marxist, constructivist, and poststructural challenges and continues to be at the center of discussions about the theory and practice of international politics. A less noticed trend in the debates about Realism has been the debate about its nature, about what constitutes Realism. The debates have continued almost in the absence of a knowledge of Realism, as Realism has become a cipher, a codeword, generally for opprobrium. The primary means of understanding Realism has been that of describing it in terms of a paradigm that seeks to present an essential set of core elements of which Realism is composed. Debate then centers on whether or not this paradigm of Realism is refuted, confuted, healthy, or in decline.[3] This book argues that this method of understanding Realism is flawed and obscures much of the value of Realism. The above quote from Nietzsche's *The Gay Science* encapsulates the spirit of this book in that its intention is to put the history and theorization of Realism in IR on the scale again, to reinvestigate the supposedly "given" nature of this central theory of international politics.

That Realism is a more complex set of ideas than is recognized within the paradigmatic approach has been illustrated elsewhere; the focus of this book, however, is to uncover the hidden history (*historia abscondita*) of Realism, and by doing so to reconfigure the debates about Realism and the wider question of the place of Realism in IR theory.[4]

Realism has been relatively well served in terms of intellectual history recently, with Roger Spegele and Brian C. Schmidt writing about the origins and development of Realism in the (primarily American) discipline of IR, while Jim George's ferocious *Discourses of Global Politics* was a full frontal historical-theoretical assault on the idea of Realism itself.[5] Other works have also appeared, for example, Jack Donnelly's primer and expanded second edition of John A. Vasquez's *The Power of Power Politics*.[6] Whereas all these works have added to our knowledge of the Realist tradition, its origins and development, they do not attempt to come to grips with what seemed to me to be the most important issue involved in understanding the nature of Realism: how did a series of complex philosophical theories about the nature of IR transform to such an extent that current representations of Realism now barely approximate the original formulations of Carr, Morgenthau, and Wight? This new entity, most commonly referred to as Neorealism or structural Realism, is a hyperstable, abstract model of international politics dominated by a concept of an international system, but is very distant from Realist forms of theorization, which were essentially critical, dialogical, and rooted in the concept of the politics of international society as a unique field worthy of study in itself, obeying its own logic rather than the idea of a system that translates across time, space, and even across disciplinary boundaries.[7]

This book attempts to recover the aspects of the Realist tradition that have been forgotten or obscured in the wake of Neorealism's rise to almost uncontested status as the ultimate form of Realism in IR. The book seeks to liberate Realist concepts, as expressed by their authors, from the stifling straitjacket of the Realist paradigm. This is not to argue that the dominant "scientific" reading of the Realist tradition is "incorrect," but rather that its essentialized version of Realism as a paradigm is too narrow to do justice to an eclectic and diverse Realist tradition; to quote Nietzsche again, "today we are at least far away from the ridiculous immodesty of decreeing from our angle that perspectives are *permitted* only from this angle."[8] This book argues for an alternative conception of how to think about Realism, to provide a counter-memory of its emergence, development, and, crucially, content.

The means to achieve this counter-memory of Realism is through a genealogical reinterpretation of Realism that uncovers the Realist tradition in a manner sufficient to answer the question of how we have got to the present state of Realist "theory," and to what extent this dominant, received notion accurately represents Realism as a whole. This notion of a single tradition of Realism is untenable and misleading; as R.B.J. Walker has argued:

> References to a tradition of International Relations theory are by no means innocent . . . particularly as they are inserted into textbooks, into passing references and obligatory footnotes—accounts of a tradition serve to legitimise and circumscribe what counts as proper scholarship.[9]

The scope of this work was limited to four authors in order to keep the project within workable parameters dictated by time and space—to go beyond four writers would have necessitated a far larger project. The selection of the four writers was determined by their usefulness in illustrating the diversity of Realism from its inception. One strain of Realism is dialogical, predicated on a profound knowledge of history and philosophy and committed to the study of politics as it occurs in both historical and contemporary international society. As representatives of this strain, I chose E.H. Carr and Martin Wight. The other strain attempts to make Realism fit into a systemic or structural framework, although as shall be demonstrated, one of my representatives of this tradition, Hans Morgenthau, has elements of the critical, historical trend in his approach to international politics. Kenneth Waltz, the creator of structural or Neorealism, is also unusual in that he turned away from the first strain in order to create an "ideal" Realism that had the effect of revolutionizing the meaning in language of the wider Realist tradition. Theoretical purity and consistency among authors is not a trait in the Realist tradition—the very diversity of which could almost count as an argument against its existence as a single "theory" of IR. To insist on a theoretical purity of Realism is to force Realism into an inappropriate evaluative space.

A key part of the reinterpretation of Realism put forward in this book is that international theory is a human science qualitatively different from natural science. As Gadamer writes:

> the human sciences are joined with modes of experience which lie outside science: with the experiences of philosophy, of art, and of history itself. These are all modes of experience in which a truth is communicated that cannot be verified by the methodological means proper to science.[10]

The book, therefore, can be seen as a project to restore (all to human) humanity to Realist thought through a philosophical-historical method, deconstructing and denaturalizing through detailed interpretation the inherited language, philosophies, and metanarratives that have contained and constrained Realism in IR theory.[11]

Realism and the Current State of IR Theory

The collective decision of the majority of practitioners of IR theory (at least in America) to surrender theory to a specific reading of scientific method, ostensibly in the name of "political science" has had a significant effect on how Realism has been understood as a theory of IR. In this decision to surrender to a standard means of operation, the content of the theory was sacrificed to the means by which it was interpreted. Thus, the historical nuance of Realism was shed in the formation of Neorealism, and in the shedding created a new perspective on Realism in which these nuances no longer mattered. Brian C. Schmidt argues that it is a presentist bias that has led to the misrepresentation of IR in the "Great Debate" models becoming accepted as uncomplicated and has preserved the simple "paradigms" of the so-called debates. Under this theoretical scheme, there are three distinct debates that have shaped the discipline: an idealist/Realist debate, a classicist/behavioralist (or positivist) debate, and the latest debate between the positivist and postpositivist wings of international theory. According to Schmidt, this entire edifice is built upon the mistaken notion of an epic history of IR, based on the ahistorical idea of overarching "traditions." This analytical tradition-based description of the discipline's past from the perspective of the present has the effect of obscuring the historical reality of IR as it was practised in the interests of an epic historical unity.[12] This has severe consequences in terms of our understanding of the theory in question. What we know about the theory, the "truth" of the theory, becomes fixed and static—an unquestioned given. As Nietzsche illustrates, this has serious repercussions:

> For that which henceforth is to be "truth" is now fixed; that is to say, a uniformly valid and binding designation of things is invented and the legislature of language also gives the first laws of truth; since here for the first time, originates the contrast between truth and falsity.[13]

The second debate, or more accurately, the transition from "classical" to behavioral standards of theory in the 1950s and 1960s represented a moment in which the "designation of things" and the "legislature of language" were transformed—the version of Realism presented as paradigmatic became canonical, unchangeable, and unchallengeable. Nowhere is this clearer than in the distinction between the truth of rationalist/scientific "theory" contrasted with the inadequate, if not mendacious, "wisdom literature" (Kaplan's term) of previous theory.[14] Something can be considered theory, therefore, only if it conforms to a prescribed way of doing things, and to the standards of truth particular to theoretical endeavor (correctly defined); otherwise, even if it contains theoretical elements of use (which Waltz recognizes that Realist thought does), it cannot *be* theory because it is not theory in the epistemological terms he endorses.[15] What has been lost sight of in this transition from thought to theory is that the transition was effected by means of a shift in perspective, that this theory, the truth of its particular age, was an intellectual construction, based upon the attractiveness of a particular type of theorization, rather than a "scientific" advance on primitive theory. The dominant means of perceiving Realism as a "social scientific" paradigm then is a social-intellectual construction that results from and reinforces a consensus about how to perform theory. It is not the sole means by which to understand the nature of the Realist tradition. The problem is that there is a lack of awareness of the plurality of truths, as opposed to the single truth of scientific method: only certain truths are admitted into the consideration of things, the acceptance of which is the precondition of recognition as a bearer of truth.[16]

Nietzsche: Historical Philosophy as an Alternative Means of Evaluation

As will have become apparent through the course of this introduction, the works of Friedrich Nietzsche have had an impact on the writing of this book. In terms of Nietzsche, the book is concerned solely with his method of evaluation—the historical-philosophical approach that begins with his analysis of perspectivism, his methods for exposing the nature of truth, and his genealogical project. While these techniques emerged in the context of Nietzsche's wider philosophical concerns, Nietzsche as moral thinker is mentioned only in passing, while Nietzsche the bombastic prophet of *Thus Spoke Zarathustra*, is conspicuous by his absence. What is of interest here are Nietzsche's critical techniques.

The interpretation of Nietzsche's works is a difficult task—one that necessitates making a choice between competing critical traditions, one that insists that there is a "true" reading of Nietzsche, and another that states that there are multiple, if not infinite, ways of reading Nietzsche's texts. The first of these approaches, typified by Martin Heidegger, maintains that there is one way of reading Nietzsche, especially in relation to the concept of the will to power. Heidegger stresses that a single meaning can be derived from Nietzsche's text, that by careful reconstruction one may "arrive at the concept and the proper use of the word" in Nietzsche's canon.[17] The other approach typified by Jacques Derrida finds any one-sided interpretation of Nietzsche ridiculous.[18] The latter approach seems the more convincing one in that Nietzsche's own works ultimately rest on the awareness of a shifting and relative perspective on truth. The intrinsic involvement of the individual in the construction of truth in reality, as opposed to the revelation of truth in the ideal, requires the exercise of the will to power in truth claims, thus the real world becomes a matter of the play and contest of interpretations.[19] Nietzsche's own testimony on the issue is rather elegant in relation to the problem of recognizing the perspectival, interpretive nature of knowledge— "the human mind cannot avoid seeing itself under its perspectival forms, and solely in these . . . Alas too many ungodly possibilities of interpretation are included in this unknown: too much devilry, stupidity, foolishness of interpretation—our own human, all too human one, even, which we know."[20] This is not to say, as has often been leveled at postmodernists, that all inter- pretations are equal. The play of interpretations is governed by relationships of power—interpretations are in a state of conflict, the truth within them must emerge from the contest, a weak theory may be exposed, a strong theory may emerge, but always in the context of a swirling universe of interpretation.

That something is an intellectual construction, rather than a single, scien- tifically derived truth, for example, in this case the Neorealist version of Realism, does not mean that it is not necessarily true, but the recognition that it is an intellectual construction, dependent upon perspective and deter- mined by subscription to an epistemologically determined set of beliefs, does enable us to recognize the perspectival element inherent in its construction. The first casualty of the recognition of perspectivism is the notion of a single truth, either about the content of a theory, or the way it is to be understood.[21] This notion of providing a definitive theorization and content of a paradig- matic Realism is the basis for the alleged superiority of the "Scientific Wing." The relationships between man, cognition, and theory are for the rationalist a simple matter of recognizing the relationship between objects and extra- polating rules and theories either on the basis of observation or logical deduction (see chapters 1 and 6). If this relationship is more complex, and Nietzsche argues it is, then the concept of truth contained therein becomes much more problematic.

This book provides a different means of understanding the development and content of Realism. It also provides an alternative means by which theory and theorization can be understood. It draws in large part on the historical- philosophical explorations of Nietzsche, in particular his "critical historical" approach, which culminates in the creation of the genealogical method of evaluation. The value-added aspect of Nietzsche's work is in his insistence that theory and modes of theorization are perpetually in the process of becoming, an evolving rather than static means of knowing the world. This shifting basis of cognition ensures that there are no eternal facts and no eternal truths, what is necessary is a "historical philosophizing" that puts ideas in the context of their emergence and development.[22] This "historical philosophizing" may be contrasted with the metaphysical certitudes that masquerade as certainties in scientific IR theory. Historical philosophizing, however, demands that we recognize that we are in the "realm of representation," and as such truth becomes a matter of how it is represented. This realm of representation is a result of humanity's creation of a world of language that exists almost as a filter through which "reality" is experienced. Man's triumph, but also his error, was to mistake the world of language for the world of reality.[23]

Truth is a much more problematic quality in Nietzsche's universe of shifting values and styles of valuation. Talking about the power of language to determine the truth, Nietzsche isolates the success of the rhetorician Hegesias:

> Such a predominance over entire centuries proves nothing in regard to the quality or lasting validity of a style; that is why one should never be too firm in one's own faith in any artist . . . The blessings and raptures conferred by a philosophy or a religion likewise prove nothing in regard to their truth: just as little as the happiness the madman enjoys from his *idée fixe* proves anything in regard to its rationality.[24]

Philosophy, positivist or otherwise, therefore, is insufficient to ground the truth, rather it can at best provide merely a linguistically limited perspective on the ideas that man has utilized in his language world simulacra of reality.[25] Indeed, philosophy without the necessary context of history is merely "monoto-theism," producing nothing but "conceptual mummies."[26] Our language world is where we make meaning, especially in relation to theory:

> It is *we* alone who have fabricated causes, succession, reciprocity, relativity, compulsion, number, law, freedom, motive, purpose; and when we falsely introduce this world of symbols into things and mingle it with them as though this symbol world were an "in itself," we once more behave as we have always behaved, namely *mythologically*.[27]

Language therefore determines meaning in a fluid sense, not as an eternal truth.[28] The power in language to create mythologies in turn legitimizes the dominant group of language users, who in themselves constitute authority, the problem here being, "as long as the world has existed no authority has yet been willing to let itself become the object of criticism."[29] Language then becomes the battleground for meaning. The role of the "good" historian is to act as a "subterranean man"—one who tunnels and mines and undermines the "prejudice of the learned that we now know better than any other age."[30] This is particularly important in the case of intellectual history as, "a good book takes time: good readers continually improve a book and good opponents continually clarify it."[31] This has important consequences for the construction of theory—clearly each age understands a good book, and, by extension, the ideas contained therein, in a different way, with meaning shifting with context, modes of theorization, and the general *weltanschauung* in which it is being interpreted. The book, in short, lives and transforms over time with its audience. What is to be avoided therefore is a dogmatic conception of truth that allows no other interpretation or possibility of constructing "truth" about the book or the ideas within—for this reason Nietzsche advises to beware of systematizers, as systems ultimately become prisons for thought and means of exclusion.[32] These forms of knowledge, even the content of theory excluded from the paradigmatic prison, become "subjugated knowledges," the historical contents of which are "buried or masked in functional coherences or formal systematisations."[33]

Truth, transitory and unfixed, lies not in the reification of concepts but in the contest of concepts and theories.[34] The epistemological basis for truth in a Nietzschean sense lies in the capacity of a theory to exert its power over other theories—the will to truth.[35] At this level, truth seeking, as opposed to an essential "truth," is the most important commitment that a thinker can make.[36] The means to seek truth then becomes important, hence Nietzsche contrasts the "pallid mental pictures" of Plato and the model approach of Thucydides, who unflinchingly engages with actuality rather than taking refuge in a metaphysical ideal.[37] Even whilst recognizing that our world of language is in itself not "reality," Nietzsche insists that we confront our existence within the experienced world, an existence that he recognizes others may identify as ugly:

> These [Platonists and other idealists] believe reality is ugly: but they do not reflect that knowledge of even the ugliest reality is itself beautiful, nor that he who knows much is in the end very far from finding ugly the greater part of that reality whose discovery has always brought him happiness.[38]

Part of the problem of knowledge of things according to Nietzsche is that philosophy since Plato has been seduced away from the world into abstract idealism, that thinkers have been unwilling "to sacrifice all wishfulness to truth, to every truth, even the simple, bitter, ugly, repulsive unChristian, immoral truth . . . For such truths do exist."[39] Plato's notion that the apparent world is merely a corruption of a real ideal world is something that has been "lyingly added," and leads to a metaphysical dead end for knowledge.[40]

Recovering Realism

Part of the problem of confronting the history of Realism is that until recently it has not been written of in consciously historical terms. The lack of a historical-philosophical sense has led to a somewhat complacent attitude. The paradigmists offer a definitive account of Realism without the transition from Realism to Neorealism being effectively charted or even recognized as a significant event, until after the event has occurred (see chapter 1). The content of Realism and the epistemology of Realism were transformed in the transition to Neorealism, yet the identification of Neorealism as Realism is almost universal: in this sense Nietzsche's observation that names are more important than things is correct, as the name stayed in place (albeit with a qualifying "neo" or "structural") and the theory was transformed—"what started as appearance in the end nearly always becomes essence and *effectively* acts as its essence."[41] In this case, the abstract rationalism of Neorealism became the content of a Realism that had determinedly eschewed abstraction and rationalism (see chapter 2). This was not so much a case of the text disappearing under interpretation as a collective failure to recognize that a shift in meaning had occurred, in Deleuze and Guattari's terms, "a power take over by a dominant language."[42]

This condition of knowledge, as being in effect a hostage to appearances and the transitory power of those who determine truth, is problematic but dynamic. Knowledge, of theory or of the past, is a question of warfare between the received ideas of our present, and thinkers resolved to determine anew the value of all things: historical philosophizing contra the present theoretical community's complacent attitude to what constitutes knowledge and theory, and the attendant "petrification of opinion" that results from the tyrannical habit of thinking in tune with the times.[43]

Genealogy

Arguably the most successful of Nietzsche's attempts to confront consensus is *The Genealogy of Morals*. This short book, a sequel to *Beyond Good and Evil*, outlines the shifts in power and language that led to the emergence of contemporary notions of morality. Previous attempts at writing a genealogy of morality, had, according to Nietzsche, put the moral cart before the historical horse.[44] What was necessary was to put history before the presumption of the utility of morals, to expose the previous genealogists as mistaken in the nature of their endeavor. In a statement echoed by Foucault nearly a century later, Nietzsche states that the "out of the blue" presentism of the English genealogist is opposed by "another colour which ought to be a hundred times more important to a genealogist of morals: that is grey—by that I mean what has been documented, what is really ascertainable, what has really existed, in short the whole long hieroglyphic text, so difficult to decipher of humanity's moral past!"[45]

In addressing the special role that genealogy plays in the context of intellectual history, Foucault states:

> It is a way of playing local, discontinuous, disqualified, or nonlegitmized knowledges off against the unitary theoretical instance that claims to be able to filter them, organize them into a hierarchy, organize them in the name of a true body of knowledge, in the name of a science that is in the hands of the few.[46]

Almost as important as the purpose of genealogies is what they are not:

> It is not that they demand the lyrical right to be ignorant, and not that they reject knowledge, or invoke or celebrate some immediate experience that has yet to be captured by knowledge. That is not what they are about. They are about the insurrection of knowledges . . . Genealogy has to fight the power-effects characteristic of any discourse that is regarded as scientific.[47]

The power-effect being, as just noted, the refusal of "science" to accord non-science a place at the table of theory. Such places must be secured through the conflict of interpretations.[48] This is a war of interpretations, an agonistic war of meaning that proceeds from an awareness that theoretical endeavors necessarily involve conflict, a special case of war: "a war without powder and smoke, without warlike attitudes, without pathos and contorted limbs."[49] It has to be demonstrated that a genealogy of Realism is capable of offering an alternative to the dominant knowledge/discourse.

One element of this conflict lies in demonstrating the weaknesses of the dominant discourse. Paradigmization (the representation of theory according to a particular reading of the philosophy of science, examined in chapters 1 and 6) seeks to place theorists under the unity of an artificial abstraction; based upon notions of fundamental similarity, a genealogy of Realism is an open-ended attempt to uncover the emergence of Realist thought and the complexity and divergences of its development. Whereas paradigmatic interpretations break down when confronted with non-conformism in the texts of the various Realists (as illustrated in chapters 1–6) and the differences between their worldviews, in the context of a genealogical approach, this dissimilarity and contention is to be expected. A genealogical approach as a means of theoretical investigation is not constrained by the dictates of the paradigmatic approach: its primary purpose is to identify and interpret, in the context of an organic intellectual tradition, the nature of Realist discourse (or discourses).

Historical consciousness makes theory intelligible by reference to antecedent thought and modes of theorization. In this regard, history becomes an effective means by which Realism in IR can be located and understood in terms of the emergence of concepts and modes of understanding. By placing the constituent parts of this theory scheme in relation to each other in the texts of Carr, Morgenthau, Wight, and Waltz, one gains a more revealing picture of the development of Realism. Crucially, one also recognizes that the principle of a path-dependent march from primitive to Neorealism obscures the potential of ideas from within the preexisting Realist forms of thought and modes of theorization.[50]

There is a need to recognize that if philosophy without history produces "conceptual mummies," then "objective" history is merely "ghostly talk in front of ghosts."[51] Nietzsche elsewhere identifies the dangers of "excess history," an inability to escape the worship of the past for the sake of it, an inability to think philosophically about history. The problem of objective history is that it attempts to mummify the past, to neuter ideas in the quest for "objectivity."[52] The context in which intellectual history occurs has also been subject to change: the nature of interpretation of the supposedly factual is fluid, not static. Objective history reifies the method of a historian and his "craft" as a fetishism of objectivity and putative fact, over and above the living reality of the presence and potential of ideas and the creative act of interpretation. This drive to objectivity produces a homogenization of interpretation, similar to that of the paradigmization of IR, which has the effect of sacrificing the historical to the objective, which in the case of Realism has led to the specifics of Realist thought being sacrificed to the creation of a tidy paradigm of Realism.[53] There is a distinct and powerful will to truth here that has recreated Realism according to a supposedly objective standard that ignores Realist thought as an organic tradition, which possesses contradictions and multiple trajectories—rendering the Realists voiceless in the drive to a simple definition of Realism. Nietzsche describes the effect of this drive to objectivity as a mania for homogeneity:

> [T]his is a race of eunuchs, and to a eunuch one woman is like another . . . [A]nd it is thus a matter of indifference what they do so long as history itself is kept nice and "objective."[54]

One might say the same about Realism, that the drive to create a paradigm of Realism has erased the individuality and value of Realist theorists.[55] An agonistic, unfixed, and plural approach to these ideas and their representation liberates them from this hermetic fetish and allows them to be reconsidered in the light of changed realities, both in terms of a contextual reinterpretation and also in terms of a changed social reality. History should not be understood as a straitjacket but should instead be seen as a means of provoking new knowledge:

> Does one have to understand a work in precisely the way in which the age that produced it understood it? But one takes more pleasure in a work, is more astonished by it, and learns more from it, if one does not understand it that way.[56]

The act of interpretation is an act of contestation, "it can only seize, and violently, an already-present interpretation, which it must overthrow, upset, shatter with the blows of a hammer."[57] What is necessary is an interpretive as opposed to definitive history of Realism. There are in any case, from Nietzsche's perspective, "no eternal facts: just as there are no absolute truths."[58] Theory is always in the process of becoming, and theorists have to interpret to infinity and to accept that one's own theory is itself subject to interpretation and reinterpretation.[59] Neorealism therefore is a moment in the development of Realism, it is not the *telos* of Realism. That it is considered a *telos* is due to the power not of its content, but rather its position as the dominant "scientific" perspective. The perspectival aspect of all knowledge and all valuations is of paramount importance—"you must learn how to grasp the perspectival element in every valuation—the displacement, distortion, and seeming teleology of horizons and everything else that pertains to perspectivism."[60] A genealogical method allows the theorist to break the chains of established theory (the recognized *image* of the past) by the employment of a radical antagonism toward received history: "man must possess and from time to time employ the strength to break up and dissolve a part of the past: he does this by bringing it before the tribunal, scrupulously examining it and finally condemning it."[61]

The return to the text has to be conducted in such a manner as to allow the texts a life outside their established representation. As such, the texts of Realist authors such as Carr, Morgenthau, Wight, and Waltz must be studied first and foremost in themselves: each of the Realists has a distinct approach to the subject of IR, species of Realism that have been lost in the paradigmization of the discipline. The purpose of a genealogy of knowledge is to denaturalize the apparent, the given, and instead to uncover difference, as such it is not a passive return to the texts, but rather an attempt to reassert the vitality of the ideas within these texts. The intention is not to introduce a new and "improved" Realism, as a genealogy recognizes that there is, in the genealogical technique, the possibility of replacing one error with another. Despite this possibility, the genealogist is still engaged in the valuable task of replacing an improbable definition with a more probable interpretation.[62] Nietzsche neatly summarizes this project of interpretation as follows:

> A thing would be defined once all creatures had asked "what is that?" and had answered their question. Supposing one single creature, with its own relationships and perspectives for all things, were missing, the thing would not yet be "defined."[63]

A genealogy of Realist meaning that uncovers the plurality of ideas hidden under the metahistorical blanket of pseudosocial science's tyrannical unification can effectively release these ideas in a process of unpacking and reorientation of knowledge.[64] An important distinction is that between descent and origin. Where the epic historians seek to create a history for Realism that extends far back into the mists of time, from Hobbes to Machiavelli to Thucydides, the genealogist is interested more in the descent of Realism, the connections and also the ruptures: again the purpose is to highlight the potential value of Realist thought in the contemporary age, not to argue the "timeless wisdom" of a Realism in the fashion of Keohane's piece on Neorealism, or Legro and Moravcsik's article, "Is Anybody Still a Realist?"[65]

As a history of the present meaning, a genealogy must enter into the representational sphere of Realism, the discursive exchanges that have led to the creation of the image of Realism currently prevalent in the form of Neorealism. This has the advantage of allowing the theorist to:

> identify the accidents, the minute deviations—or conversely, the complete reversals—the errors, the false appraisals, and the faulty calculations that give birth to those things that continue to exist and have value for us, it is to discover that truth or being does not lie at the root of what we know and what we are, but the exteriority of accidents.[66]

It is for this reason that genealogy requires a commitment to study the emergence of Realism in the texts of Realist authors. A genealogist of Realist thought cannot accept as given the depictions of the texts of Realist authors or Realist thought.[67] More often than not, these contain significant errors that are the result of insufficient attention to detail. This is not to argue in Straussian terms that it is possible to know the "true" mind of an author, but it is necessary to read more than *Politics among Nations* in order to realize that Morgenthau had a deep suspicion of rationalism as it was applied to politics in general and IR in particular. Two of the more prominent attacks on the Realist tradition (albeit from very different angles), Vasquez's *The Power of Power Politics* and George's *The Discourse of Global Politics*, are united in one thing, neither lists *Scientific Man versus Power Politics* or *Science: Servant or Master?* in its bibliography. This lack of attention to the descent of Realism can only be rectified by a genuine commitment to study Realist texts and the developments between, within, and among Realist works. Michael Mahon, following Foucault, defines one of the central tasks of the "Foucauldian" genealogist as the provision of a counter-memory, what I refer to as the hidden history of Realism, "in order to recreate the forgotten historical and practical conditions of our present existence."[68] This book performs the challenge to the established version of history implicit in any genealogy, but also seeks to build a more historically accurate understanding of the Realist tradition(s) that a counter-memory can provide.

To this end, the theorist who employs a genealogical method must also trace the eruptions of emergence within the discourse of Realism, the moments of mutation: when Realism changes shape, focus, or direction. These ruptures do not present any form of linear progress, but rather the effect of different modes of theorization based essentially on epistemological perspectives and ontological arrangements. The analogy I use is one of a chess game in which multiple players engage in a game in which rules and fashions, and sometimes the board, change but that is characterized by the persistence of a general agonistics of discourse. Realist concepts may be compared to pieces: not all pieces are used at any given time, nor are all the concepts in play at any given time (some have been captured or sacrificed) but most pieces can once again be placed upon the board when the situation permits and requires.[69]

This book is not another statement of Realism in the sense that it insists on a particular reading of Realist texts, it is not in itself essentially "true," in fact that would be counterproductive as the book's significance lies in demonstrating that there are a number of ways at looking at the nature of Realism: the idea is not to use genealogy as a means of instituting a new Realism, but rather to remove Realism from the cyclopean gaze of its more dogmatic interpreters.[70] The effect of removing Realism from dogma is dramatic, as it results in the liberation of Realism from the paradigmatic prison, it is in Foucault's words: "A sort of attempt to desubjugate historical knowledges, to set them free, or in other words to enable them to oppose and struggle against the coercion of a unitary, formal, and scientific theoretical discourse."[71] In order to free Realism, it is necessary to see how it became ensnared in science and to provide an escape route through an alternative counter-memory of its meaning.

CHAPTER 1

Square Pegs and Round Holes: Forcing Realism into a Paradigm and Keeping It There

The first act of any genealogy of knowledge is to problematize received notions of a metatheoretical nature. Nietzsche established his radical reinterpretation of the genealogy of morals by contrasting the utilitarian theories of late-nineteenth-century mental and moral science with a more historically and etymologically correct examination of the emergence of a moral sense in antiquity, and the subsequent transvaluation of the first expression of moral being in the Judaeo-Christian valorization of the morality of the self. It was in this way that the modern conception of moral being, so uproblematically endorsed by the English utilitarians, came to dominate our conception of "correct" moral attitudes.[1] Nietzsche's purpose in highlighting the descent of morality was to illustrate the limitations and the negativity of the foundations of modern morality, and to suggest a way of going beyond our current understanding of morality. Der Derian characterizes this aspect of the genealogical approach as "to act on a suspicion, supported by historical research" that the present meaning of a concept (in his investigation "diplomacy") does not reflect the true complexity of that concept and that the present must be challenged by an "interpretative history."[2]

The aim of this chapter is to problematize received notions of Realism, both positive and negative, that are derived from an uncritical acceptance of the metatheory of science in IR theory. I argue that this uncritical acceptance of a notion of a constitutive and legitimizing scientificity leads to a deeply flawed understanding of Realism and IR in general. After a brief account of how the scientific approach to theory entered, and then began to dominate the theory of IR, I then examine the validity of the paradigmatic approach to IR and Realism.

Enter the Scientist: The Metaphysics of an American Discipline

International Relations is a discipline characterized by discord. Almost from its inception as a separate discipline it has been riven by internal revolt. The most important of these have become known as the "Great Debates" of the discipline, the first of these so-called Great Debates occurred in the 1930s with the Realist revolt against the prevailing orthodoxy of liberal internationalism (see chapter 2). The second of these so-called debates occurred in the 1950s and 1960s and centered on issues of approach and methodology in IR theory.

The debate began in earnest with the publication of Morton Kaplan's *System and Process in International Politics*. This book represented the culmination of postwar American response to the problems of international politics—in particular the problem of war and security. What differentiated Kaplan and his generation from their predominantly European predecessors was an approach that stressed not the classics of political thought (or the scant few classics of IR), but rather a new process of theorization based upon the notion of creating a genuine science of IR.

The established theorists in the field vigorously opposed the theoretical innovations of the new "scientific" wing of IR theory. As early as 1946, Hans Morgenthau, who was to become the exemplar of the Realist school with the publication of *Politics among Nations*, wrote, in his first major work in English, *Scientific Man versus Power Politics*, that earlier, liberal attempts to conceive of IR in terms of science as a practice that "perverts the natural sciences into an instrument of social salvation for which neither their own the nature nor the nature of the social world fit them."[3] The core of the problem as perceived by Morgenthau was the assumption that both the political and natural world are subsumed under the unifying force of a scientific reason, which is basically inadequate and inapplicable to the task of interpreting the social world. Scientific reason is simple, consistent, and abstract, whereas the social world is complicated, incongruous, and concrete.[4]

The centerpiece of the "debate" however was not the exchange of one generation against another, but of two relatively new writers forcefully expressing their views in the pages of *World Politics*: Hedley Bull and Morton Kaplan. Unease had already been growing about the increasing encroachment of scientific method in the academic realm of IR before their 1966 "debate," with Stanley Hoffman describing the "scientism" of Kaplan's systems theory as a "huge misstep in the wrong direction . . . only those problems that are relevant to the systems are being considered, whatever their relevance to the field."[5] The attempt to reduce IR to a series of laws from which a theory would be built is for Hoffman "based on a misunderstanding, by social scientists, of the nature of laws in the physical sciences; these laws are seen as far more strict and absolute than they are . . . the reduction of our field to a system of laws, even if it could be done, would be an impoverishment."[6]

Bull's indictment of the scientific school built upon Hoffman's identification of the inapplicability of the natural science method to the purpose of IR.[7] The language of the scientific school is one of its strengths argues Bull, as it employs a persuasive set of concepts that taken at face value are an attempt to construct a rigorous system of IR, which although not pretty is nonetheless powerful in its exposition. It is the modelization process that lies at the heart of the new approach that is singled out by Bull as the most pernicious and misleading element of the scientific theorists' approach. The abstraction of political reality to a series of axioms and theorems is for Bull an error to be deplored.[8] The illusion of "intellectual completeness and logical tidiness of the model-building operation [which] lends it an air of authority which is often quite misleading as to its standing as a statement about the real world" is the problem with scientism in IR, as ultimately it is based upon a false premise of what Hoffman condemns as a shortcut to knowledge. Kaplan's remarks are, according to Bull, "either tautological extensions of the definitions he employs, or are quite arbitrarily formulated empirical judgements that do not belong to the model at all."[9] Perhaps the most important of Bull's critiques given the subsequent history of IR and the paradigmization of the discipline is his observation that:

> the practitioners of the scientific approach, by cutting themselves off from history and philosophy, have deprived themselves of the means of self-criticism, and in consequence have a view of their subject and its possibilities that is callow and brash . . . an uncritical attitude toward their own assumptions.[10]

Kaplan's reply, *The New Great Debate: Traditionalism vs. Science in International Relations*, is important in that it cast the Bull article in terms of a debate, with Kaplan offering a refutation of Bull's position. It becomes apparent from the outset that Kaplan's definition of "science" is exclusive of a wider definition as he accuses Carr of being the most important of the leading proponents of the anti-science school, despite the fact that Carr himself was anxious to stress the scientific nature of his own work.[11]

Systems theory lies at the heart of Kaplan's approach to IR. The political sphere of IR is based on the interaction of units within a system composed of various units: states, international organizations, economic bodies, and so on. These systems in turn can be understood in terms of models, that can approximate reality and thus make the international environment understandable by using theories, explanations, and tools that are different from those of the physicist but form "part of the general arsenal of science."[12] Kaplan refutes Bull's accusation that the physical sciences neglect intuitive processes by arguing that intuition is largely unconscious, but argues that it is the techniques of science that prepares the base on which new intuitions are formed. Traditionalist (by which he means nonscientific) theory is characterized by its inchoate nature, which to Kaplan is unacceptable as a form of science— "a great mass of detail to which absurdly broad and often unfalsifiable generalizations are applied."[13]

It was Kaplan's clarion call for a new method of IR that created the conditions for the legitimization of the scientific approach to IR. Scholars in the discipline were offered the options of an incoherent mass of detail in the shape of traditional theory or, alternatively, a progressive theory based upon a new analytical framework that promised to unlock the secrets of international politics. Revisiting the debate 18 years after denying the validity of the scientific approach, Stanley Hoffman attempted to account for the transformation of IR into a quasi-scientific discipline. According to Hoffman, the success of the scientists was attributable to their location in postwar America, where confidence in scientific method and the prestige of the exact natural sciences was high.[14] He attributed this confidence to American faith in the power of science and instrumental reason, what he terms the "national ideology" of America. Hoffman claimed that it was the success of economics in becoming the exemplar social science that others were to aspire to was also crucial in creating the conditions in which a scientific approach to IR would flourish. Postwar America became the crucible of IR in theory and practice. Without a tradition of international involvement, the Americans were forced to rely on the Enlightenment ideology of reason and its nineteenth-century successor—positivistic science— as the key to effective, rational practice in IR.[15]

The adoption of the scientific method by the American academic community of IR had profound consequences on the nature of theorization in the discipline. The language of IR became colonized by the philosophy of science and by scientific discourse itself. Where before theorization was based upon philosophy or history, the eclipse of these disciplines in IR (as predicted by Bull) occurred within a generation in America. Classical theorists such as Morgenthau and Kennan, though respected, became dislodged by a generation of theorists for whom science was the only way of conceiving IR. Modelized systems of analysis such as Allison's bureaucratic model, Keohane and Nye's neoliberalism, and Kenneth Waltz's Neorealism became the dominant features of the new conceptual map of IR theory.

As the reliance on science and scientific method continued to grow in IR, the concept of paradigm became the key to reading IR. Imported from the history of science, the term was initially used in IR as a form of compartmentalization. Theories that had previously been rather freeform in composition became rigidly defined by the new impulse toward science.

The scientific approach was then applied retrospectively to the classics of IR theory. A typical attempt to critique a classical theorist by a theorist committed to scientific theory using the concept of a paradigm was Oran Young's "Aron and the Whale: A Jonah in Theory." In this piece, Young defines a paradigm in the following terms: "it is used here to convey a general meaning without necessarily carrying all of the specific connotations ascribed to it by Kuhn."

According to Young, Aron's work was riddled with unscientific assumptions and processes. Aron's terms, concepts, and variables are imprecise and the theorization that resulted from these premises were "vague and open-ended." The problem for Young being that Aron's thought was composed of a "large and confused thicket of partial paradigms . . . rather than a coherent, systematic and distinctive paradigm of his own."[16] This attempt to create a scientific approach to IR has continued with particular emphasis upon the nature of the Realist paradigm often being presented as the paradigm to be improved upon by placing it on a scientific basis or replaced entirely by a new paradigm. The following section presents a number of these criticisms.

Representations of the Realist Paradigm

One of the most persistent critics of the Realist paradigm since the 1970s has been Robert O. Keohane, one of the founding members of the neoliberal school. Keohane's critique centers on the lack of scientific clarity in theoretical terms. Although invaluable as a sophisticated framework of questions and initial hypotheses, according to Keohane, "Realism does not provide a satisfactory theory of world politics, if we require of an adequate theory that it provide a set of plausible and testable answers to questions about state behaviour under specified conditions."[17]

Three "fundamental assumptions" of Realism are produced:

1. State centrism
2. States are rational actors
3. Power as the aim of states.[18]

For Keohane, Realism lacks an adequate basis in scientific terms, its vagueness and ambivalence leading to a lack of clarity that is unacceptable according to the Lakatosian definition of theoretical purity.

John A. Vasquez is also a long-time critic of Realism in IR. His criticism is, like Keohane's, based upon the unscientific nature of much Realist IR theory. Vasquez's system of appraisal is based upon the philosophy of science, with the influences of Kuhn and Lakatos central to his project of determining the adequacy of Realism in IR. *In Search of Theory: Toward a New Paradigm for Global Politics* (with Richard Mansbach), Vasquez and his coauthor maintain that their propositions were developed with an eye to the principles of falsifiability, a concern for measurement, and a belief in parsimony.[19]

Vasquez defines a paradigm thus: "the concept of paradigm, then, would be stipulatively defined as the fundamental assumptions scholars make about the world they are studying."[20] Like Young, Vasquez clarifies that his paradigm is not entirely identical to that of Kuhn— "the use of Kuhn's concept of paradigm can be very problematic given the ambiguity of his definition . . . [t]he definition employed here reflects a revision of Kuhn's concept."[21] In *The Power of Power Politics*, Vasquez outlines how to judge a theory: it is a simple matter of determining the number of corroborated hypotheses and rejecting those theories that contain anomalies. The best theory is the one with the most corroboration and the fewest anomalies—the purpose of science is served by employing this theory.[22] By employing such a process of inquiry, IR become more systematic.

After a preliminary historical account of the development of IR from an original paradigm based upon principles of liberal internationalism, Vasquez isolates Hans Morgenthau as his exemplar of the second, Realist paradigm that had been reinforced and systematized by Morgenthau, Kennan, and Carr.[23] According to Vasquez, Morgenthau "best expressed, promulgated, and synthesized" the work of these writers (the original Realists such as Niebuhr and Carr).[24] The Realist text *par excellence* is Morgenthau's *Politics among Nations. The Struggle for Power and Peace*, a work described by Vasquez as "comprehensive, systematic and theoretical."[25] Vasquez derives three core assumptions from *Politics among Nations*: (1) that nation states or their decision makers are the most important actors for understanding IR; (2) that there is a sharp distinction between domestic and international politics; (3) that IR is a struggle for power and peace.[26] Morgenthau's delineation of international politics correlates to a Kuhnian starting point from which scientific inquiry may proceed.

Vasquez is, however, very careful to distinguish the Realist paradigm from a broader power political framework. The Realist paradigm is a technical term and refers only to the three delineated fundamental assumptions, which adherents of Realism (or power politics—the wider framework) happen to have made—but "without their conceptual baggage or their explanations." In support of his thesis that *Politics among Nations* is the exemplary work of Realism, Vasquez uses a survey conducted by Richard Finnegan to confirm that 46.7 percent of a random selection of IR theorists replied Hans Morgenthau when asked to list the scholars they felt had made a great contribution to the study of IR. Further, 35.5 percent of respondents offered *Politics among Nations* as the most important text.[27] Other important Realists include Carr, Claude, Waltz, and Aron. All these writers exhibit the fundamental assumptions of the Realist paradigm.

In evaluating Realism, Vasquez makes "the ability to produce knowledge," the ultimate criterion for the judgment of a theory's truth or utility. This ability to produce knowledge is dependent upon the "empirical content of its theories, that is, the number of theories that have failed to be falsified."[28]

The first part of the book concludes that the Realist paradigm is failing as many of its central hypotheses are falsifiable in Vasquez's opinion.[29] The failure of Realism lies in its inability to provide a body of empirically sound theory from which IR can develop as a true science, one that conforms to a model of scientific development, whether it be in a Kuhnian or a Lakatosian scheme. Realism, is according to Vasquez, operating as Kuhnian normal science, in the final analysis it is a degenerating rather than progressive paradigm—the proof of which is found in its continual emendation in the face of challenges, which he terms a degenerating tendency. A progressive paradigm, according to Vasquez, does not emend in response to challenges to its worldview causing both inconsistency and a lack of clarity.[30]

Moravcsik and Legro's "Is Anybody Still a Realist?" further explores the lack of purity in Realist thought, highlighting recent authors' lack of Realist orthodoxy and extrapolating from this the redundancy of Realist thought. This article was written partially in response to Vasquez's *The Power of Power Politics*. Like Vasquez they concentrate upon the paradigmatic reading of Realism, the point of difference between the two works being their statement that emendation is not necessarily a sign of degeneration. They define a paradigm as "a family of theories . . . or a 'basic theory' 'research Program' 'school' or approach . . . We do not mean to imply more with the term 'paradigm' than we state."[31]

The utility of the paradigmatic notion enables the meaning of Realism in IR. This meaning is dependent upon the unity of the Realist paradigm, a unity that is observable through the existence of "a series of shared core assumptions." Where Vasquez judged paradigms in relation to the debates among Kuhn, Toulmin, and Lakatos, Moravcsik and Legro assess it according to two criteria, (a) coherence and (b) distinctiveness.

The authors describe coherence as the absence of internal logical contradictions. Deviations from the core assumptions of Realism have the effect of lessening the internal logic of Realism, contradicting its status as a unified paradigm.[32] No less important is the category of distinctiveness. A paradigm's assumptions must be clearly differentiated from recognized theoretical alternatives—"A paradigm is only as powerful and useful as its ability to rule out plausible competing assumptions and explanations about the world."[33]

The Realist paradigm, according to Legro and Moravcsik, has a familiar triad of assumptions:

1. The nature of the actors: rational, unitary political units in anarchy.
2. The nature of state preferences: fixed and uniformly conflictual goals.
3. International structure: the primacy of material capabilities.

Of these, the most important in terms of the cohesion of the Realist paradigm is the recognition of the centrality of material power constituting a "fundamental reality." The error of recent Realist scholarship is its "slide" into non-Realist theory, "extraneous and contradictory to Realism."[34] This slide beyond paradigmatic boundaries has led to Realism being "stretched, beyond all recognition or utility."[35]

The Problem with the "Paradigm" of Realism

It is obvious that the idea of paradigm is an essential part of the armory of the scientific IR theorist. It is the adherence to this principle that distinguishes him from his classical forebears and their "woolly" and "effete" brand of theorization.[36] Upon investigation, however, the relationship between IR theory and the philosophy of science is more problematic than presented by those professing the paradigmatic approach to IR.

The first and most serious problem is that of incompatibility. The paradigm concept was developed by Kuhn in order to account for the development of the physical sciences, not IR theory. Implicit in all the paradigmatic interpretations presented above is an unquestioned belief that IR in some way constitutes a science similar to physics and the other natural sciences. At the very least, Thomas Kuhn, the foremost twentieth-century analyst of the paradigm concept, had expressed grave concerns at exactly the kind of theory banditry that the scientific wing of IR theory and their counterparts in other social sciences has been practising almost from the time he expressed the idea of the paradigm in *The Structure of Scientific Revolutions*. So vexed was he at this misappropriation of his idea that he wrote in clarification:

> [I]f some social scientists take from me the view that they can improve the status of their field by first legitimating agreement on fundamentals

and then turning to puzzle solving, they are badly misconstruing my point.[37]

As befits a theory developed within the sociology of knowledge, Kuhn's paradigm is as concerned with the practitioners of the theory as with the theory itself. A paradigm is not a pure environment, it is contingent upon those who work within it. Again, Kuhn clarifies this point in the second edition of *The Structure of Scientific Revolutions*:

> On the one hand, it stands for the entire constellation of beliefs, values, techniques and so on shared by the members of a given community. On the other, it denotes one sort of element in that constellation, the concrete puzzle-solutions which, employed as models or examples, can replace explicit rules as a basis for the solution of the remaining puzzles of normal science.[38]

IR theory and Realism in particular satisfy none of the criteria of a paradigm as defined by Kuhn. Two of the founding fathers of Realism, Carr and Morgenthau, shared no common beliefs, values, or techniques beyond an identification of the role of power in IR, and disagreed even on that one issue. The same may be said of other notable Realists, from Wight to Waltz. There is no commitment to shared rules and standards that Kuhn isolated as a necessary element of paradigmatic practice.

In the second element of the paradigm as isolated by Kuhn, the element of concrete puzzle solutions, these solutions do not exist in IR. There are no equivalents to validated scientific solutions or explanations of phenomena, such as Cockroft and Walton's experiment that splitting the atom provided concrete evidence of Einstein's theories. IR remain putative, not definitive. There is not even a method for describing international society as a process in the same way as photosynthesis may be described in terms of a biochemical equation. This is the fundamental error made by successive generations of theorists in IR: the desire for science is not mirrored by a commensurate amount of progress in the field. IR is necessarily fluid and contingent, its qualitative theorization is dependent upon incomplete and unscientific information. The reality it engages with is imprecise, subjective, and fundamentally moot. It can never achieve the precision of Newton's *Principia*, and the system of scientific progress and the accumulation of knowledge as described by Kuhn in *The Structure of Scientific Revolutions*, of anomalies contradicting the established body of fact culminating in a paradigm or gestalt shift (as in the case of the paradigm shift in physics from Newtonian to quantum physics); this can never occur as there is no established body of observable fact against which anomalies may be discovered. The discipline of IR contains too many species of truth with competing bodies of facts for such a method to succeed.

No knowledge accumulation has occurred, therefore, not because of a lack of data, but rather because of the incommensurability between data and process. There is nothing that has been said in mathematical or scientific terms that had not been said in so-called classical terms. An example of this is Vasquez and Mansbach's attempt to assess American and German foreign policy in terms of rank order of actors involved in the decision-making process—it is a statement of fact and poorly executed quantitative history rather than a system that sheds light on anything other than the fact that the United States and West Germany have relationships with both non-state and state actors. That these countries have relations with non-state actors is then construed to prove that the Realist paradigm is decaying. This "proof" however is dependent upon the reader accepting their definition of the Realist paradigm: their critique is based not upon an empirical fact or deduction but rather on a tautologous system of auto-suggestive artificiality.

Kuhn again stresses the inapplicability of his research in the second edition of *The Structure of Scientific Revolutions* by decrying the misappropriation of the paradigm idea. What is crucial in the following quotation is his statement that his technique was itself borrowed from history, and is not the product of scientific research:

> A number of those who have taken pleasure from it [that is, the book] have done so less because it illuminates science than because they read its main themes as applicable to many other fields as well . . . their reaction has nevertheless puzzled me. To the extent that the book portrays scientific development as a succession of tradition-based periods punctuated by non-cumulative breaks, its theses are undoubtedly of wide applicability. But they should be, for they are borrowed from other fields. Historians of literature, of music, of the arts, of political development and of many other human activities have long described their subjects in the same way.[39]

The paradigm idea, at least in its original form, is not a scientific one, but a historical attempt to explain the development of science. Kuhn's conception of the paradigm bears little resemblance to the rarefied "scientific" fundamental assumption model of those who were to use the paradigm concept. Kuhn's concept is more sophisticated than the "fundamental assumptions" approach of the scientific wing: the paradigm notion was seized upon by the scientists as an article of faith and a system of categorization to create a new method of theorization based upon nonpermeable categories or international thought. This end was achieved *via* the abstraction of existing theory to new "scientific" theories of IR, that is, neoliberalism and Neorealism.

The "paradigmists," have not applied the Kuhnian concept of paradigm in their writings, rather they have reduced Realism in IR to a series of axioms.[40] These axioms serve to limit the intellectual space occupied by Realism, constraining it within a boundary of which its originators knew nothing. It is a rich irony that Morgenthau, who vigorously opposed the use of scientific method in IR, should be portrayed by Vasquez as the progenitor of the scientific wing of IR.[41] These axioms are based not upon the ideas and texts of Carr, Morgenthau, Wight, Waltz, and others but are based upon distilled abstractions of these authors' ideas. It is a synthesized theory of Realism based on a particular reading of the philosophy of science.[42]

Having uncovered the axiological nature of the scientific wing of IR theory and Realist critics, the question that remains to be asked is whether or not these axioms are accurate portrayals of Realist theory. According to some (but by no means all) of the scientific wing, the most "scientific" method for investigating theoretical validity is through the principle of falsification developed by one of its gurus, Sir Karl Popper.

Popper's falsification principle is an attempt to resolve the limitations of empirical investigation. According to Popper, the solution lies not in a continuous series of verifications, but rather in attempting to falsify theories. If upon examination the statements or predictions of a theory are found to be false, then that theory is invalidated of falsified.[43] Expressing the theory in layman's terms, Popper wrote: "[T]o falsify the statement 'All ravens are black' the inter-subjectively testable statement that there is a family of white ravens in the zoo at New York would suffice."[44]

Taking Popper as a guide, we first have to isolate the Realist theory of IR as expressed in terms of a paradigm or unified theory—Vasquez, Legro, Moravcsik, and Keohane. As state centrism is the one feature that all those who cast Realism as a paradigmatic category have in common, it is fitting that any attempt at falsification should begin with this idea.[45]

Paradigmatic Representations of the State as an Actor in International Relations

The role of the state is paramount according to the paradigmatic reading of Realism. According to Vasquez, the state or its decision makers is the most important actor for the Realist paradigm. For Moravcsik and Legro, one of Realism's core beliefs is that the state is rational and unitary. In Keohane's reading of Realism the state is the center of IR and like Moravcsik and Legro maintains that states are rational actors. In all cases the authors stress that power is the ultimate aim of the state within the Realist "paradigm."[46]

Attempts at falsifying the theory must be located in the texts of prominent theorists identified as Realists by the paradigmists. In this section, two of the theorists presented by Vasquez as archetypal Realists, E.H. Carr and Hans Morgenthau, are examined in terms of their compatibility with the "paradigm" of Realism.

Carr and the State

The depiction of Carr as the archetypal Realist was in no small part a result of the role he played in the so-called first great debate of IR theory—that between idealism and Realism. In *The Twenty Years' Crisis*, Carr devotes a lot of time to exposing the inadequacies of liberal/utopian international theory, which, claimed Carr, was a product of the juvenile nature of the "science" of IR.[47] But the depiction of Carr as a Realist in the classic mold is understandable as evidence abounds that this was a major component of his thought. The best evidence that Carr was a Realist in the Mansbach–Vasquez mold is found particularly in *International Relations between the Two World Wars*.

International Relations between the Two World Wars deals largely with the diplomatic history of the period 1919–1939. Carr's primary aim is to describe the series of events that created the conditions for the relapse into war in the late 1930s. In order to do this, Carr creates a drama on which nations play the role of actors, with Europe and the wider world providing the stage on which these actors operate. It is the contract between the states in the peace settlement of 1918–1923 that arranged the architecture of IR in this period—"Almost every important political event of an international character in the period between the first and second world wars was the direct or indirect product of this settlement."[48]

The most important relationship during the *interbellum* was that between Germany and France, it is around this dyad of an aggrieved revisionist power and a victorious but anxious power that Carr constructs that most Realist of scenarios—the security dilemma. Carr presents the relationship between France and Germany as a historically constructed battle for supremacy with France as the older power fading in comparison to a younger competitor "whose natural resources were far greater . . . which France could not hope to rival." France had become "morbidly conscious" of her inferior power relative to Germany.[49] As a consequence of the failure of the peace settlement to create a genuine mutual security system (which Carr attributed to the failure of the Americans to become involved in postwar international politics and of the British to provide adequate security guarantees to France), France was left with no option but to plan against the possibility of German irredentism. French security was to be achieved by seeking a system of treaty guarantees and a series of alliances.[50] Revealingly, Carr dispatched the first element of French policy in less than three pages, declaring that the tradition of encirclement of enemies by allies as a security device was "more congenial to French temperament and tradition."[51]

It is this relationship between allies that creates the international system in Carr's conception of IR. Motive is always dealt within terms of the power dynamics of the participants, who act in accordance to the maxim "my enemy's enemy is my friend." Chief among France's allies was Poland, which Carr paints as a potentially unstable and "quarrelsome" (not to say belligerent) power anxious to assert itself in its newly independent statehood.[52] The other French ally was The Little Entente (Czechoslovakia, Romania, and Yugoslavia). This grouping, as presented by Carr, was a motley collection of France and the newly created states, which were riven with internal strife between their various component races and antipathetic toward each other or to other powers (Yugoslavia and Italy, Poland and Czechoslovakia, Hungary and Czechoslovakia). Carr presents the relationship among France, Poland, and the Little Entente as a simple power matrix of interest accommodation, with an implicit guarantee of assistance at moments involving their very immediate security dilemmas.

The other side of the dyad was composed of the revisionist powers, which were united by a sense that their position in the international hierarchy was incommensurate with their previous position or their current standing. Chief among these powers was Germany. Carr reinforces the notion of entrenched enmity with the observation, "[t]he years of French supremacy were also the years of Germany's deepest humiliation."[53] After the period of internal chaos, 1918–1923, the appointment of Gustav Streseman as foreign minister and France's realization that peace through force would lead to financial crisis and a split with Britain, led to the normalization of international politics. It is interesting to note that although Carr maintains that whereas the domestic politics of Germany were hugely important, having a "direct influence on the international situation" (this distances Carr from Mansbach and Vasquez), throughout the text both the democratic Weimar and Nazi Germany pursued the same ends in IR, namely the repudiation of the Versailles Treaty. The methodologies of the two regimes are vastly different, in that the Weimar government sought to reestablish German power in the new forum of international legal structures, while Nazi Germany sought to reestablish Germany's power by threat and use of force. The implication of this goal-oriented approach to the conduct of IR by two governments at opposite ends of the political spectrum is that Carr again conforms to Mansbach and Vasquez's definition of Realism.

The third element of the Mansbach–Vasquez definition is that of the repetitive and systemic nature of an international politics that is animated by power and peace. The power political nature of IR between the wars is clear from the description above of France's fear and Germany's desire to reclaim her place at the forefront of European nations. In this regard, postwar politics were little different from the antagonistic nature of previous centuries. A persistent feature of *International Relations between the Two World Wars* is the use of the phrase *amour propre* to describe the fundamental mentality of nations operating in the international environment. Nations are located on a power hierarchy, with all powers seeking to secure or extend their position in this hierarchy in the aftermath of World War One. In this regard, Carr again fits the paradigm of Realism suggested by Mansbach and Vasquez.

Carr then would seem to be a Realist, fulfilling all parts of the Mansbach–Vasquez "model" of Realism. But what would the implications be if the totality of Carr's international thought contained elements that transcend this traditional interpretation of Realism? Does this render Carr a "non-Realist" or is the definition of Realism that is most commonly accepted inadequate to the task of encompassing what is a tradition rather than a "scientific" paradigm?

Even in this most narrowly (one might even say cynically) Realist of his works Carr finds the space to present alternatives to the state-centrism of the traditional Realist school. Carr does not attack the principle of the League of Nations, but denounces its origins in the "tainted document" of the Treaty of Versailles.[54] The ultimate failure of the League is traced to the incommensurability of its political philosophy and its regional bias. The failures of the League in relation to the Italian bombing of Corfu and the inadequate response to the Japanese invasion of Manchuria undermined the claims of the League of Nations to act as an effective means of arbitration. The failure of the League and of conciliation in general is a result of the persistence of the antagonistic stance of nations remaining in the Hobbesian condition of being "in continuall jealousies, and in the state and posture of Gladiators."[55] Despite the rhetoric of the period, the unsuccessful end of the Disarmament Conference demonstrated that Realism had intruded into the logic of the legal structures that had been posited as its successor, in a reversal of the Clausewitzian dictum, politics had become war by other means. The fault clearly lies with nation states and their individual psychologies, the League was merely an inadequate solution to the entrenched problem of the relations between sovereign states.[56] Having described the events, actors, and system of IR in *International Relations between the Two World Wars*, in the more theoretically ambitious *The Twenty Years' Crisis*, Carr attempts to analyze the mechanism of IR. In terms of the state, however, Carr's most important work is *Nationalism and After*.

It is in *Nationalism and After* that Carr attempts to interrogate the nature of possible change in IR moving him further away from the supposedly "fixed and conflictual" aims of the paradigmatic reading of Realism. Having established the historical progression of the concept of nation from the singular nationalism of monarchism to the mass nationalism of modern political culture, Carr assessed the prospects of internationalism. In an attack on the concept of nation state (supposedly a fundamental assumption of Realism), Carr maintains that the age of the nation state is over, "they are an anomaly and an anachronism in a world which has moved on to other forms of organization."[57] For Carr then, the nation state, the mainstay of the "social science" of IR, is an irrelevance, only power and its distribution within an *indeterminate* system remains relevant throughout the history of global politics. Veering into Mitrany territory, Carr attempts a proto-critical approach to IR: the emancipatory nature of his theory of functional Realism is evident from his invocation that in future IR should be predicated upon "the value of individual human beings, irrespective of national affinities or allegiance and in a common and mutual obligation to promote their well-being."[58] Realizing the impracticability of world government, or of any narrowly legal approach to the question of international politics, Carr states that intermediary bodies based on extending military and economic organization could provide the vector by which international comity could be established. The creation of a system based on interlocking loyalties, is, according to Carr, the only alternative to "sheer totalitarianism."[59] (See chapter 3 for a more detailed discussion of these themes.)

Carr and Power

Carr concludes *The Twenty Years' Crisis* with his synthesis of morality and power, an understanding of these terms may assist in the comprehension of Carr's ultimate statement on the nature of IR. Power has multiple meanings for Carr. The primary relationship in *The Twenty Years' Crisis* (as in *International Relations between the Two World Wars*) is that between France and Germany—around this relationship Carr draws a theoretical schema devoted to explaining the power dynamics within the parameters of satisfied and dissatisfied nations. The rational egotism of France's security needs contends with Germany's "need" to rebuild her military and industrial strength.

The machinations of both countries in the pursuit of these power political aims are presented as the effective motor of IR. The relationship is determined by the location of each in a hierarchy of power. Carr's presentation of this hierarchy (it is important to note that there is a hierarchy, not a strict anarchy of power relations in Carr's work) is revealing in that power dictates morality, a morality that Carr maintains is separate from the morality of individuals. The dialectical relationship between morality and power is revealed as peculiar to Carr in that thesis and antithesis, or perhaps more accurately, factor P and factor M are causally linked in that morality in IR, which is an aspect of power, a consequence of the will of the status quo powers finding justification in an appeal to a morality that is in itself a product of political reality. State morality is in any case not analogous to the morality of the individual being more pugnacious and derived from the group rather than individual perspective. The highest moral virtue becomes loyalty to the group, thus creating a self-reinforcing loop around which the morality of the nation's acts should be judged.[60] This synthesis seems to be a form of reflective Realism, an attempt to understand the workings of the international system by reference to a sophisticated political philosophy combining elements of Hegel, Marx, and Mannheim. Carr transcends the concerns of the descriptive Realism of *International Relations between the Two World Wars* by seeking to go beyond the ontological questions of who, what, and when and into the more epistemological realm of why and how international politics work the way that they do.

The final section of the *Twenty Years' Crisis* is peculiar in that Carr's synthesis of power and morality comes to a conclusion based upon the accommodation of morality and politics. Contemporary Realists may have excised morality from IR, but it was also incontrovertible that nations accept the existence of a comity of nations, and as a result have obligations to this comity. In his treatment of world society Carr states, "there is a world community for the reason (and for no other) that people talk, and within certain limits, behave as if there were a world community."[61] The verbal signification of "community" had come to exist in an intersubjective sense. In this regard, Carr anticipates Bull and Wight's concept of international society and the alternative systems that they developed to explain the coexistence of power politics and international society, but goes beyond either into the realms of linguistic relativism; the influence of Mannheim allows Carr to adopt this approach to the language of community and power while retaining the sentiments of his earlier statements regarding international peace during the 1920s as a result of the free flow of capital across the Atlantic. Perhaps the most significant feature of the synthesis of power and morality is the admission that peaceful change is possible. Every solution to the problem of political change for Carr is linked to the placement of moral concerns in the power network of international society, the success of moral causes linked firmly to the political and military resources applied to their implementation.[62] The transformative effect of power in the international environment is linked to the possibility of legislative alternatives to international anarchy. Peaceful change equates to an alternative mechanism to war: the struggle has been transformed from one in which power is the single stake and method in a single system to one stake in a system composed of new structures and methods.

It should be clear from a reading of Carr's texts that his conception of the state's role in IR is more complex than that of the paradigmatic reading and is at least in part a falsification of the theory that Realism is state-centric. It also brings into question the nature of power in IR, for Carr power is more than simply the ability to dominate others. It has both an oppressive and emancipatory element (derived from the limited autonomy for moral and ethical concerns inherent in the dialectic of power and morality) that the paradigmists in the drive to parsimony have chosen to ignore. Far from being static and repetitively antagonistic the power dynamic in Carr's conception of IR has a quasi-dialectical momentum and the capacity for qualitative change.

Morgenthau and the State

It could be objected that Carr has been mislabeled all along and that he was not in fact a Realist. This is the opinion of some theorists in the United Kingdom.[63] But what of Hans Morgenthau, Vasquez's arch-Realist? What was his position vis-á-vis the state in IR? Surprisingly, he too professed an attitude toward the role of the state that is far more ambivalent than the paradigmists allow for Realist theory:

> While the Realist indeed believes that interest is the perennial standard by which political action must be judged and directed, the contemporary connection between interest and the nation state is a product of history, and is therefore bound to disappear in the course of history. Nothing in the Realist position militates against the assumption that the present division of the political world into nation states will be replaced by larger units of a quite different character, more in keeping with the technical potentialities and the moral requirements of the contemporary world.[64]

This profession that the state is not a timeless entity at the core of IR was also the subject of an introduction that Morgenthau wrote for the 1966 edition of Mitrany's *A Working Peace System*. Morgenthau goes beyond the position expressed in *Politics among Nations*, drawing close to Carr's position regarding the redundancy of the state, stating that the state has no useful role to play in a technologized world.

Modern technology has rendered the nation state obsolete as a principle of political organization; for the nation state is no longer able to perform what is the elementary function of any political organization: to protect the lives of its members and their way of life.[65]

In terms of rationality, the decision makers of states are not pursuing the preservation of the nation state at all costs as they would under the paradigmatic definition of Realism (cf. Keohane), but rather:

The more enlightened statesmen of Europe and Africa are aware of the contradiction between this fragmentation and the rational requirements of the age, which call for the amalgamation of nation-states into larger supra-national entities. The attempts at creating a united Europe testify to this awareness; so do many—albeit abortive—initiatives at merging a number of African states into larger units.[66]

These statements suggest that Morgenthau's theoretical position regarding the state's role in IR is far removed from the simple state-centric model of which he is supposed to be the progenitor.[67]

Morgenthau and Power

Although Morgenthau is more concerned with the origins of power in terms of human nature, which he expresses as a need to dominate, there is a subtle distinction in his work between power as an immutable desire in man and the role that power plays in the international scene.

Morgenthau's conception of power is rooted in the idea of tragedy and human nature. For Morgenthau, all political decision making involves a deviation from moral principles—"As soon as we leave the realm of our thoughts and assumptions, we are inevitably involved in sin and guilt . . . The very act of acting destroys our moral integrity."[68] This is where Morgenthau deviates from the standard interpretation of Realism's position regarding the centrality of power. Where the standard interpretation and indeed neorealism state that power is analogous to money in that money and the profit motive is the foundation upon which the entire edifice of economic theory is built, Morgenthau states that power is subject to a "curious dialectic" with morality.[69] The issue of morality in IR is difficult to determine according to Morgenthau due to the morally compromised means–end relationship. It is this compromise that makes harmony between an ethical standard and human action impossible:

In order to achieve it, one must weigh the immorality of the means against the ethical value of the end and establish a fixed relationship between them . . . The means end relation itself therefore has no objectivity and is relative to the social vantage point of the observer.[70]

The key to understanding this dialectic lies in the distinction between power as bio-psychological drive manifesting itself in a will to dominate, which Morgenthau attributes in a distant sense to Augustinian concepts of sin and guilt and power as it is practised in the international environment. Where lust for power is a biological imperative, immutable and ever present in the human psyche, power in the international realm is subject to a counterforce of morality in the shape of civilization.

Civilization is the apex of an irenistic reaction to the will to power. This tradition, represented by thinkers such as Locke, creates awareness that there is a threat to humanity in the lust for power and engenders "a revolt against power which is as universal as the aspiration for power itself."[71] In the domestic sphere power politics are kept in check through normative systems of morality, mores, and law. These normative systems are based on a civilization impulse that Morgenthau casts in sociologically instrumentalist terms:

> What we call civilization is in a sense nothing but the automatic reactions of the members of a society to the rules of conduct by which that society endeavours to make its members conform to certain objective standards, to restrain their aspirations for power, and to domesticate and pacify them in all socially important respects.[72]

Although weaker than the domestic civilizing impulse, Morgenthau maintains that it exists in the international sphere also. Statesmen are not amoral in their pursuit of power. In a statement that distances him from the normal interpretation of Realism, Morgenthau maintains that even when it would be rational to conduct a policy of outright extermination, states and their representatives do not conduct such rational, expedient acts.

> They refuse to consider certain ends and to use certain means, either altogether or under certain conditions, not because in the light of expediency they appear impractical or unwise but because certain moral rules interpose an absolute barrier. Moral rules do not permit certain policies to be considered at all from the point of view of expediency.[73]

Power is not a single cause in IR, analogous to money and the profit motive in the thought of Morgenthau, rather it is a part of the continuing dialectic of power and morality that mankind plays out in both domestic and international politics (Morgenthau does not make a sharp distinction between the two). Vasquez and others who seek to simplify the complex nature of

Morgenthau's thought in the name of parsimony are guilty of removing vital elements of his *weltanschauung*, and are misrepresenting the dialectical subtleties of a book the full title of which is *Politics among Nations. The Struggle for Power and Peace.*

Conclusion

The multifaceted nature of Carr and Morgenthau's theorization of IR cannot be accommodated within the parsimonious, pseudoscientific reading of IR. Attempts by theorists such as Young to critique authors like Aron for a lack of scientific clarity and a confused paradigmatic approach to IR fall into a category of error of misinterpretation. To criticize Morgenthau, Carr, and other classical Realists for a lack of science is equivalent to criticizing George Best and Pele for being poor rugby players or to stress Michael Jordan's incompetence as an ice hockey player. The pseudoscientific interpretation of IR was not their language game. To attack them for not playing by rules developed after their involvement (especially in the case of Carr) is as inappropriate as placing them within that framework.

As demonstrated above, the notions of falsifiability and parsimony are not useful in relation to theories of IR. Although Carr and Morgenthau expressed the opinion that empirical evidence was necessary in a pragmatic sense as a confirmation of their theories, neither of them had a positivistic approach to scientific proof. For Carr and Morgenthau, events were historical in nature and existed within the dialectic of power and morality, not within a simple, rationalized system based upon the abstraction of IR to the single means and unit of power. Power in their conception is far more complex and multifaceted.

The inappropriacy of techniques of presentation and analysis (often mistakenly) derived from the philosophy of science, which presents Realism as a series of axioms under the cover of paradigm and then analyzes it on these straw-man notions, robs Realism of its complexity and value, distorting and debasing a Realist tradition marked by flexibility and a sophisticated understanding of the role of power, morality, and change. It also begs a vital question: if the philosophy of science is inadequate to the task of presenting and critiquing Realism, what is the alternative to this method? I propose that to understand a theory based not upon a chimera of science, a text-based process of understanding the complexities of Realism that integrates rather than excises difference and complexity such as genealogy, is necessary in order to understand what Realism is and how it can progress in the post–cold war environment.

CHAPTER 2

Realism as Contramodern Critique

> Thinking back on Kant's text, I wonder whether we may not envisage modernity as an attitude rather than as a period of history. And by "attitude," I mean as a mode of relating to contemporary reality; a voluntary choice made by certain people; in the end, a way of thinking and feeling; a way too of acting and behaving that at one and the same time marks a relations of belonging and presents itself a task . . . [R]ather than seeking to distinguish the "modern era" from the "premodern" or "postmodern," I think that it would be more useful to try to find out how the attitude of modernity, ever since its formation, has found itself struggling with attitudes of "countermodernity."
>
> Michel Foucault, "What Is Enlightenment?"[1]

In "What Is Enlightenment?" Michel Foucault introduces two important concepts. The first of these concepts is that one needs to recognize that we are to some extent historically conditioned by modernity as a process that has determined how we view the world. The second concept is that of an attitude, which orients itself against the progressive teleology and certainties of the modern mindset. Foucault characterizes this contramodern attitude as "an attitude, an ethos, a philosophical life in which the critique of what we are is at one and the same time the historical analysis of the limits that are imposed on us and an experiment with the possibility of going beyond them."[2]

The aim of this chapter is to provide the first step toward the creation of a genealogical counter-memory of Realism that recognizes this contramodern attitude of the Realist tradition (at least in the writings of Carr, Morgenthau, and Wight—Waltz comes to embrace modern rationalism as the sole means of theoretical justification and legitimization—see chapter 6). This chapter concentrates on two key texts that challenged the dominant conception of international politics in the 1930s and 1940s: E.H. Carr's *The Twenty Years' Crisis* and Hans Morgenthau's *Scientific Man versus Power Politics*. These texts revolutionized IR's conception of human nature, the meaning of power, and for the first time attempted to demonstrate the limits of the modern, Enlightenment project as a means of understanding political being and the implementation of order in international politics. In this sense, Carr and Morgenthau are symptomatic of a general undercurrent in the wider field of political thought that criticized the pretensions of modern (and, in particular, Enlightenment-based rationalist, liberal) forms of thought.[3]

It is not a coincidence that Realism emerged at the same time as the international system began to collapse as a result of the ascent of Fascism and the inadequacy of the League of Nations to effectively restrain the revisionist powers. As an effective science, Realism emerged in order to make sense of a world that was suffering a crisis of meaning. The purpose of this chapter is to concentrate on Carr and Morgenthau's systematic attack on the bases of liberal international thought that dominated international theory in the 1920s and 1930s. Realism's emergence lies in a "negative" sense with its refutation of a liberal internationalist mindset: from this refutation they created the space to develop "positive" approaches to IR in order to counter or even to go beyond the possibilities of the modern, liberal international system.

The Utopian Vision

Recent work on the history of IR theory has correctly identified the "myth" of the First Great Debate in IR—that between the Realists and the utopians. As Brian Schmidt writes, "It is almost impossible to read an account of the history of IR that does not begin with the writings of the 'interwar idealists'. According to the conventional wisdom, the genesis of the field was rooted in an idealist moment when scholars were apparently more concerned with finding utopian solutions to the problem of war and peace than with analyzing the cold hard facts that constitute the daily practices of politics among nations."[4] This representation of the first generation of international theorists is misleading, especially in relation to relatively hardheaded analysts such as Alfred Zimmern and Norman Angell; the first generation of those working in IR theory was motivated by one central concern, the elimination of war from the international arena and the establishment of a stable international system. Theories abounded as to how this would best be achieved. From the perspective of international law, Philip Noel Baker argued for a complete recasting of the international legal system: a structural initiative that would have had the effect of fundamentally altering the form and logic of international political activity. Alfred Zimmern argued for a cultural approach, claiming that international conflict was at root a consequence of political and cultural ignorance that could be solved by education and cultural awareness programs combined with pragmatic solutions to poverty and inequality. Perhaps the most widely promulgated liberal approach to IR was that of Sir Norman Angell who argued in 1912 that large-scale war between the great powers was irrational due to the interdependence of world markets and industry. No war would be profitable, wrote Sir Norman, therefore no war should occur although this did not mean that war could not take place. The appointment of Zimmern to the position of David Davies Chair of International Politics at Aberystwyth gave a clear signal of intent from those "in control" of the discipline that the role of international theorists was to find a solution to the war problem and that the way ahead was to be mapped by those informed by a liberal approach.[5]

With the great powers of the world excluded or abstaining from the Versailles international system, liberal theorists struggled to account for the failure of their world vision to materialize. Noel-Baker, convinced of the power of public opinion, was instrumental in organizing the Peace Ballot of 1935, in which 11 million voted for the preservation of peace. Angell, in his 1932 edition of *The Great Illusion*, warned against the rise of atavistic tendencies toward violence in Europe.

As the international system lurched nearer to the disaster of 1939, E.H. Carr published *The Twenty Years' Crisis: An Introduction to the Study of International Relations* in the last month before World War Two. The first part of the book is a thorough examination of the failure of international theory to understand international events, due to an excessive attachment to modern modes of thinking, and the second part concentrates upon the prospects for a new form of IR and a global politics based on alternative principles recognizing the centrality of power in international politics.

A Heretic of Power: E.H. Carr as Radical Skeptic of Modernity

The first part of Carr's *Twenty Years' Crisis* exposes the tenets of liberal internationalism to close critical scrutiny.[6] Whether there was uniformity of opinion or not among the utopians is unimportant in the context of Carr's critique in that his target is not individual thinkers per se, but rather the concepts of liberal rationalism as applied to IR theory. The utopians, as Carr dubs the liberals, have made a series of category errors in their analysis, which have led not merely to specific failures of analysis, but to a fundamental misunderstanding of international politics. Carr attributes the failure of liberal IR theory to the fact that IR is "a science in its infancy."[7] He identifies the utopians as the first generation of IR theorists and draws a direct parallel between them and the alchemists who predated the modern chemists. The first chapter of *The Twenty Years' Crisis* is concerned with the creation of a dialectic relationship between utopia and Realism—the fluid synthesis of which later forms Carr's foundation for the effective study of IR.

Carr's theory is basically dialectical, and is essentially opposed to the universal claims of modern "reason." The distinction between observer and observed, between the thing to be examined and the subject/examiner is the first point of departure from the utopians. The Utopians' theories were intrinsically linked to the Enlightenment ideal of rationality illuminating the individual separate from his environment. Carr, influenced by Mannheim's theories on the contingency of knowledge, rejected the validity of the observer/observed separation and instead posited the theory that fact, thought, and action are interdependent.[8] Political science must, therefore, be recast from the original Enlightenment mold: this could be achieved by the combination of two categories, utopia and Realism, the dialectical tension between the exuberance of utopianism counteracting the barrenness of Realism, with each as a corrective to the other. This would create a lens through which international politics could be experienced, reflected, and also examined.

By erecting a dialectical relationship, Carr removes IR from the uniperspectival bind, which he attributes to the predominance of nineteenth-century liberal thought.[9] Carr's critique of the harmony of interests is a direct refutation of liberals such as Angell, who, confident of utilitarian reason, saw the extension of international trade networks as a "natural" and progressive trend that would promote international harmony in both economic and political spheres. The intrusion of Darwinism into the economic sphere in the late nineteenth century, copper fastened the belief in a self-regulating mechanistic international society, similar to contemporary economic theories emphasizing the survival of firms.

Carr rejects the principle of harmony of interests, especially a harmony of interests dependent upon the principle of *laissez-faire* economics, describing it as "the paradise of the economically strong."[10] This leads to another of Carr's critical techniques, that of locating ideology within the interests of dominant groups. Paralleling Gramsci, Carr claims that the "conditioning of thought is necessarily a subconscious process," a process dictated by the powerful, whose interests are expressed through the dominant ideology.[11] Utopianism, claims Carr, is revealed as a disguise for the unconscious reflections of national interests, usually in favor of the status quo.[12] The universalizing tendencies of the Enlightenment's discourse on knowledge came to clothe the naked self-interest of individual states. Thus could the fiction of a harmony of interests between rich and poor countries be constructed in the liberal mind.[13]

Carr begins an investigation of national motive in IR by reference not to the universal morality of nations, but by reference to their power capacities.[14] Economically satiated powers or "welfare powers" possess sufficient arms and war materials for their security needs, therefore they favor the maintenance of peace as the continuation of the status quo.[15] Analyzing the pre–World War One political world, Carr states that it is the economic rather than the military powers that wielded the greatest influence in world affairs. One of Carr's major themes is the centrality and indivisibility of power in IR: "[P]ower . . . is an element of all political action, [it] is one and indivisible . . . economic power cannot be isolated from military."[16]

Attacking the principle of validation through public opinion as a manifestation of effective propaganda (itself a form of power) rather than as an autonomous moral force, Carr effectively removes a central plank of the presumed universal morality cited by liberals as a central element of their program for an agreed world order. Such is the desire for an effective propaganda machine that nations and press develop ever-closer links forming what Carr terms "the nationalisation of opinion." The League and Comintern for Carr represented the zenith of modernity's capacity for self-delusion. Under the banner of internationalism, both promulgated a vision of international society rooted in nineteenth-century conceptions of effective international community relations, one liberal the other Marxist. The "reality" of the situation was not one of promoting free trade or the international workers' revolution as the propaganda stated, but rather the extension of national interests when rhetoric and national interests ran parallel—ideology as a justification rather than a cause of IR.[17]

The role that ideology plays in IR is essentially an oppressive form of indoctrination in that dominant powers impose a favorable ideology upon weaker nations; the powerful not only evolve opinions favorable to the maintenance of their privileged position, they also impose upon the weaker nation that ideology through a myriad of forms, not least the economic and the military. There is room for dialogue here between Carr's concept of power as international agent of oppression of difference and Gramscian theories of hegemonic consciousness. Perhaps this convergence is unsurprising given their common utilization of Marxian concepts.

Carr recognizes a limited autonomy of language that affords some possibility of a virtual realm in which the principle of an international morality created from a common stock of ideas may occur. This is different however from a liberal conception of IR in that the liberal international conception of the international society is one in which law embodies a concrete legally recognizable entity in which the rule of law is absolute and binding.

Virtual Morality

The question of morality in IR is according to Carr, "the most obscure and difficult problem in the whole range of international studies."[18] Carr creates a referential shorthand in his assessment of international morality, in which the "ordinary person" or the "common man" is deployed as a base level of interpretation of law and morality. This rather specious technique leaves Carr open to the charge of deliberately deflecting from the validity of liberal internationalism and the reader is left with reservations about the method Carr employs.

Carr goes on to stress the importance of the creation of virtual identities in international law and politics as vital in the form of IR, for example, obligations by treaty being attributed to "nations" rather than to individual politicians.[19] The personality of a state becomes a "necessary fiction" in IR, part of the referential thought world in which individual states and nations act, each one employing a shared stock of perceptions in order to rationalize and predict the international actions of its fellows.[20] According to Carr, individual diplomats are subsumed into accepting the given norms of state personification—the belief in moral obligation creates the virtual reality of state morality. International morality and international law are the fictitious products of what is ultimately a fictitious system based upon convenient imagined entities.

Carr, operating at the critical level, undercuts the logic of liberal internationalist aspirations for the extension of international government between nations as a pipe dream, claiming that these aspirations were based upon an excessive faith in the abilities of an imagined community to go beyond the preexisting fictions of individual nations. Legal responsibility within the international society cannot be compared to the domestic as they are two different realms, the domestic society being clearly recognizable, hierarchic, and governable. The international society in contrast was the product of an overextension of the society principle from the domestic to the international, as international society was composed of an anarchic series of units of varying power with nothing in common but their perception of each other as different from each other—the illusion of an international society being created by the elite charged with the rationalization of this peculiar political space. It is international lawyers such as Grotius who created the idea of an international society of states—not the inexorable rules of progress from the aristocratic to the bourgeois or the teleologies of liberal or Marxist history.[21]

This is one of the more intriguing aspects of Carr's international theory, the role of the virtual and the role of perception. According to Carr, following the creation of the international comity in the writings of Grotius, further developed by Pufendorf and the writers of the Enlightenment tradition, all nations began to accept the existence of a comity of nations and rights and duties within this comity.

It is in the humanist/enlightenment intellectual revolution of modernity that contemporary international morality was conceived and developed. It is the concept of instrumental reason via natural law that liberated Europe from absolutism but which also created the valorization of the individual, projected onto the international sphere in the shape of the sovereign nation state. The international morality of the state system, already revealed as the ideology of the dominant powers, is thus further entrenched within the patterns of thought most closely associated with those powers.

Carr demonstrates the instrumental application of international morality by citing the Nazi appeals to justice in their attempts to reclaim land lost to Germany under the terms of the Versailles Treaty, the severity of which Carr attributed to the new post-Darwin morality and reason of IR:

> One reason for the unprecedented vindictiveness of the peace treaties and in particular of their economic causes, was that practical men no longer believed—as they had done fifty or a hundred years earlier—in a moderating harmony of interests between victors and defeated . . . The object now was how to eliminate the competitor, a revival of whose prosperity might menace your own.[22]

International morality then is a virtual phenomenon in Carr's scheme; malleable and subject to profound shifts in emphasis, it cannot be relied upon as the absolute foundation for a working peace system. The Nazi claims to justice, founded upon sound modern principles of self-determination, sovereignty, and public opinion, although at the same time inimical to the international society from which these claims had grown, demonstrated the negative aspect of an international society predicated upon the notion of a legal order in turn dependent upon the instrumental reason of natural law.

Carr's distinction between individual morality and state morality is crucial in that there is a qualitative difference between the two. Although state morality was created by reference to individual morality and informed by its vocabulary of values, the collective identity of the group person, for example, Germany, is different from individual morality. The morality of an individual is rooted in the great religions and on an absolute scale of virtues and vices, the morality of nations is rooted in a separate imperative, that of self-preservation. This state logic of morality is therefore relative and more pugnacious, often resulting in actions morally reprehensible to the individual but laudable from the group perspective. The Machiavellian dictum of ends justifying means remained valid. Loyalty to the group person or patriotism becomes the key virtue of the modern citizen within the secular state, especially under arms.[23] Thus a self-reinforcing loop develops between values of state and citizen in which the citizen's ultimate moral duty lies not in the personal but in the collective. Far from being an atavism, extreme nationalism is a product of the Enlightenment.

The utopian ideal of a League of Nations united in preserving the existing order ignores the nature of the relationship between the satiated and unsatiated powers. According to Carr, there is only one genuine solution, negotiated change of the international order.[24] It could be argued that Carr gives no basis for the nature of this negotiation, which replaces a virtual morality with a perverse one dictated solely by the capacity to create mayhem on the international scene. This is one of the problems with the Realist system of analysis created by Carr, which I shall return to later in the book.

Law as the Expression of Power

The final assault upon the liberal conception of IR that Carr employs in *The Twenty Years' Crisis* is the position of international law. I have already discussed the relationship among morality, law (and by extension), modernity, and the Enlightenment in Carr's writings, but his identification of the political derivation of all legal norms is crucial in that it demonstrates that the dialectic of morality and power in IR is not straightforward. Carr quotes Berber's belief that law is the expression of a community as the starting point of his concluding synthesis. This synthesis is created through the location of the dialectic of morality and power in law where the dialectic finds its resolution. Carr resolves the dilemma in an unusual and individualistic fashion, concluding:

> Every system of law presupposes an initial political decision . . . as to the authority to make and unmake law. Behind all law there is this necessary political background. The ultimate authority of law derives from politics.[25]

The significance of this lies in the dialectical relationship between the supposed thesis and antithesis, power and morality (expressed through law). In Carr's scheme, the antithesis is merely an aspect of the thesis. The synthesis of the two therefore can only be one in which power remains the fundamental category of IR. It follows from this that all attempts to reform the international environment must recognize the absolute centrality of power in structure, process, and logic. This is precisely the failure of the utopians, that they did not recognize the centrality of power, but rather assumed that the structure of IR could be reformed without recourse to an appreciation of power-based motives in IR. Carr spends a great deal of time undermining the principle of moral obligation in treaties in favor of the political obligation of treaties in illustration of this point, for example, demonstrating the hypocrisy of Britain castigating the Germans for nonfulfillment of treaty terms, while themselves reneging on treaty obligations to repay their American war debt. Relative power, economic or military, is what determines observance of a treaty between contracting parties, not the moral obligation of observance of that treaty.[26]

The failure of international law to deal with the complexities of IR lies in the nonimplementation of an alternative to war. By trying to enclose the defeated parties of 1918 in an artificially constructed subordinate position under international law, the allies had forced the crises of the 1930s. Although unstated in the book, Carr's theory scheme revolves around a notion of a hierarchy of power capabilities. States occupying lower rungs in the hierarchy may rise and vice versa, with conflict being the result of an international environment without a necessary system of recognizing the de facto change—power and morality collide due to the inability of law to act as an attractive alternative to war for rising powers.

Morgenthau: Antirationalist

Morgenthau concentrated on the location of the development of liberal internationalism in the scientific mindset of the nineteenth century, and subsequently demonstrated the inadequacy of that thought. Morgenthau's critique of international liberalism proceeds from a German origin in the distinction between *Geisteswissenschaften* and the natural sciences. His refutation of liberal IR as the product of the modern fetish for science closely parallels that of Gadamer. An awareness of this wider problem of philosophy underpins Morgenthau's first major work in English, *Scientific Man versus Power Politics*. Morgenthau begins his analysis of international theory with a wider definition of modern philosophy, which is in essence that the modern world has an excessive faith in the powers of science to explicate not only the scientific realm, but also the social and political:

> [Philosophies are] . . . largely unconscious intellectual assumptions by which the age lives, its basic convictions as to the nature of man and society, which give meaning to thought and action.[27]

Philosophy then has a central role in composing the system of IR. Modern philosophy, by heroizing the concept of instrumental reason, and the unit of experience under this reason leads to a marked degree of blind acceptance of scientific and deductive reason. This uncriticality of the modern world leads to entrenchment in the thought world of the time, quenching the possibility of alternatives beyond that particular *zeitgeist*.[28] Morgenthau identifies rationalism as this age's dominant mode of thought, which he claims, "has maintained the unity under reason of the social and the physical world and the ability of the human world to mold both worlds through the application of the same rational principles."[29]

The crucial issue is that of the molding of events in the political world under the interpretative power of scientific rationalism. This belief in science and scientism is central to liberal and Marxist nineteenth-century thought. In addition to misunderstanding the nature of man as biological and spiritual as well as being rational, scientism, which Morgenthau relates to liberalism as the dominant political ideology of the age, "perverts the natural sciences into an instrument of social salvation for which neither their own nature nor the nature of the social world fit them."[30]

The core of the problem as perceived by Morgenthau is that the philosophy is basically inadequate and inapplicable to the task of interpreting the social world. Scientific reason is simple, consistent, and abstract, whereas the social world is complicated, incongruous, and concrete.[31]

The Rise of Liberalism: Morgenthau's Critique of the Substitution of the Particular for the General

Morgenthau attributes the rise of liberalism to the success of Grotius in isolating a series of laws separate from the divine and prerational. Similar to Carr, Morgenthau identifies these laws as products of rationality and constitutive of the secular worldview essential for the development of liberalism and rationalism, the philosophy and mindset of the bourgeoisie, who were becoming the dominant social category. The legal system, similar to Carr's interpretation, was merely an attempt to guarantee middle-class rationalization and liberal ideologies. Through the mastery of the physical world and the triumph of science over superstition (and by extension over the *Ancien Regime*) in such controversies as the heliocentrism debate, modern man gained confidence in the transformative powers of reason.[32]

For Morgenthau, modern international thought illustrated the sterility of the modern mind: the legalist trend in particular coming in for heavy criticism—"they attempt to exorcise social evils by the indefatigable repetition of magic formulas . . . they act like St. Louis when it is necessary to act like

Talleyrand."[33] A corollary of this legalism that Morgenthau does not explore is the faith in the institutions created by international law, the UN and the Bretton Woods institutions, not to mention the League of Nations. This is an important methodological difference between Carr and Morgenthau: Carr's critique of liberalism is based on a clearly inductive, historical reading of international politics and the particular problems of the *Twenty Years' Crisis*; Morgenthau however attacked the liberals primarily on the lacunae and flaws in the assumptions underlying their argument.

Morgenthau and Carr agree on the issue of liberalism's projection of domestic successes of the nineteenth century to the international scene. In a more coherent fashion than Carr, Morgenthau relates how politics was diminished in favor of the economic as the theory of *laissez faire* and natural law decisively influenced the principle of nonintervention. There was an optimistic trust in the harmonizing power of the "course of events," "natural development," and the laws of nature as a justification for international inertia.[34] Although not an explicit critique of Angell's *The Great Illusion*, Morgenthau's identification of liberal attitudes to war as being an aristocratic atavism and an unproductive bad investment are clear sign postings to the liberal logic involved in their derivation. Violence and force may be unacceptable to the specific morality/rationality of the modern middle classes, but this is a specific, not universal or eternal, truth. The importation of modern, liberal theories of economics and science into the international arena failed because they tried to apply liberal ideas and institutions (the instruments of domestic domination, judicial, and economic) to a non-liberal political space. In the case of *laissez-faire*, Morgenthau quotes McIlwain who regarded it as "surely one of the strangest fantasies that ever discredited human reason."[35] The contradiction between universal morality and international politics becomes clearer in individual moments when war becomes good, for example, wars of national liberation or unification, resistance against oppression, and so on.

Modern liberalism, according to Morgenthau, has degenerated into a decadent form that is incapable of thinking beyond its central mantra: democracy = good, autocracy = bad. Morgenthau claims that the liberals gave this "opposition a non political and absolute meaning." Political action was becoming dependent upon the tenets of philosophy in an unthinking reactive fashion. In essence, the actors on the international stage were becoming bound by the assumption of an association between democracy and peace.

Drawing close to Carr's identification of the specificity of the supposedly universal value of liberal economics and their relationship to the preservation of peace, Morgenthau claims they were valid only under certain political and social conditions.[36] The "One World" technologists, confident of the transformative effect of technology, are also confronted with the cynicism of international politics:

> The "One World" of technology has made it possible to circle the globe in a few days. It has also made it possible for human beings to sail from port to port for months without being allowed to disembark anywhere.[37]

The problem seems to lie in modernity's confusion in relation to the nature and purpose of politics. Morgenthau attributes this to the Western world's failure to develop an effective concept of politics. This seems to imply that politics is not an autonomous activity in IR, but rather the modern mind seeks to interpret it by scientific means and then relate it to economics.

It is this privileging of the rational, rather than the accomplishing of the possible, that enables the modern mind to persist in the false partition between an emancipatory discourse (liberalism) contra the atavism of war. The edifice of IR, particularly in the post–World War Two Period, is based upon the liberal presupposition that economic solutions can be applied to political problems, with the Bretton Woods institutions being the manifestation of the economic perspective's solution to problems in international politics.

This thinking is isolated as typical of single cause theorization, described by Morgenthau as an arbitrary abstraction from a multitude of actual causes, with the production of one solution. The single cause explanation and solution may be sound logically, but according to Morgenthau, the solution of today often becomes the fallacy of tomorrow.[38] Unsurprisingly, the diminution of political consciousness has resulted in an unsatisfactory form of theory, resulting in—"the substitution of scientific standards for political evaluations and ultimately, the destruction of the ability to make intelligent political decisions at all."[39] This lack of intelligence lies in the category error of assuming that scientific truth could be carried over from science to the realm of politics, which, according to Morgenthau, is the realm not of truth but of power.[40] Attempts to change international politics by reference to a truth (which may be one among many), attempts to work at an inappropriate level. This results in the cause and effect mentality of the modern mind becoming lost in questions of power, where motivation is enmeshed in the human and subjective, rather than the supposedly "separate" subject/object scientific perspective of cause and effect.

Faced with its inability to "command" the sphere of IR, liberalism is forced into a compromised version of its philosophy. The "grand structures" of international politics are forced into recognizing the realities of power politics in their negotiations with powerful nations. Morgenthau attributes the lack of interventive politics in IR to the importation of the domestic *weltanschauung* of liberalism. The domestic sphere is characterized by a system in which actors act according to the rules of a clearly identifiable system. In the international sphere, "no such community of rational interests and values exists . . . at least not permanently or universally (which would be necessary for the effective working of such a system)."[41]

To treat international society as analogous to the domestic is to misidentify the political space of IR for Morgenthau. The error lies in not recognizing the domination of the bourgeois as a refined Leviathan that can manifest its will in the domestic sphere through its control of both ideology and legal structures. The failure of liberal internationalism in the 1930s, symbolized by Chamberlain's scrap of paper, was attributable to the belief in the miraculous power of legal formulae to govern IR and to counter evil by the inherent qualities of these legal formulae.[42] These legal formulae could not be successful in the absence of a Leviathan, refined or otherwise.

Whereas liberalism fails in its attempt to graft domestic liberal morality and ideologies into the international political space, scientism mistakes the methodology of the natural sciences as applicable to the social environment of international politics, the great questions of which scientism does not even recognize as legitimate problems.[43] A further difficulty results in the non-transferability of cause and effect diagnostic approaches of science to the social and international, where scientific conditions do not prevail and where a multiplicity of causes may have a multiplicity of effects. The economic *rationale* of the economic man, acting in a detached maximizing sense cannot be transferred either, as the conditions cannot be reduced to the source of economic theorization. Group dynamics are such that they cannot be contained within scientific practice. The aim of social sciences, according to Morgenthau, should be to "deal with the interminable chains of causes and effects, each of which, by being a reacting effect, is the cause of another reacting effect, and so on *ad infinitum*."[44]

The Inadequate Science of International Liberalism

The reified image of science current in Morgenthau's time was in any event a discredited stereotype rather than a genuine description of science, which had developed a more sophisticated awareness of itself, probably due to the effect of quantum physics and the discovery of fallibility in science. Morgenthau dubs this heroization of science: "a kind of folklore of science which receives its authority from tradition and from the longing for intellectual as well as actual security."[45] Advances in scientific theorization, especially the Heisenberg principle, undermine the subject/object dichotomy of "scientific" philosophy.[46] The academic observer is so rooted in the supposed "object" of IR that he becomes part of the object in terms of his engagement of it. This is another similarity with Carr, in that it closely mirrors the influence of Mannheim on Carr (not surprising given his exposure to Mannheim and others linked to the Frankfurt School when he attended Frankfurt University).[47] The relationship is not one of discrete categories, but rather of two linked phenomena, the subject creating the object's significance through perception. In Morgenthau's words:

> The social scientist as such stands in the streams of social causation as an acting and reacting agent. What he sees and what he does not see are determined by his position in those streams; and by revealing what he sees in terms of his science he directly intervenes in the social process.[48]

The social world is also characterized by its rational impurity: human reason is "surrounded, interspersed and underlaid with unreason, an island precariously placed in the midst of an obscure and stormy sea."[49] It is in this way, by addressing the contingent and irrational, that Morgenthau attempts to integrate the irrational into international politics.

Morgenthau draws close to Carr in his identification of the malleability of reason that is dependent upon other forces in terms of application. Interests, rather than abstract reason, are what determine the mode of perception and the process of rational inquiry, which in turn makes reason the instrument of the interests applying it. "Rationality" is a socially conditioned quality rather than an a priori point of reason, and it is here that Morgenthau locates the greatest failure of rationalism: social scientists are conditioned by forces that are not "rational" but social, and force the social scientist into an unsolvable dilemma of trying to accommodate rational ideologies and methodologies to an irrational environment. The problem is huge, but the blindness of the majority of social scientists to the problem, due to their faith in method and rationalism, is such that they are incapable of recognizing this blindness. The core of the problem is that science has become the new metaphysics for the modern world, with the corollary that forms of thinking beyond this lie beyond the ken of rationality becoming heresies of the brave new world.[50]

The Morality of the Lesser Evil: The Tragedy of Power

As mentioned earlier, the greatest difference between Morgenthau and Carr is in their attitude toward morality. While both are aware that morality is created, generally in the service of the dominant powers, Morgenthau argues that a new morality is necessary for the mitigation of international conflict.

The current liberal morality of the greatest happiness for the greatest number is excessively quantitative and leads to the conclusion that moral and successful actions are coterminous. This has the effect of ensuring that god is always with the stronger battalions, with the party who wins elections, and with those who have the means to affect change to their position through funding, force, and the like. Politics, for Morgenthau, exists in a curious dialectic with morality, introducing a relativistic quality that Carr would recognize, but also the admission that politics must remain moral to some degree.[51] The problem lies not so much in the infusion of morality, but rather in the nature of the relationship between absolute ethical standards and human action that Morgenthau declares is impossible:

> In order to achieve it, one must weight the immorality of the means against the ethical value of the end and establish a fixed relationship between them . . . the means-end relation itself therefore has no objectivity and it is relative to the social vantage point of the observer.[52]

The tragedy of political behavior provokes Morgenthau to declare that "as soon as we leave the realm of thought and aspiration, we are inevitably involved in sin and guilt . . . The very act of acting destroys our moral integrity."[53] It is this quasi-Augustinian element of sin and guilt that accounts for Morgenthau's couching of the actor-result relationship in negative terms. The contingencies of history deflect the actor from the original intention, and can create evil results out of initial good intentions. It is these "accidents" of history, which cannot be placed in the teleologies of liberalism and Marxism, that create the conditions for immorality, or perhaps more accurately, the perversion of intent in IR.[54]

In addition to the contingent, the actor is placed in the position of necessarily deciding between two "causes" both of which are couched in moral terms, "we must do evil while we try to do good; for we must abandon one moral end in favor of another."[55] Not only can intentions be corrupted in the world of actuality, but it can also be corrupted at source. Ultimately, man is forced to recognize that he is compelled to choose between himself and others—"It is here that the inevitably of evil becomes paramount."[56] Man must be selfish in order to survive, survival being the greatest morality, therefore muddying the clarity of selfish/unselfish dichotomy. The will to power, not morality, lies at the heart of human interaction, man's primary needs may be satisfied but the lust for power could only be fully satisfied if the last man became the object of his domination.[57]

Modernity's loss of insight into the tragic nature of politics in the inevitable and "evil" lust for power has resulted in a worldview incapable of addressing this lust for power. He is scathing about liberal attempts to reform structures and institutions—"[t]he age has nothing better than a narrow and distorted formulation of the problem and a sentimental and irrelevant solution in the spirit of political reform."[58] Morality enters the international equation only in terms of the lesser evil, which forms the sole basis for ethical decisions in IR.

Attempts to alter perception and to create a new morality based upon the acceptance of difference and toleration, such as those proposed by Zimmern, are doomed to failure because education and cultural awareness are not the panacea for international conflict. To see conflict in these terms is to render the social sphere one in which conflict is analogous to social stupidity.

The "scientific" approach to international politics failed because the collation of facts as a bedrock of data from which hypotheses can be created is not applicable to the social world. In a telling contrast, Morgenthau states that solving the peace problem and the development of the air-cooled engine are not the same process.

Morgenthau closes *Scientific Man versus Power Politics* by declaring that man is caught in a perennial human tragedy, experiencing the contrast between the longings of his mind (reason) and his actual condition (necessity and lust for power). In sacrificing natural knowledge derived from observation of social and historical events for the techniques of science, man places himself in the condition of one who:

> sees but does not comprehend, touches but does not feel, measures but does not judge . . . scientific man errs when he meets the challenge of power politics with the weapon of science, and the freedom of man is challenged to renew the fight with other means.[59]

The other means by which Morgenthau attempted to reconstruct the mode of thought in relation to international politics is the subject matter of his most famous work, *Politics among Nations. The Struggle for Power and Peace.* I examine Morgenthau's attempt to create a new system of interpretation in chapter 4 of this book.

CHAPTER 3

E.H. Carr and the Complexity of Power Politics

The current wave of interest in E.H. Carr has culminated in several articles: a special edition of the *Review of International Studies*, two biographies, and a critical reintroduction, providing evidence of Carr's enduring importance to a discipline, International Relations, that has accorded him iconic status.[1] This chapter tries to build on the achievements of previous commentators on the works of Carr, not by seeking to rescue Carr's theory from the clutches of Realism or by making it serve as the foundation for a more emancipatory discourse of IR, but by examining Carr's theory on its own terms as a highly complex and individualized dialectic of power and morality. In doing so, one begins to develop an awareness that this most foundational of Realists in IR theory creates a more nuanced political philosophy of power than the paradigmatic Realism with which he is often associated. The singularities of Carr's approach mark the emergence of Realism as a social theory of change in IR, something he shared in common with Morgenthau; however, where Morgenthau feared the future, Carr embraced it. Methodologically, Carr also introduced a dialogical element to IR theory, which attempts to place theory in the context of a continuing debate between utopianism and Realism. It is this methodology that constitutes Carr's positive theory of IR, a theory that is based not on being in international politics, but of becoming. As such, Carr's theories are the antithesis of static, modelized Realist theory that do not accept the notion of structural change.

The chapter has four sections. In the first section, I examine the conceptual apparatus of Carr's theory of IR, uncovering the philosophical derivation and structure of *The Twenty Years' Crisis*, including the all-important synthesis of

Realism and utopianism. *The Twenty Years' Crisis* was not, of course, Carr's last word on IR. The second section of this chapter concentrates on Carr's later works—much of the richness of his insights into IR is lost if one neglects such important works as *The Future of Nations: Independence or Interdependence?, Conditions of Peace,* and *Nationalism and After*—in which Carr employed the dialectic of power and morality to posit a theory of international transformation. In the third section, I examine reactions to Carr's writings, ranging from the immediate response of those criticized in *The Twenty Years' Crisis* to attempts to understand Carr's contribution to international politics from a wider, more historiographical perspective. The chapter concludes with a section on relativism and reason and the condition of knowledge in international theory as Carr conceived it. This section also examines Carr's standing as a progenitor of critical or post-positivist approaches to IR, and the opening of the discipline of IR to new conceptual avenues and methods.

Delving into the works of Carr, one becomes more aware of the inadequacy of textbook definitions of Realism when compared to the complex theory presented by Carr in *The Twenty Years' Crisis* and developed throughout his later works. Far from creating a rigid, axiomatic theory of IR, Carr's primary aim in writing *The Twenty Years' Crisis* was to demonstrate the fatal shortcomings of the liberal worldview: it is perhaps the first book in IR that works at an advanced critical level to attack modernity's pretensions to political understanding. With globalization and other theories of interdependence predominant in international discourse after the end of the cold war, Carr's exposure of the pretensions of rationalism, liberalism, and modern international politics in general remain as relevant now as they were in 1939.

The Philosophical Derivation of The Twenty Years' Crisis

It is Carr's stated aim in the preface to the first edition to add a dimension to the study of IR lacking in the many historical and descriptive works of the period 1919–1939. His goal, he declares, "is to analyze the profounder causes of the contemporary international crisis." One of the most striking aspects of *The Twenty Years' Crisis* is Carr's powerful, though unobtrusive, command of modern philosophy. Carr had a double first in Classics from Cambridge, so one would expect him to have a thorough knowledge of classical philosophy and to develop an interest in political philosophy during his career as a diplomat and academic. What is surprising about *The Twenty Years' Crisis* is the presence of other, more contemporary, philosophical concerns such as Mannheim's sociology of knowledge, and the extent to which the book is an empiricist polemic against a priori abstraction. In a sense, it is a paean to induction and the value of practical over abstract reason. Another of the notable conflicts in *The Twenty Years' Crisis* is Carr's analysis of utopia and reality as facets of the debate between voluntarism and determinism; he argues that utopianism is essentially voluntarist while Realism is essentially determinist.

As Carr wrote in an autobiographical sketch, *The Twenty Years' Crisis* was influenced by Marx but was not Marxist in nature.[2] This magpie-like attitude toward theory makes Carr's international thought difficult to unpack and decipher.[3] Throughout his career, Carr adopted a purposive, tactical approach to knowledge. The provenance of a system or an idea was of little concern to him; he was content to use elements of Soviet, Marxist, and liberal ideologies, theories, and structures in order to assemble a system of thought that would respond effectively to whatever problem he was attempting to solve. Perhaps the only consistent feature of Carr's IR career is an attachment to pragmatism and a rejection of a priori rationalism. The significance of Carr's devotion to an inductive approach is crucial in that it has profound implications for the kind of theory Carr was attempting to create. Carr constantly stressed the need for a practical, pragmatic approach to IR, one that generated awareness of the realities of international politics, rather than one that placed these realities in an abstracted artificiality.

Carr quotes from Bacon's *On the Advancement of Learning* and *Novum Organum* with the intention of clearly signposting his position in the wider debate between inductive and deductive approaches to knowledge. Bacon's dismissive comment that the discourses of the philosophers "are as the stars which give little light because they are so high" is echoed throughout *The Twenty Years' Crisis*. Carr quotes Hegel's *Philosophy of Right*: philosophy "always comes too late."[4] Bacon's second position on the relationship between practice and knowledge, that "it is safer to begin and raise the sciences from those foundations which have relation to practice. And let the active part be as the seal which prints and determines the contemplative counterpart," underpins Carr's attempt to place IR in a pragmatic, inductive context. Carr's subscription to the empirical over the deductive was such that he described the idea of a *homo politicus* who pursues nothing but power to be as unreal a myth as the *homo economicus* who pursues nothing but gain.[5] Thus the wider debate between induction and deduction has a crucial part to play in the origins of Carr's approach to IR. His opponents (primarily the liberal wing of IR) subscribed to the wrong kind of theory, being excessively concerned with the development of reductive theories of IR, limiting the problem to a simple cause-and-effect dimension. They failed to appreciate the multifaceted dimensions of IR.

Carr's theory on the progression of science (not to be confused with positivist definitions of science, understood as the "physical sciences" by Carr)[6] has something in common with that of Kuhn, as both subscribe to the notion that discoveries dislodge existing orthodoxies. This also corresponds to one of the vestiges of liberal thought in Carr's own conception of history: that history is progressive (but not teleological; in Carr's words, "yet it moves"). Carr wastes little time in foregrounding the primacy of pragmatism as the root of effective science. He invokes Engels's position on technical need as the true motor of scientific progress, with the clear implication being the relative importance of need-based problemsolving over airy abstract deduction. The concrete, problemsolving approach is the oldest form of intellectual endeavor, claims Carr, citing the practical ends of geometry in ancient Greece as an early and crucial example of needs-based thinking.[7]

The benefit of the concrete, purpose-driven approach to knowledge is contrasted with the abnormality and barrenness of thinking for thinking's sake. In addition, as a further implication of deduction's lesser status, Carr identifies the role of purpose in human approaches to knowledge. Purpose, whether we are conscious of it or not, is a condition of thought and as such plays a vital role in how we determine both problem and solution. Drawing a clear distinction between the natural and the human sciences, Carr maintains that the essential difference between them lies in the fact that purpose, analysis, and prescription are inseparable in the human sciences. Tellingly, Carr alludes to the human sciences as a realm of persuasion: the "desire" to interpret and therefore to change the significance of these presumed "facts" relating to human behavior plays an important part in altering the role of these facts in the complex problem–solution equation, first in the mind of the investigator and then in the mind of his audience.[8]

Carr, at least at this stage, was an opponent of the *ideal* of objectivity, which he perceived as an unachievable chimera.[9] This subjectivist position underpins the polemic strategies that Carr employs throughout *The Twenty Years' Crisis*. Carr's depiction of the harmony of interests has been cited as the most obvious of these strategies: by erecting this strawman notion he identifies as typical of the liberal school, Carr then proceeds to demolish it as a self-serving fiction of the satiated powers, those powers that benefit from and dominate the status quo. Tim Dunne refers to Carr's polemic strategy as the use of "theories as weapons," further arguing that Carr's Realism is the negation of utopianism, rather than the unreflective, conservative Realism that Carr dismantles in the chapter entitled "The Limitations of Realism."[10] The purpose of this rhetoric, as Charles Jones has illustrated, was to allow Carr to place his policy prescriptions, especially appeasement as a means of measured change, at or near the core of his analysis. In order to accomplish this goal, he had to argue contrary to the arguments of leading liberal thinkers.[11] Rather than take their ideas individually, he places them all together and proceeds to dismantle the collective identity rather than the individual theories of the various writers involved. It is the ideology of modern liberalism that is under attack, not individual liberal theorists. Carr's use of Marxism in the *Twenty Years' Crisis* is similarly derived from his essentially tactical approach to the question of knowledge in IR, and the related aim of debunking his liberal opponents. In his autobiographical sketch, the appeal of Marxism is clearly marked out: "I've always been more interested in Marxism as a method of revealing the hidden springs of thought and action, and debunking the logical and moralistic façade generally erected around them, than in the Marxist analysis of the decline of capitalism."[12]

The rhetorical occlusion of individual liberal ideals under the rubric of "utopianism" is relatively unimportant, however, as the position of the utopians within the *Twenty Years' Crisis* is merely window dressing, as is equally the case in the depiction of the few Realists mentioned. Carr's aim is to distil elements from both camps. His approach is essentially eclectic, an incorporation of various parts of theories that are applied to concrete puzzles. His aim is the creation of an insight into IR, not the creation of a theory as an end in itself. Theory is not to be judged by parsimony or theoretical consistency but by the production of a solution to a problem, or in the case of *The Twenty Years' Crisis*, the production of an effective means of conceiving the international system and a modus operandi for its transformation.

Carr's stated aim of uncovering the deeper causes of international affairs necessitated a reinterpretation of the "facts" by reference to his system of pragmatic international thought, thereby effecting a reconstitution of the problem itself. To Carr this was not surrender to the immanence of power, as his international theory was described by Morgenthau; rather, it was an assessment of international politics reached through an empirically logical (if eclectically idiosyncratic) and systematic approach to the problem of conflict in international affairs. One of Carr's most penetrating insights in terms of the development of his theory of international politics was his identification of the interdependence of political thought and action: "every political judgment helps to modify the facts on which it is passed. Political thought is itself a form of political action."[13] This allowed him to adopt a purposive approach to his work that, though polemical, was nonetheless a cogent and brilliantly conceived orchestration of disparate elements.

The "Synthesis" of Utopia and Realism in The Twenty Years' Crisis

According to Charles Jones, Carr is merely using the dialectic framework as a rhetorical device, placing two unsatisfactory options before the reader and then presenting him with another, more reasonable "third way."[14] While this would be a problem if his system of thought was restricted to this cunning use of dialectics as camouflage, Carr's subsequent development of an IR theory based upon the synthesis of the two categories seems to be more progressive than the smuggling of reform into a *realpolitik* framework. The elastic nature of Carr's epistemology may be inferred from the influence of William James on his thought as signified by his use of the utopian/Realist dyad on the same page as he gives an extended footnote to James's binary typology. A more nonprogressive, Heraclitean reading of the conflictual relationship between ideas than the necessarily progressive dialectics of Marx or Hegel, this may account for the state of persistent tension between the two categories of utopianism and Realism.[15] The reference to one of America's leading pragmatist philosophers may also explain Carr's extensive and positive use of the word "pragmatism" throughout *The Twenty Years' Crisis*. Carr used some form of binary system that employed aspects of Hegelian, Marxist, and Jamesian methodologies, with a Freudian twist. To this end, Carr presents utopianism as immature and Realism as the sterile product of old age and the negation of political thought and action. Carr isolates three types of theory—utopian/immature, Realist/sterile, and "balanced"/mature. Mature thought (i.e., Carr's) harnesses the best aspects of the two essential facets of political thought, combining "purpose (utopianism) with observation and analysis (Realism) . . . Sound political thought and sound political life will be found only where both have their place."[16] Carr's privileging of his own analysis, which purports to accomplish the optimal integration of utopia and reality, is described in the second chapter in the following terms: "All healthy human action, and therefore all healthy thought, must establish a balance between utopia and reality, between free will and determinism."[17]

This synthesis of utopianism and Realism forms the basis of Carr's positive theory of IR. The nature of the synthesis is both fluid and unresolved due to the identification of morality as an expression of power rather than a discrete dialectical counterpart. Once this insight has been acknowledged by Carr, he sets about applying it to contemporary politics and the possibility of change in IR. The location of the synthesis within the text is an important chapter entitled *The Nature of Politics*. This synthesis is, to some extent, a reiteration of the initial proposition that utopianism and Realism must be combined. In a further illustration of the dyadic nature of human interaction at the individual level within society, Carr creates another series of Jamesian binary oppositions:

> Coercion and conscience, enmity and good will, self-assertion and self-subordination, are present in every political society. The state is built up out of these *conflicting aspects of human nature*. Utopia and reality, the

ideal and the institution, morality and power, are from the outset inextricably blended in it . . . The utopian who dreams that it is possible to eliminate self-assertion from politics and to base a political system on morality alone is just as wide of the mark as the Realist who believes that altruism is an illusion and that all political action is based on self-seeking.[18]

It is important to note that Carr, like his counterparts, Morgenthau and Wight, believes that, at root, all political action is derived from human nature, or more precisely from competing aspects of human nature. This is essentially a social-determinist argument and provides evidence of Carr's essentially Realist attitude—if man cannot be saved from his aggressive instincts and self-serving cupidity by his rationality, then he has to face the issue of his political existence in the light of both vice and virtue. Hence the dialectic of power and morality is an eternal aspect of human social organization and, by extension, of IR.

The primacy of the political has the effect of rendering the utopian's hope for moral conduct in IR little more than a pipe dream. The political derivation of international law demonstrates that the logic of IR is conditioned by power rather than by morality. Where morality comes into the equation, it is merely as a counterpoint to the dominant factor. This is Carr's central insight and provides the key to understanding his IR theory. The very morality produced by the exigencies of power is designed to perpetuate the power struggle, favoring "Us" over "Them."

Carr's ultimate statement on the nature of IR, as expressed in the final section of *The Twenty Years' Crisis*, leaves him far closer to the Realist end of the spectrum than the utopian. His finding that the primacy of power in IR is an unassailable condition only slightly mediated by the opposing factor of morality would seem to leave little room for a philosophy other than power-centric Realism.[19] Yet there are significant differences between textbook Realism and Carr's international theory; as such, it is necessary to examine in more detail the complex workings of the relationship between power and morality and the logic that led Carr to advance appeasement of Germany as an ad hoc policy of practical power politics.

The Historical Inevitability of Change in International Relations

Carr's theory of IR revolves around the idea of progressive change as an inevitable feature of the international environment.[20] Carr embarks upon a justification of violence and revolution as the means by which progress occurs in world history. The progress of IR is intrinsically linked to the revolutionary impulse. Without revolution there can be no redress of injustice, resulting in a static international environment and the irremediable exploitation of the weak by the strong. Mechanisms that have removed the need for conflict in the domestic sphere, for example, legislation in parliaments ("a legal revolution" according to Carr), are absent from the international society. In the absence of a world state, there can be no peaceful change, analogous to domestic change, through legislation.

Appeasement and the creation of a culture of conciliation, based on the threat of violence in the first instance, is Carr's initial attempt to propose an alternative to war. By doing so he recognizes the centrality of power in creating the conditions for the "moral" conduct of IR. This synthesis is based upon the utilization of an analogy between workers and employers in the developed world: "have-not" confronting "have," with the ultimate weapon of the strike:

> The "have-nots" of most countries steadily improved their position through a series of strikes and negotiations, and the "haves," whether through a sense of justice, or through a fear of revolution in the event of refusal, yielded ground rather than put the issue to the test of force . . . If we could apply this analogy to International Relations, we might hope that, once the dissatisfied Powers had realized the possibility of remedying grievances by peaceful negotiations (proceeded no doubt by threats of force), some regular procedure of peaceful change might gradually be established and win the confidence of the dissatisfied . . . [C]onciliation would become a matter of course, and the threat of force, while never formally abandoned, recede further and further into the background.[21]

Carr declared that this synthesis of moral aspiration and power politics would only be verified if it stood the test of experience. In the early years of the war, as his prescription for peaceful change by accommodating Hitler seemed a failure, Carr attempted once more to reanalyze the nature of the international crisis and to offer a solution once again incorporating the dyad of power and morality—it is important to note that it is the policy prescription rather than the mode of analysis that changes in Carr's treatment of IR.[22] The most important of these works are *Britain: A Study in Foreign Policy from the Versailles Treaty to the Outbreak of War* (published at the same time as *The Twenty Years' Crisis*), *Conditions of Peace*, and *The Future of Nations: Independence or Inter-Dependence?* A further, though less pronounced, shift in perspective is witnessed in *Nationalism and After* and the short piece *Democracy in International Affairs*.

The key issue throughout all these works is society, domestic and international, in transition. This transition is of a fundamental nature, played out in a revolutionary era in which old certainties are caught in the maelstrom of cultural-historical change. The intellectual locus of this *zeitgeist*-defining conflict between regressive and progressive forces is the concept of democracy. By late 1939, Carr was adopting a critical attitude to the foundations of democracy, arguing, "democracy is an attitude of mind, not a set of rules."[23] By casting democracy in this light, Carr enabled a series of revisions to the concept of democracy and the role of that idea in IR that would culminate in his advocacy of the complete transformation of the structure of international society.

The transformation of attitudes toward democracy and international society was first broached by Carr in the 1941 pamphlet, *The Future of Nations. Independence or Interdependence?* The problem was that democracy had become "inert." It no longer served as an adequate political philosophy in domestic or international politics. In its nineteenth-century liberal-democratic form it could not respond to questions of greater political importance than those of the ruling middle classes, chained as it was to the intellectual processes and morality of these classes. In the international sphere, the extension of specific liberal-democratic ideals of the English-speaking countries, in particular the ideas of *laissez faire* and self-determination, further exacerbated, rather than solved, the problem of international conflict:

> The crisis of self-determination is parallel to the crisis of democracy. Self-determination, like democracy, has fallen on evil days because we have been content to keep it in the nineteenth century setting of political rights, and have failed to adapt it to the twentieth century context of military and economic problems . . . there is no task which imposes itself more urgently on those engaged in formulating the outlines of the new world which must emerge out of the war.[24]

The problem of international conflict was not aided by the imposition of a Western idea of democracy on the post–World War One states of Eastern Europe. Western conditions of closely integrated political communities held together by the joint principles of nationality and self-determination were almost wholly irrelevant.[25] The failure of the makers of the peace to integrate these countries into the economic and military systems of Europe is attributable to the peacemakers of 1919 "living in a past world, whose transient conditions they assumed as a postulate of the peace settlement."[26]

A Democracy Incompatible with Security: The Anachronism of Self-Determination

The irony of the liberal-democratic peace solution was that this insistence on self-determination, a trope of liberal democracy and a Wilsonian ideal, created insecurity rather than security. The reason for this, according to Carr, was that its time had passed: the postulates of political existence, domestic and international, had changed irrevocably. Overriding concerns of security, not nineteenth-century ideals of national self-determination and *laissez-faire* economics, dominated the political life of the *interbellum* years.

The fallacy of security through the proliferation of independent states was demonstrated through the serial violation of the principle of neutrality by German forces during World War Two. In an example of the Realism applied by Carr to the outbreak of the war, the Athenian position in the Melian debate, of the weak suffering what they must, while the strong do what they will, was updated to the occupation of Holland and Denmark by the invading Germans and exposed the hollow claims of independence of action sanctified by the peace treaties. In military terms, the only option open to small powers was that of alliance with larger powers, in a necessarily subordinate position.[27]

In the economic sphere, the situation was worse. Self-determination had failed in its basic task of creating prosperity, as the lives of ordinary people in areas such as Eastern Europe had failed to improve after World War One. Smaller nations must "subordinate military and economic policy and resources to the needs of a wider community."[28] Yet Carr did not entirely underplay the significance of self-determination in contemporary Europe. He was aware of a prevailing trend of peoples to associate according to heritage or language. His solution to the problem was to propose a separation of powers and identity, a divorce of the "cultural nation" from the "state nation." By integrating the two opposing forces, one obviates the need to choose between conflicting loyalties, creating a process of both centralization and devolution.[29]

Conditions of Peace: *The Radical Political Economy of Transforming the International System*

If *The Twenty Years' Crisis* is the location of Carr's dialectic and the foundation of his theory of IR, *Conditions of Peace* is the work in which he most fully explores the ramifications of this theory.[30] In this book, the synthesis of morality and power becomes the foundation of a logic of IR that has as its endpoint the radical transformation of international society.[31] The attack on modern modes of thought, and abstract, a priori reasoning, present throughout *The Twenty Years' Crisis*, is expanded in *Conditions of Peace*. The entire edifice of modern thought—economic, diplomatic, moral—is revealed as bankrupt and anachronistic. This constitutes the most important problem to be solved in IR: how to effect a solution to the international system's flawed logic.

Carr's method throughout is historico-cultural, in which the clash of ideologies plays the most important role in animating international politics. The influence of Hegel is prevalent, as the intellectual conflict between forms of democracy and political organization dominates the core of the book. Hegel's conception of history as the inevitable progress of liberal democracy is mirrored in *Conditions of Peace*, but Carr's aim is to demonstrate the redundancy of Hegel's liberal-democratic state as the termination of history.

The practical and theoretical means that Carr identified as necessary for the solution of IR was the restoration of both the political and the economic elements of the international political economy. Carr reformulated the problem of IR from his original position in *The Twenty Years' Crisis*, in which the problem of international conflict was addressed by the measured, healthy expedient of peaceful change. *The Twenty Years' Crisis* was a book that stressed the centrality of political thought and diplomatic action; *Conditions of Peace*, while retaining the dialectic structure and methodology of *The Twenty Years' Crisis*, offers a completely different perspective on the problem of creating a peaceful world: revolution, not evolution, is the key.

The most important dialectic in this work is that of progressive versus regressive powers in IR, the dynamic Germany contrasted with the sedentary and satisfied liberal democracies. Carr employs the Hegelian notion of history in order to depict World War Two as a revolutionary war, the crucible in which the revolutionary forces of anti-liberalism confront the inert and calcified forces of the liberal-democratic, English-speaking countries. Although describing Hitler and Nazism as "negative" and "destructive," Carr draws a direct parallel between Hitler and Napoleon, arguing that both performed the essential function of "sweeping away the litter of the old order."[32] Revolutionary consciousness inevitably manifests itself in war and conflict. Quoting the Greek maxim attributed to Heraclitus, Carr states that war is the "father of all things": violent action exposes the contradictions inherent in the international system and change occurs as a result.

Carr is always careful to couch his ideas in terms of a wider ideological conflict, or sociohistorical cultural "moment." Thus the extension of democracy and "political rights" and their subsequent decline are the backdrop for his international theory. The epistemic crisis of modernity was that of the fundamental inappropriateness of liberal democracy for the needs of mass democracy. Economic needs had eclipsed the political rights secured by the bourgeoisie in the nineteenth century: the attendant alienation of the governed from the government that this eclipse occasioned led to increased support for the radical politics of Nazism, Fascism, and Soviet communism.[33] These forces are, for Carr, the agents of history, forcing the redevelopment of politics into a new sociopolitical framework. They work by exposing the fact that our most valuable abstractions no longer apply; we act by their precepts but no longer believe in their inherent value:

> Our conscious thought has begun to reject the abstract ideas which characterized the past 200 years of history—the belief that progress is infinite, that morality and interests coincide, and that society rests on a natural and universal harmony of interests between men and nations. Yet without consciously believing these things, we still unconsciously take them for granted and see other things through them. Hence our thought is confused, and our speech unclear. We repeat ritual words that no longer have any vital meaning.[34]

In Nietzschean terms, liberal democracy was dead and we had killed it, but what would make us worthy of this deed? According to Carr, the fundamental issue of international politics was moral and required a new ontology of collectivity rather than the bankrupt foundation of individualism:

> Shorn of its moral foundation in the harmony of interests, individualism, as Nietzsche had demonstrated, could lead only to the doctrine of the morally purposeless superman. Shorn of the same foundation, nationalism, as the history of the last twenty years has shown, could lead only to the doctrine of the morally purposeless super-nation or *Herrenvolk* . . . The twentieth century has brought an ever growing recognition that "patriotism is not enough"—that it does not provide an intelligible moral purpose and cannot create a cohesive international society.[35]

According to Carr the only way to achieve the moral aim of creating a cohesive international society was to recognize the necessity of structural change in the international system itself. If the moral imperative is the creation of a peaceful international society, the means by which this society would be created lay in the fusion of political will with economic power. Perhaps Carr's most noticeable error lay in his overestimation of British power after the war. He should not be judged too harshly for this, however, as he cannot be expected to have been able to foretell the economic ruin that would fall on the victors of World War Two. In fact, Carr's prognostications are more often characterized by their success than their failure. These prognostications are an essential element of his attempt to provide an alternative basis for international society.

In a chapter entitled "The New Europe," Carr outlines a vision of a functional-Realist future.[36] European reconstruction would have to have a purpose more radical than the mere restoration of the old system, and more

Realistic than the retention of the war economy. In order to create the new Europe, various bodies would be necessary: a European Relief Commission, a European Transport Corporation, and the European Reconstruction and Public Works Corporation. At the head of these would be the European Planning Authority (EPA), the master key of the European settlement that "should be encouraged to develop into the ultimate authority responsible for vital decisions on 'European' economic policies."[37] The role and function of the EPA would be all-embracing, with the economic power "to intervene in those fields of economic life where the misconceived and unqualified independence of the national unit has proved so fatal to the peace and prosperity in the past twenty years."[38] To this end, Carr predicted the necessity of a European bank and a common currency system (at least of exchange).[39]

The increasingly utopian sentiments in Carr's analysis in *Conditions of Peace* are best represented by his conclusion that the "nucleus of power on which the European Planning Authority will depend will no doubt be drawn in the first instance from the English-speaking countries and Russia."[40] Carr at this stage was increasingly unwilling to recognize the most unpalatable but vital insight of Realism, that conflict is just as likely as cooperation in IR. Perhaps the prescriptive quality of *The Conditions of Peace* accounts for the more optimistic tenor of this work.

Carr's attempt to escape the implication of Realism is to return to the task of creating a new utopia. This task was first expressed in *The Twenty Years' Crisis* and fleshed out in *Conditions of Peace* and *Nationalism and After*.[41] As described in chapter 1, it is in *Nationalism and After* that Carr writes of nation states, "they are an anomaly and an anachronism in a world which has moved on to other forms of organization."[42]

Carr's final involvement in the thought world of IR was his engagement with the question of democratic ideology and a quest for a Realistic moral foundation for international affairs. The short lecture entitled *Democracy in International Affairs* begins this phase: its purpose was to juxtapose the revolutionary and the status quo versions of democracy as the ideological battleground of the agencies of regression and progress in domestic relations and IR. While partisans of both approaches profess their aim as the promotion of democracy, their definitions of it are based on fundamentally different premises. Anglo-Saxon democracy is based on the idea of individualism and the harmony of interests and a belief in the self-regulation of markets and the natural order of things. Contrasted with this system is Soviet democracy, which is based upon a collective rather than individual identity. The tension between the two ideologies will animate the international system, which will remain in a constant state of flux as the realm of ideas transmutes.[43] Perceiving the progress of history in utilitarian terms, for Carr the democracy that extended to the most number of people in the most meaningful sense, that is, economic and political freedom, liberty and equality, was necessarily progressive. Carr concludes his analysis with the exhortation that democratic leaders in the English-speaking world should not rest on their laurels but rather "seek new social and economic spheres of action for the application to the democratic principle."[44] Carr's "error" was that he believed that the Soviet Union was the agent of progress, the actions of which would dialectically force the creation of a new regime in IR, although arguably in the creation of welfare states and European integration the Soviet presence was a spur to Western development.

Initial Moral and Philosophical Responses to Carr

The significance of Carr's place in IR theory has grown in the telling.[45] Initial reactions to *The Twenty Years' Crisis*, although acknowledging Carr's brilliance, nonetheless were almost uniformly hostile. The idea of a first great debate in IR between idealists and Realists may have been a myth, but the appearance of *The Twenty Years' Crisis* and subsequent works provided both a vocabulary and a dialogue that continues to have a huge impact on international theory. Those who felt most slighted by the assault upon liberal internationalism (Zimmern, Angell, Woolf) all reacted to *The Twenty Years' Crisis*. This provided them with an opportunity to counter the claims of Carr and to highlight the flaws in his analysis of their positions. As such, their critiques are a valuable insight into the complexities of the liberal-Realist dialogue. Reaction to *The Twenty Years' Crisis* may be divided into two overlapping categories: moral and philosophical condemnation (Morgenthau, Woolf, Richard Crossman as "Richard Coventry," Zimmern, Wight) and critiques of his methodology (Hayek, Zimmern, Stebbing).

Carr's works, especially *The Twenty Years' Crisis*, have often been criticized for their moral and philosophical positions on the nature of IR and the necessity of placing considerations of power at the center of analysis. Condemnations of his position are further complicated by Carr's unwillingness to provide a clear, systematic definition of that philosophy.[46] Faced with this lack of definition, many commentators created a philosophy for Carr, and then proceeded to focus their criticism on misconceptions of his theory. Perhaps the most famous attempt to critique and condemn Carr's philosophy was that of Leonard Woolf, described by Martin Wight as an essential corrective to *The Twenty Years' Crisis* itself.[47] Woolf's primary criticism was of Carr's mendacious rhetoric, in particular his implication "that the failure of the League [of Nations] and of the attempt to reconstruct a peaceful Europe was 'inevitable' only because it was a failure."[48] The second prong of Woolf's attack was the argument that Carr's policy of appeasement was also a failure and by implication that his thought processes were as faulty as those of the idealists.

Despite its reputation as a stunning riposte to Carr, Woolf's "Utopia and Reality" is ultimately unconvincing. One of the major problems with the piece is its failure to identify the technical nature of Carr's idiom. There is a very particular etymology to words such as "science" and "utopia" in Carr's discourse. Utopia and utopian ideology are not the simple derogatories that Woolf depicts; rather, they have a specific meaning derived from Mannheim's *Ideology and Utopia*. The misunderstanding of these terms and the failure to appreciate the role of dialectics in *The Twenty Years' Crisis* leaves Woolf's criticism floundering at the outset. He is mistaken also in his critique of Carr's assault upon the League of Nations. Carr's analysis of the failure of this institution was based upon its inadequate bases in the postulates of nineteenth-century theories of world government—the League was a symptom of wider problems of political thought. In a little-known section of the relatively obscure *Britain: A Study in Foreign Policy from the Versailles Treaty to the Outbreak of War*, Carr writes that the British government was merely trying to create a peaceful solution to the problem of German strength in Europe, taking practical considerations of political will and military preparedness into account: appeasement was an immediate solution to an immediate problem, not the product of a grand design for peace reasoned from a priori principles. The problem was not the policy of appeasement, but the lack of German sincerity and measuredness. Hitler had made the mistake of Clemenceau at Versailles, using maximum force and brutality in order to achieve his aims.[49] Callously dismissing the fate of Czechoslovakia as an unreasonable war aim, Carr argued that Britain would not have gone to war with Germany had concessions been made earlier in more propitious circumstances than faced Chamberlain, that Britain could not have gone to war due to military unpreparedness in 1938, which made conciliation the only "practical" option, and (ironically using Woolf's later logic) just because the policy of appeasement failed did not mean that it should not have been tried.[50]

Woolf's assertion that Carr believed power was more "real" than interests and beliefs is also false. Carr believed that power was the source of beliefs and morality, and that power and morality operated in tandem. Carr did not attack the "reality" of the harmony of interests; he attacked the belief that the harmony of interests was universal and that it could serve as the basis of an international order.[51] Woolf also ignores Carr's position regarding Realism: the complexities of a progressive dialectic are rendered into a simple dichotomy between Realism and idealism. In his defense of the idea of harmony of interests, Woolf attempted to demonstrate the inapplicability of

Carr's notion of conflict being a dominant factor by using the example of France and Britain cooperating, beginning in the 1890s. What Woolf fails to mention was that both countries perceived the threat emanating from Germany to be of far more significance than any threat they posed to each other. Fear, not a quantum leap in diplomatic psychology, provoked their cooperation.

By means of an extended analogy to Hobbes, Richard Crossman, writing as Richard Coventry, was somewhat more successful in highlighting the moral *problematique* and practical shortcomings of Carr's IR: "it analyses International Relations with the same ruthlessness and something of the same detached relish in the supremacy of things evil, which inspired Hobbes to write *The Leviathan*."[52] The analogy is particularly striking, according to Coventry, in that both have successful power analyses, but also "nonsensical" practical conclusions: despotism in the case of Hobbes, appeasement in the case of Carr. The question of the moral void in *The Twenty Years' Crisis* was further addressed by Alfred Zimmern, who declared that "the thorough-going relativism—not to say scepticism—here revealed undermines the force of his expert criticism."[53] The most damaging moral critique is that of Morgenthau, possibly because he best understood Carr's intentions in writing *The Twenty Years' Crisis*. Similar to other commentators, Morgenthau applauds Carr's achievement in highlighting the failures of contemporary political thought, but Carr is himself a product of an age in which political thought was in decline and his work "points up in its own shortcomings the extent and the import of the disease."[54] Morgenthau understands Carr's dialectic of morality and power because he recently and independently had been engaged in a similar dialectical process; however, where Carr placed his faith in an unformed future, Morgenthau reluctantly placed his in providence, a force outside history. For Morgenthau, Carr's discovery of the centrality of power in IR forced him to seek a new utopia: "all his subsequent thinking becomes the odyssey of a mind which has discovered the phenomenon of power and longs to transcend it."[55] Works such as *Conditions of Peace* and *Nationalism and After* are attempts to go beyond this phenomenon, but the solution evades Carr because he

> has only the vaguest idea of what morality is . . . the philosophically untenable equation of utopia, theory and morality, which is at the foundation of *The Twenty Years' Crisis*, leads of necessity to a relativistic, instrumentalist conception of morality . . . Mr. Carr, philosophically so ill equipped, has no transcendent point of view from which to survey the political scene and to appraise the phenomenon of power.[56]

This lack of moral insight is neatly summed up by Morganthau's epithet: "It is a dangerous thing to be a Machiavelli. It is a disastrous thing to be a Machiavelli without *virtu*."[57]

Though fewer in number, methodological and epistemological critiques of Carr are more serious than the moral critiques. Alfred Zimmern was the first to point out that Carr's polemic was ranged against too wide a series of targets, rather than a single identifiable group of "utopians." Pacifists, free traders, lawyers, the League of Nations, defenders of the status quo, and exponents of ethical values are at various times lined up for criticism by Carr. Such a range of targets detracts from the power of Carr's analysis, as this disparate group of people had such differing aims that the strength of Carr's observations was diluted. Hayek's branding of Carr as a totalitarian, comparable to the Nazi philosopher Carl Schmitt, in thrall to the expediency principle, is one of the most damning of all commentaries on Carr. Hayek, an instinctively socially conservative liberal, also condemned Carr for the "fatalistic belief of every pseudo-historian since Hegel and Marx [that] this development [revolution] is represented as inevitable." He objects strongly to (and misrepresents) Carr's theory of revolution and insurrection as the means of justice in international affairs. The failings of Carr's totalitarianism and the dialectic inadequacies of his epistemological foundations were exacerbated by Carr's lack of economic theory:

> Professor Carr is not an economist and his economic argument generally will not bear serious examination. But neither this, nor his belief characteristically held at the same time, that the importance of the economic factor in social life is rapidly decreasing, prevent him from basing on economic arguments all his predictions about the inevitable developments or from presenting as his main demands for the future the reinterpretation in predominantly economic terms of the democratic ideals of "equality" and "liberty."[58]

Norman Angell's reply to Carr, "Who Are the Utopians? And Who the Realists?" has the same angry tenor as Leonard Woolf's, but is far more accurate in its criticism of *The Twenty Years' Crisis*. Angell is one of the few commentators to hoist Carr by his own rhetorical petard, employing history and fact in order to undermine Carr's position as an empirically sound pragmatist. Angell's approach is to undermine Carr's claims to pragmatism: Carr's system is unworkable, argues Angell, because "we are left in the dark as to the manner in which, and the proportions in which, we are to mix our utopianism and Realism." The book is also conceptually flawed, argues Angell, in that

Carr's conflation of the League of Nations with *laissez faire*, under the rubric of utopianism, in fact, combined two mutually exclusive policies. According to Angell, it was the utopian advice to take action earlier against revisionist powers, opposed by the Realists, that was borne out by events not the Realist policy of appeasement. Carr's own position regarding the postwar world was undermined by his strange choice of political bedfellows. Whereas the utopians such as Zimmern, Noel-Baker, or Toynbee would support Carr's vision of the future, it was unlikely that Conservative backbenchers or the Realists of the Beaverbrook or Rothermere press would support any radical change as expressed by Carr in the chapter "The Prospects of a New International Order."[59]

The most severe methodological criticism of Carr came from an unexpected source, L. Susan Stebbing, a noted historian of science. Attacking the basis of Carr's utopian–Realist dyad, she maintained, "it is strictly nonsense to assume that to have ideals is equivalent to *being a visionary*, i.e., one who builds ideal schemes which have no relevance to the facts and are *therefore* incapable of being achieved."[60] Carr's claims to science are undermined by terminological indecision, especially as to what constitutes Realism, which is so confused that Carr falls into contradiction. The problem lies in Carr's lack of scientific method; Stebbing says, "his method is so unscientific that he nowhere clearly defines these terms [utopianism and Realism], but uses them in a vague, popular sense."[61] Assuming Carr to be a Realist in the Machiavellian mold, she attacks the basis of Realist thought, arguing that moral judgment penetrates political decision making, even in such an archetypal Realist as Bismarck.[62] The evil means employed by a Bismarck, Hitler, or Stalin in pursuit of a particular worthy end are not political decisions, but ethical ones—the Realist himself judges the means by which he achieves his end and political expediency is merely "an excuse for the use of means antecedently judged to be evil."[63] The nature of Carr's synthesis also makes little "scientific" sense: "since Prof. Carr has opposed power to morality, as a pair of contradictories, it follows that power cannot be moralised nor morality made powerful; just as it follows that black cannot be whitened, or white blackened . . . Prof. Carr's conclusion is nonsensical and reveals that something is seriously wrong with his scientific analysis."[64]

While these criticisms provide an essential corrective to the more mendacious and poorly thought out details of Carr's system as developed in *The Twenty Years' Crisis*, they share one thing in common. The fundamental problem with all of Carr's early critics is their inability to detect the dialectical framework employed by Carr; none of them seems willing to look beyond the polemic of *The Twenty Years' Crisis* and see that Carr was trying to create a system of thought for the interpretation of international events. Realism and

Utopia were merely elements of a dialectical process whose momentum was dependent upon both having their place. White can be blackened, and black whitened, producing the new color gray: that is the basis of dialectical thought, which Carr retained in his analysis.

Assessing Carr's Place in International Relations

After the initial impact of *The Twenty Years' Crisis*, interest in Carr's system of IR began to fade. Insofar as he featured in the discipline, it was as a hard-line Realist, placed in the same category as Morgenthau and Kennan. As a historiographical object, *The Twenty Years' Crisis* was regarded as the Realist *coup de grace* against the idealist position in the so-called First Great Debate of IR.[65] The first attempt to investigate the totality of Carr's thought was Whittle Johnston's article, "E.H. Carr's Theory of International Relations: A Critique." The basic premise of this chapter is that Carr did not have a unified theory of IR, but two theories of international conflict that were unrelated to each other in a consistent fashion.[66] It is Johnston's contention that Carr changed from a moral position in *The Twenty Years' Crisis* to a systemic methodology in *Nationalism and After* and later works. Johnston's primary bone of contention was Carr's anti-objectivist stance, which, Johnston argues, cannot provide the means by which historians can judge the morality of historical events.[67] Johnston's error is a failure to recognize Carr's eclecticism, but also the essential unity of his work. Although Carr uses elements of Hegel's philosophy of history, he does not subscribe to it in totality. Carr's "reason" is also not that of Hegel or other Enlightenment thinkers: reason for Carr is the use of intelligence to make (subjective) sense of the world, not the means by which history will inevitably gain its end. Carr's idea of progress is also different from that of Hegel and Marx—he described their attempts at creating a goal outside of history as "eschatological."

Graham Evans's reply pointed out some of the flaws in Johnston's interpretations of Carr. In response to Johnston, Evans states that it would have been impossible for Carr not to change his mind as the twentieth century progressed from one set of political conditions and crises to another, but that these changes do not necessitate the charge of inconsistency.[68] Arguing against Morgenthau and Stebbing, Evans contends that Carr was acutely aware of the need for a moral basis for international affairs, and throughout his works attempted to offer a moral vision for world politics.[69] *Conditions of Peace* was clearly, according to Evans, the heir of *The Twenty Years' Crisis* in that the centrality of power was the dominant motif of the book, the moral findings of which were clearly related to the fact that they were power dependent. Johnston failed to recognize another element of continuity in Carr's work: in his historical and political works on IR, Carr is determined to illustrate that the failure of political elites to address the problems of the international arena with appropriate intellectual tools is bound to lead to disaster, as it did with the failure to recognize the collapse of the nineteenth-century belief in an international harmony of interests in *The Twenty Years' Crisis* and the fragmentation of the political philosophy of nationalist self-determination of the nineteenth century in *Nationalism and After*.[70]

Hedley Bull, in his guise as a historian of the discipline, painted Carr as an irremediable Realist in his article "*The Twenty Years' Crisis* Thirty Years On." In his survey of the discipline from 1919 to 1969, Bull describes Carr as brilliant and provocative, but like his fellow first generation of Realists, fundamentally redundant.[71] Bull is one of the few commentators willing to examine the consequence of Carr's use of the sociology of knowledge in *The Twenty Years' Crisis*, but Bull downplays the significance of the insight that moral and legal positions in IR are historically or socially contingent, arguing that this does not mean that they do not have independent causal force in international politics.[72] Like Morgenthau, Bull attributed the moral failings of Carr to his relativism and his instrumentalist take on international law and the norms of international society.[73]

The true significance of all Carr's interlocutors is that it is through their interpretive acts that the world has come to know Carr.

Carr, Relativism, and Reason—E.H. Carr as Post-Positivist?

The key issue of Carr's relativism was revived by Michael Joseph Smith in his study of Realism, *Realist Thought from Weber to Kissinger*. According to Smith, Carr's relativism was the unfortunate corollary of his use of a "crude" sociology of knowledge. Smith's particular criticism of Carr is that he does not examine the nature of this system and does not attempt to answer hard questions about the process of conditioning of thought. Smith accounts for Carr's superficial use of a sociology of knowledge approach as a tactical attempt to debunk the utopians, rather than a fully conceived system of thought.[74] Carr's belief that IR was the product of underlying social and economic forces manifesting themselves in the political sphere leaves no autonomy for the realm of thought leading to a thoroughly destructive relativism that Smith (quoting Carr himself) believed could be "pressed to the point where the debunker is himself debunked."[75]

Smith is one of the few commentators to understand Carr's conception of power as a means, an end, and as "a master key for understanding" international politics.[76] Drawing close to Stebbing's earlier critique, Smith maintains that without a more meaningful definition of power, Carr's theory of power centrality is of little use, being, in effect, "an unhelpful platitude." Smith claims that the other element in Carr's international thought, that of morality, is based on inadequate foundations in his "intuitive" interpretation of morality represented by "the man in the street." This specious argument by Carr has been described as a tactical attempt to undermine the position of the utopians by contrasting their airy concerns with the immediate reality of everyday life.[77] As Smith correctly points out, Carr had no monopoly on intuitive readings of morality. It was Carr's moral relativism (derived from his "crudely materialist sociology of knowledge") that led to his failure to distinguish between revisionist powers and Nazi Germany: Carr's instrumentalist morality would not allow him to see that Germany was not a simple "have-not" power that would become a pillar of international society once its reasonable needs were met.[78] Echoing Morgenthau, Smith concludes that "in the hands of E.H. Carr Realism ultimately becomes an agnostic relativism of power."[79]

The moral criticisms of Carr, based upon his relativism, are well founded from the perspective of the modern, liberal, Enlightenment-inspired epistemic community of IR scholars of both Realist and liberal schools, but Carr did not belong to that community. Carr was acting on an entirely different rationale: as worked out in *Conditions of Peace* and *Nationalism and After*, his quasi-Marxian reinterpretation of rights and obligations of citizenship and his belief that mass society had outstripped the efficacy of bourgeois democracy placed him in a separate political space from his contemporaries.

Relativism as a product of the sociology of knowledge held few terrors for Carr, and the "relativistic, instrumentalist conception of morality" decried by Morgenthau was exactly the form of morality that Carr was trying to promote—the notion of an absolute morality, based on eternal a priori principles was anathema to Carr, and demonstrated the very bankruptcy of modern thought in dealing with the problem of international conflict. Carr's position regarding determinism was made clear in his defense of Mannheim:

> He struggled hard against the imputation of "relativism," arguing rightly enough that the charge can be made good only by those who accept a priori an absolute standard. He believed that the essence of reality is dynamic, and that to seek any static point within it from which to deliver "timeless" judgments is a fundamental error. The individual's apprehension of this ever-changing reality is necessarily partial and relative. He can see it only from the perspective of time and place in which he finds himself; and even this partial view is of something which is in process of continuous change as he looks at it. It makes no sense to describe the one as "relative" to the other. Reality consists in the constant interaction of subject and object, of man and his material environment.[80]

Drawing a clear distinction between this form of "relativism" and the relativism of "absolute scepticism," Carr comes to a clear statement on the nature of social knowledge: "The first answer is that the right view is the one which enables us to understand and cope with reality in its existing (and *ex hypothesi* transient) form . . . We know it is the right key because it fits, and because we see the man with the wrong key battering helplessly at a closed door."[81] This finding has enormous consequences for our understanding of Carr's own interpretation of IR. In terms of *The Twenty Years' Crisis*, the man battering at the door could be either a utopian or a Realist trying to unlock the door of IR. He is failing because he is addressing the problem with the wrong kind of key. In both cases, the door batterer is employing a static form of knowledge based on "timeless principle," persisting in his mistaken system rather than acknowledging the inefficiency of his method. The key to opening the door is one of recognizing that one must solve the problem on its merits, not according to "principles."

We also learn in this chapter of Carr's interpretation of reason and rationality in the work of Mannheim and, we may infer, in his own works. Mannheim had torn "the gaudy and long tattered garments of the Enlightenment" but had unconsciously (Carr imputes this from his writings rather than quoting directly from Mannheim) developed a notion of "supratemporal Reason . . . not to be invoked except as a last resort, in the background of human affairs."[82] Carr's own desire for an ultimate means by which to judge the vagaries of existence is coming to the fore in his analysis of Mannheim, and may be his attempt to escape the charge of relativism leveled at him by his critics.

The most recent in-depth attempt to assess Carr's place in international theory has been Charles Jones's *E. H. Carr and International Relations: A Duty to Lie*. Mannheim, according to Jones, provided Carr with a "distinctively post-positivist, social-scientific methodology that would mark him off from the dominant positivism of the Anglo-Saxon world of his day."[83] It is this post-positivism that enables Carr to eschew Enlightenment rationalism and "naïve" empiricism. In *The Twenty Years' Crisis*, Carr was "neither a historian, nor a positivist, but a social scientist of some sophistication, espousing a form of pragmatism tempered by structuralism."[84] This degree of post-positivism is important in terms of any attempt to portray Carr as the progenitor of a critical discourse of IR, as it provides the basis for a dialogue with other forms of post-positivist thinking in international theory.

In addition to Jones, R.W. Cox has identified Carr as one of the leading forebears of critical theory in IR as his historical method ensured that Carr was "sensitive to the continuities between social forces, the changing nature of the state and global relationships."[85] As a philosopher of history and as an

IR theorist, Carr, through the "historical mode of thought . . . [delineated] the particular configurations of forces which fixed the framework of international behaviour in different periods and [tried] to understand institutions, theories and events within their historical contexts," providing a sign posting to a more critical approach to international theory.[86] As an example of Carr's awareness of structural transformation, Cox cites Carr's incorporation of industrial workers into the status quo as a new social force affecting the international system by creating the conditions for a populist, jingoistic imperialism and economic nationalism, ultimately leading to a more antagonistic form of international society.[87] Jim George takes a different interpretation, firmly identifying Carr as a positivist. Carr and his Realist followers "have never seriously confronted his (or their own) one-sidedness, intolerance, and analytical silence."[88] The problem lies in Carr and other traditional/classical Realist thinkers being rooted in a positivist/modernist ontology, which creates the logic of Realism that continues to frame the problems of IR "in terms of the phenomenalist and nominalist perspectives on knowledge."[89] That Carr can produce such a disparity of opinion among his numerous commentators is testament to the complexity of his thought.

His attitude of skepticism toward the claims of Enlightenment rationalism and liberal ideology seems to have been derived from his reading of Russian intellectuals, Dostoevsky in particular. The influence of Dostoevsky on Carr's intellectual development has been highlighted by Jonathan Haslam in his recent biography. This influence was particularly important in persuading Carr (at this stage a convinced liberal) of the limitation of rational thought processes—in *Dostoevsky* he describes rationalism as "an orderly blight."[90]

The discovery of an entirely different mindset on Europe's doorstep, and the rejection of Western norms by the Russian intelligentsia, seem to have opened the doors of perception for Carr: "I now perceived for the first time that the liberal moralistic ideology in which I had been brought up was not, as I had assumed, an Absolute taken for granted by the modern world, but was sharply and convincingly attacked by very intelligent people living outside the charmed circle who looked at the world through very different eyes." In his biography of Dostoevsky he salutes the author of *Crime and Punishment* for piercing "the hollowness of the attempt to base ethics either on egoism or on rational altruism," the two means by which modernity has attempted to rationalize ethical behavior.[91] The influence of the Dostoevsky epiphany on Carr is clear from his statement that the "quality in Dostoevsky which gives him his permanent place among the great writers of all time is his faculty of creating for us a new world, of lifting us on to a new plane of existence, where our old standards, hopes, fears, ideals lose their meaning and are transfigured for us in a new light."[92] The Russian critic Rozanov is singled out by Carr for his early identification of "the relative and hypothetical character of human thought . . . the reality of existence is not identical with what can be conceived by the reason."[93] As further evidence of Carr's anti-positivist stance in *The Twenty Years' Crisis*, he locates the failure of international theory in its being "strongly colored by the mathematical and natural sciences" (the lodestones of Enlightenment thought), which Carr considered inappropriate to the study of international politics. In what amounts to a critique of the blindness of liberal/utopian thought, Carr places international politics firmly in the category of an infantile science where "thought has been at a discount."[94]

Carr's later works, *Conditions of Peace*, *Nationalism and After*, *Democracy in International Affairs*, *The New Society*, and *The Moral Foundations of World Order*, are all attempts to transcend the modern nation state, and, however misguided on occasion, speak of a desire to go beyond this central project of modernity. Carr's achievement in IR theory was to create an open-ended, fluid theory that rested on eclectic foundations in history, philosophy, economics, and political theory. As an analysis of the IR of the interwar years, *The Twenty Years' Crisis* was, as Carr admitted in the preface to the second edition, "a period piece," but the insight provided by his dialectic of power and morality, and the effect it had on IR theory was immense, in that it provided a critical philosophy to what had previously been a discipline lacking a true appreciation of the complex role played by power in the international sphere. He is the creator of reflective Realist logic, a Realism aware of the complex relationship between morality and power, but also aware of the origins and implications of his theory. Carr's Realism is the product of dialectical thought and pragmatic problemsolving. His insights are a response to the challenge of IR rather than an attempt to close IR in a strictly utopian or Realist box.[95] The dialectic is not a tidy, neat modern dialectic however, as Carr clearly favors Realism over utopianism, both as a corrective and as an epistemological vantage point—*l'esprit de contradiction*.

CHAPTER 4

The Realist Truths of Hans Morgenthau

As the title of his 1970 essay collection suggests, *Truth and Power: Essays of a Decade*, Morgenthau's career revolved around a commitment to discovering the "truth" of international politics and an assertion of the primacy of power in IR. His incessant toil in the fields of history and political theory were intended to provide the means for the discovery of this truth. Morgenthau rejected existing liberal and scientific theories of international politics in *Scientific Man versus Power Politics* for precisely this reason—they did not produce a true theory of international politics, but rather subsumed it in a scientific philosophy and methodology that obscured rather than revealed the harsh realities of international existence. For Morgenthau, the truth about international politics was intrinsically bound to power, so much so that a commitment toward examining the central role of power in IR dominates his work. The primacy of power is the ultimate reality and truth of international politics as it permeates the social and political fabrics of human existence. During the course of the chapter, I demonstrate the degree to which power dictates both the practice of power and the structure of international politics.

Politics among Nations has become the classic text of American Realism—a book that defined the field of IR in America for generations after World War Two. In this work, he proposes a theory of international politics that is designed to make the international arena less complex and understandable to the student of international politics. It does this by delineating a theory of truth about the nature of power and the practice of power in international politics. The aim of this delineation is to create the foundations for a science of international politics that would provide a rational approach to understanding global politics. Yet this marked somewhat of a breach in Morgenthau's own work, especially *Scientific Man versus Power Politics* in which he had previously attacked the shortcomings of rationalist liberal and Marxist attempts to create a science of international politics.

The purpose of this chapter is to trace the phases of Morgenthau's changing accounts of truth in international politics, from his early critical attitude and skepticism toward "scientific" international theory, to his commitment to a "rational" theory in *Politics among Nations*, to his rejection of the rational as a basis for truth in the late 1960s and 1970s.

Morgenthau serves as an effective counterpoint to his contemporary E.H. Carr. Although Morgenthau also adopted a dialectical approach, in this case to the relationship between power and morality, Morgenthau was committed to the development of a singular theory of Realism, which, although not being rationalist, nonetheless lacked the dialogic element of Carr's approach. It is this "lack" of theoretical dialogue that forced Morgenthau to shuttle between Nietzschean radical skepticism and Weberian ideal form theorization.[1] Morgenthau thought "truth" could emerge from only one place, and that technique could uncover it. For Morgenthau, Realism was eternal and true, and largely unchanging as a philosophy of power: individual situations may be different, but ultimately Realism could uncover the social logic of any given international community.

As the key purpose of this section of the book is the creation of a countermemory of Realism, one of the central aims of this chapter is to demonstrate that despite the lack of a dialogic aspect, Morgenthau's Realism is vastly different from the dominant representation of Realism. The complexity of his ideas in relation to power, morality, and the civilization impulse in international politics and his skeptical attitude to rationalism in social science distinguish Morgenthau from the paradigmatic Realist.

Determining "Truth" in International Relations

Morgenthau, Rationalism, and Empiricism

In the earliest phase of his career in America, Morgenthau was committed to the notion of truth derived from observational experience combined with a rational approach to the systematization of knowledge. Setting himself against the dominant European modes of thought of deduction and positivism, Morgenthau developed a thoroughgoing skepticism toward the functional blindness of the social sciences. As early as 1940, Morgenthau was decrying the baleful influence of pseudoscientific rationalism, as the following attack on legal positivism demonstrates:

> If an event in the physical world contradicts all scientific forecasts, and thus challenges the assumptions on which the forecasts have been based, it is the natural reaction of scientific inquiry to re-examine the foundations of the specific science and attempt to reconcile scientific findings and empirical facts. The social sciences do not react in the same way. They have an inveterate tendency to stick to their own assumptions and to suffer constant defeat from experience rather than to change their assumptions in the light of contradicting facts. This resistance to change is uppermost in the history of international law ... Not unlike the ancient sorcerers of primitive ages, they seek to exorcise social evils by the indefatigable repetition of magic formulae.[2]

Morgenthau's main complaint with rationalism is its misunderstanding of the nature of social knowledge. Rationalist models are described as "idols," the product of seventeenth-century rationalism's desire for an order analogous to the order perceived in the natural world, a vision of science hopelessly outdated in the twentieth century. Echoing Carr, Morgenthau states that the social scientist "stands in the streams of social causation as an acting and reacting agent. What he sees ... [is] determined by his position in those streams."[3] The multiplicity of causes and effects that characterize politics and IR are poorly served by the "arbitrary abstraction" of the single-cause pseudoscientism of the liberals and Marxists who attribute all the ills of the social world to the distribution of wealth and resources in the international environment. This form of "single-cause" theorization is derived from the rationalist mode of thought typical of the Enlightenment and is responsible for erroneous readings of international politics that cannot be expected to be relevant for more than a short period of time.[4]

But Morgenthau does not dispense with the category of the rational in its entirety: he is far too conservative a thinker for such an approach to knowledge. To this end there is a clear distinction in his works between rationalism and rationality. Where rationalism provides merely an illusion of control over knowledge derived from a traditionalist interpretation of science, rationality is an effective approach to knowledge, it is what makes knowledge possible in IR in that the enormous range of contingencies inherent in the social world is provided with a "measure of rationality if approached with the expectation of Macbethian cynicism."[5] Although expressed here in terms of social planning, this argument of rationality giving meaning to the social world is the foundation of Morgenthau's approach to the formulation of the six principles of political Realism. The rational anticipation of potential trends, which are detectable via a set of assumptions about the world (in this case Morgenthau's Macbethian cynicism), provides the key to an approximate (or satisfying) solution to a specific social problem.[6] In terms of *Politics among Nations*, this approximate and tentative approach to the "problem" of IR leads to a theoretical position that is formulated on the basis of large-scale political probabilities.

The method of such a technique of determining the rationality of political behavior in IR is determined not by the mere facts of history: in the clearest statement of intent that Morgenthau provided of his technique, he states that "we must approach historical reality with a kind of rational outline, a map that suggests to us the possible meanings of history . . . It is the testing of this rational hypothesis against the actual facts and their consequences which gives meaning to the facts of history and makes the scientific writing of political history possible."[7] Morgenthau opposed the excessive empiricism of the American foreign policy elite, claiming that in the absence of a coherent theory of political behavior, empiricist approaches to individual power jeopardized foreign policy as a whole. Facts, according to Morgenthau, do not exist outside their social context:

> Facts have no social meaning in themselves. It is the significance we attribute to certain facts of our sensual experience, in terms of our hopes and fears, our memories, intentions and expectations, that create them as social facts. The social world itself, then, is but an artefact of man's mind as the reflection of his thoughts and the creation of his actions. Every social act and even our awareness of empirical data as social facts presupposes a theory of society, however unacknowledged, inchoate and fragmentary.[8]

This phase of Morgenthau's career, in which he targeted the failings of positivist social science, reached its culmination in the publication of *Scientific Man versus Power Politics*, a text that ranks alongside *The Twenty Years' Crisis* as a searing exposure of the failings of modernity to form the basis of a reliable science of international politics. Modern philosophy, by heroizing the concept of instrumental reason, leads to a marked degree of blind acceptance of the scientific and deductive reason. This uncriticality of the modern world leads to entrenchment in the thought world of the time, quenching the possibility of alternatives beyond that particular *zeitgeist*. Morgenthau identifies rationalism as this age's dominant mode of thought, which he claims:

> has maintained the unity under reason of the social and the physical world and the ability of the human world to mould both worlds through the application of the same rational principles.[9]

The crucial issue is the molding of events in the political world under the interpretative power of scientific rationalism. Rather than being a truly objective exercise, rendering politics into a scientific form is an act of will, imposing an interpretation onto a foreign discipline. This belief in science and scientism is central to liberal and Marxist nineteenth-century thought. In addition to misunderstanding the nature of man as biological and spiritual as well as being rational, scientism "perverts the natural sciences into an instrument of social salvation for which neither their own nature nor the nature of the social world fit them."[10]

The core of the problem as perceived by Morgenthau is that modern thought is basically inadequate and inapplicable to the task of interpreting the social world. Thinkers within the Enlightenment tradition had substituted science for political thought leading to the eclipse of power (the basis of political thought since Machiavelli) and the erection of an artificial standard for politics in science. Unsurprisingly, the emasculation of political consciousness resulted in an unsatisfactory form of theory, resulting in "the substitution of scientific standards for political evaluations and ultimately, the destruction of the ability to make intelligent political decisions at all.[11] This lack of intelligence lies in the category error of assuming that scientific truth could be carried over from science to the realm of politics, which, according to Morgenthau, is the realm not of truth but of power.[12] The science of international politics required a more substantial basis than the imported criteria of science. Morgenthau found his basis for a "truthful" science of politics in the reality of power.

A "True" Science of International Relations

Morgenthau has a very particular notion of what constitutes "science," which rests on the distinction between being rational as opposed to rationalistic. If political cynicism and skepticism are the keys to understanding IR, the role of scientific analysis is to prune down national objectives to the measure of available resources. Economics, the most significant of the social sciences in terms of prediction, serves as a model (though not explicitly) for a science of IR as passages such as the following demonstrate: "No nation has the resources to promote all desirable objectives with equal vigour; all nations must therefore allocate their scarce resources as rationally as possible." A species akin to *Homo economicus* and the related conceptual universe forms a partial basis for the theoretical understanding of the political world in *Politics among Nations*, but Morgenthau does not remain fixed to this idealization throughout.[13]

Morgenthau's position should be clearly differentiated from positivistic attempts to create a quantitative science of IR, a project he derided for being responsible for the replacement of genuine "theory" (here understood as the empirical and inductive mode typical of political thought in the period dating from Machiavelli) by "dogma." Those who followed the inductive path created a theory that was designed to maximize rationality: the "new" theories in attempting to create a "pervasive" rationality made reality ontologically subordinate to theory, which has the effect of undermining its functionality, "their practicality is specious since it substitutes what is desirable for what is possible."[14] Perhaps realizing the incongruity of the historical development of IR and economic logic, Morgenthau retreated from his earlier emphatic deployment of economics as the model for the development of a theory of international politics. This withdrawal from the economic path was probably a reaction to the attempted quantification of the discipline of IR by the behaviorists (themselves following in the economists' wake) in the 1950s and 1960s. By the time of the publication of *Science: Servant or Master?* Morgenthau had determined that "good" science was the separation of truth from falsehood, an attempt to understand reality in a systematic and theoretical fashion. The failure of the "new" theories was that that they told nothing of "the real world" and perpetuated through their language the metaphysics of utopianism: "much of the social sciences ends up in a kind of secularized Talmudism, an afunctional social game with methodology and terminology accessible only to the initiated . . . irrelevant for the systematic, theoretical knowledge of a truth worth knowing."[15] Truth, the most important of concepts for Morgenthau, was to be found not in formulae, but in the prudential judgment that originates in philosophy and history.

Truth and Theory

For Morgenthau, the essential task of political science is to isolate the truth of political experience: as truth is the transcendent value that gives science meaning. This task is not easy, however, as "[w]hat parades for truth in matters political is but a delusion of self and of others . . . masking interests of class and the desires of the self," and the role of the theorist is to determine what is and what is not truth.[16] It is a recurring feature of the works of Morgenthau that he identifies the problematization of the concept of truth. The end of metaphysical certainty as a consequence of the breakdown of the grand structures of rationalism in the nineteenth century was the source of this problematization. The effect of Rousseau's, Nietzsche's, Marx's, Kierkegaard's, and Freud's works was to render the received systems of thought empty, relegated to the position of mere ritualistic incantations, ideological justifications, and rationalizations.[17]

The "problem" of truth is further complicated by the relationship between the observer and the observed as "the perspective of the observer determines what can be known and how it is to be understood. In consequence the truth of political science is of necessity a partial truth."[18] If Morgenthau is aware of the partial nature of political truth, what status are we to accord to his own "truth"? Throughout his career, Morgenthau operated on the assumption that "the truth of political science is the truth about power, its manifestations, its configurations, its limitations, its implications, its laws."

If truth is socially conditioned by the perspective of the theorist, then surely the same applies to Morgenthau's version of the truth? Morgenthau, however, states that his truth is universal and valid for all times and circumstances. The apparent contradiction is resolved by Morgenthau's identification of an eternal "objective" truth of political science as otherwise the insights of a Jeremiah, Plato, or Hobbes would be meaningless to the contemporary world. The fact that these "truths" are accessible to us proves their "objectivity" and thus escapes the "relativist dilemma" at the heart of political science. Morgenthau's preference for political cynicism blinds him to the fact that his position is untenable, if he is to accord truth to one set of philosophers then he must accord truth to the others. Morgenthau recognizes this in *Politics among Nations* when he casts the thinkers of civilization against the philosophers of power. Political science must uncover the truth behind the ideological postures. The truths are perennial, but the methods by which these truths are uncovered and articulated are specific to that particular time and place, it is the lag between political reality and political theorization that accounts for the inaccurate analysis of political society by political theory.[19]

The discovery of truth is dependent upon the form of theory employed: only a pragmatic theory derived from the observation of political action (which is ontologically prior to political thought in Morgenthau's conception of the relationship between political thought and action) can hope to predict the future course of events and by being conscious of the past and present condition of political being uncover the objective truth of political experience. The antinomian counterpart of this form of theory is ideology, an intellectual refuge from the "metaphysical shock" of the collapse of the grand narratives of Enlightenment rationality. Faced with the existential crisis of his own absurdity, Man recreates reality by subjecting it to rationalized, abstract thought.[20] In order to achieve truth, Man must recognize that he is fundamentally in conflict with reality. It is only when the conflict becomes apparent that Man has the capability of discovering truth: the condition of suffering, therefore, is the precondition of genuine consciousness, which in turn is necessary for the discovery of truth.

Politics among Nations: Enunciating a Realist Theory of Power

Morgenthau's disparate writings on the philosophy of knowledge, theory, and the political experience of IR are distilled in his most famous work, *Politics among Nations. The Struggle for Power and Peace*. The purpose of this book is to uncover the "objective truth" (in Morgenthau's meaning of the word) of IR through the discovery of underlying principles that can make political activity "knowable" through scientific theory. It is in *Politics among Nations* that Morgenthau makes clear his philosophy of power and the logic of its operation in the international environment. The combination of a rational outline and the attempt to draw lessons from the historical record typify the approach of Morgenthau in *Politics among Nations*. There are a number of problems with Morgenthau's method that originate in his initial proposition that IR (in the political sense) may be contained within a theoretical framework of six fundamental principles. This is discussed in the following sections.

The Six Principles of Political Realism

Morgenthau has a precise idea of the purpose of theory, which is "to bring order and meaning to a mass of phenomena which without it would remain disconnected and unintelligible." This is a revealing statement of intent by Morgenthau as it demonstrates that he is confident of his ability to uncover a method of understanding IR by the deployment of theoretical strategies and the capacity of language to bring order to the chaos of IR. Crucially, such a theory must be "consistent with the facts and with itself."

The theoretical space in *Politics among Nations* is demarcated between two political positions, liberalism and Realism, cast them in terms of antitheses of each other. The synthesis of utopianism and Realism, so important to Carr, is left relatively unexplored by Morgenthau in this phase of his analysis of international theory, when he does so it is generally in terms of the failures of both to provide answers to the fundamental problem of IR, and that of international conflict. In "The Machiavellian Utopia," he clearly identifies the failure of existing theory, both liberal and Realist. The Wilsonian vision of the League of Nations was heroic and futile, while the framers of the United Nations at Dumbarton Oaks (dismissed as the "visionless epigones" of Machiavelli) are criticized for producing a solution less heroic, but no less futile.[21] Prior to *Politics among Nations*, Morgenthau was content to limit his analysis to a critique of IR theory and practice, rather than to propose a theory of IR.

The six principles of Realism arise out of the initial juxtaposition of Realism and liberalism in Morgenthau's opening theoretical salvo. The battleground in this war of theories is clearly marked. On one side is liberalism, which is essentially rational and has as its aim further progress toward a moral political order. Its foundations are universally valid, abstract principles reasoned deductively from an a priori basis. It takes as its foundational assumption the essential "goodness" of human nature: the failure of the social order is a failure to live up to rational standards, and the means by which to create order is through education, reform, and occasionally coercive violence. On the other side lies Realism, which Morgenthau characterizes as rationally imperfect, a fault that is the result of human imperfection. The world is not composed of a single vision, but is instead composed of a multiplicity of opposing and conflicting interests. Moral principles, far from being universal, can never be fully realized and can at best attain an approximate morality based on the lesser evil rather than the greater good. Underpinning the Realist worldview is a form of reason based not upon the a priori, but rather the uncertain and imprecise knowledge gained from historic precedent. Importantly, Morgenthau maintains that to improve the world one must work with the forces that result from the imperfections of human nature rather than against them.[22] Morgenthau does not state that the Realist school is better than the liberal, but this is the implication that may be derived from his singling it out as the theory that is concerned "with human nature as it actually is, and with the historic processes as they actually take place." The purpose of the contrast is to reinforce in the reader's mind the pragmatic and grounded nature of Realist theory in contrast to the abstract, rationalistic theorization of international politics already dismissed by Morgenthau in *Scientific Man versus Power Politics*.

In what seems a peculiar decision, Morgenthau declares that it is not his intention to attempt a "systematic exposition" of the political philosophy of Realism, but rather to restrict his analysis of Realism to the presentation of six principles, "which have been frequently misunderstood."[23] The first and most important of these principles concerns the very nature of human knowledge about political behavior. Political Realism, according to Morgenthau, states that politics is governed by "objective" laws that have their roots in human nature, which he claims has remained the same since the classical civilizations of India, China, and Greece first attempted to analyze them. This statement has implications for regard to the type of theory that Morgenthau is trying to create. The first of these is that the theory is based upon the assumption that human nature and the laws that are the corollary of human nature are immutable. This is necessarily a determinist argument and implies that the mode of analysis is essentially restricted to the single element of human causation and its effect on the international environment.

The concept of law is important in the overall scheme as it posits the notion that human behavior in the context of political society is fixed.

The assumption that laws can be discovered that may be employed to govern the realm of political knowledge is indicative of Morgenthau's intention to create a unitary truth of political existence. Morgenthau is aware that the laws of politics are difficult to conceive and express, "Realism . . . [m]ust believe in the possibility of developing a rational theory that reflects, however imperfectly and one-sidedly, these objective laws."[24] Morgenthau is caught between that which is being observed and the imperfect nature of human observation, rationalization, and expression. He attempts to circumvent the problem of theoretical relativism (a fault he denounced in Carr) by creating a distinction between truth and opinion. Truth is both objective and rational and is supported by evidence and reason. The truth of a theory is determined by the dual test of reason and experience—it is reason that "gives" meaning to political fact. Political knowledge, expressed in terms of a political theory of IR, is gained from the product of testing rational hypotheses against actual facts. Morgenthau restates his position on eternal truth in a piece originally written for the *Encyclopaedia Britannica*:

> The consistency of patterns beneath the variety of historic manifestations makes both historic understanding and theoretical analysis of International Relations possible . . . By detecting in the International Relations of different cultures and historic periods identical responses to identical challenges, we are able to develop certain theoretical propositions about International Relations that are true regardless of time and place.[25]

Morgenthau attempts to combine two forms of knowledge in his search for the political truth of IR, a rational approach based upon his conception of science as systematic and coherent theory and a peculiar reading of history that may (for want of a better phrase) be described as a historico-empiricicalist approach. The problem here is one of conceptual "fit": if the form of the theory is based on rational hypotheses, how can it stand the rigors of falsification in the empirical "reality" of historical events?[26]

Throughout *Politics among Nations*, Morgenthau cites countless examples in support of his theory of IR, but seems unaware that this data is in fact specific not general, one example that contradicts his theory of international politics is enough to falsify his assumptions of the "timelessness" and immutability of human behavior—except at a level that expresses everything and nothing. It is this lack of a truly rational outline to history that ultimately convinced him of the need to disown Realism as he had expressed it in *Politics among Nations*.

Morgenthau makes no effort to contextualize the writings of Thucydides, Machiavelli, Kautilya, Hobbes, and others, he merely subsumes them within his concept of the notion of truth to which he subscribes. The decision to use them is made on an a posteriori basis: the writings are used in an instrumental fashion in that they validate Morgenthau's particular theory of truth rather than being seen as products of specific time and place. Morgenthau therefore approaches history with the intention of discovering his truth rather than with the intention of allowing the texts to be understood in terms of their argument. This may be useful "social knowledge" in terms of the development of Morgenthau's vision of Realism, but it is a misunderstanding of the nature of history.[27]

Truth and Power

Morgenthau had a complex understanding of power that was rooted in an existential understanding of man's "loneliness." Man turns to the lust for power as a consequence of the failure of man to achieve a universal love.[28] The second of the six principles asserts that the concept of interest expressed as power is the "main signpost that helps political Realism to find its way." This idea of the pursuit of power (expressed as the national interest) as the fundamental reality of politics is the link between the conceptual world of IR and the world of practical politics. It is this universal lust for power that creates a logic that gives form to international theory, the initial theoretical point that serves to encapsulate international politics within the logic of Morgenthau's worldview. Without this central concept, a science of international politics would be impossible, states Morgenthau, as it is this concept that allows the theorist to bring "systematic order to the political sphere . . . and thus makes the theoretical understanding of politics possible."[29] Morgenthau's conception of theory in *Politics among Nations* is based upon an almost Platonic notion of rational (as opposed to rationalist) foreign policy being "good" foreign policy—Morgenthau makes a point of highlighting the inevitable gap between a rational foreign policy and foreign policy as it is actually practised.

The concept of national interest provides the actor in international politics with the necessary rationale for his actions, what Morgenthau refers to as the "rational discipline" that in turn creates "that astounding continuity in foreign policy [which makes] . . . foreign policy appear as an intelligible rational continuum, by and large consistent with itself, regardless of the different motives, preferences, and international and moral qualities of successive statesmen." This belief in the immutability of foreign policy objectives is prominently stressed throughout *Politics among Nations*, with the persistence of Russian imperialism, from the Tsarist to Soviet eras being the prime example of this "astounding continuity." It is the identification and articulation of the concept of interest expressed as power that creates the possibility of theorization.[30] Already, the reality and the theory of international politics are being expressed in terms of the theorist's ability to create a constrained model of the international sphere.

The virtuality of this knowledge is implicitly recognized by Morgenthau in his use of the phrase "appear as an intelligible rational vacuum." In a piece of theoretical *leger de main*, Morgenthau separates political Realism from political reality (its supposed *raison d'etre*) by introducing the contingencies of history as a deviation from the "rational course" of international politics (following one of his earliest influences, Max Weber). Democracy in particular is singled out as an impairment of rational foreign policy, as the need to garner support from the populace (characterized by their emotions) inhibits rational diplomatic action. This rational action requires a distinction between the desirable and the possible. In essence, this is a conservative position in that Morgenthau privileges the possible (i.e., the present state of affairs) over the desirable. This is a further narrowing of Morgenthau's theoretical horizons and serves to further limit his Realism to the descriptive realm. There is also an implicitly static moral position inherent in this evocation of the preservation of the status quo as the rational purpose of international politics. The deviations from "rational" (i.e., conservative) foreign policy in the modern world are such that Morgenthau proposes investigation into the possibility of creating a "counter-theory of irrational politics, a kind of pathology of international politics."[31] This psychopathological theory of IR would have at its core the analysis of the refusal of the modern political elite to recognize the flaws in their theoretical understanding and the substitution of the abstract a priori model for empirical reality.

The function of Realist political theory is to highlight the rational *essence* of a policy, to "present the theoretical construct of a rational foreign policy which experience can never completely achieve." This is further evidence of Morgenthau's seeming inability to recognize the disjunction between his stated aim of relying on the empirical for evidence as the basis for theoretical form and his reification of what amounts to a rationalist theory. The peculiarly Weberian nature of Morgenthau's worldview is best exemplified by his statement on the proper relationship between theory and reality: "reality, being deficient . . . must be understood and evaluated as an approximation to an ideal system of balance of power."[32]

The third principle of political Realism is a further statement on the nature of interest and power. Interest is, according to Morgenthau, "an objective category which is universally valid" but with an unfixed meaning. The actual interest is determined according to the specific historical and cultural context in which foreign policy is formulated, which includes all possible variations of policies. For Morgenthau, power is concerned with the control of man by man and is that which can be used to compel acquiescence to the controller's will. In what seems a nod toward Freudian interpretations of social interaction, Morgenthau claims that power is present in all social relationships that revolve around this submission/domination principle, including IR.[33] The means by which interests are gained, power, is also determined by the political and cultural environment in which it can be exercised. This can lead to situations where material power is usurped by the contingent situations of history, Morgenthau refers to this as the impotence of power. In two important essays, he outlines the irrelevance of the status of the United States as a superpower. The first of these concerns the inability of the United States, to use its plenitude of military power to prevent Cuba from pursuing a foreign policy inimical to the interests of the United States, nor can it enforce behavior more in accordance with its own principles from its allies. In addition to these difficulties, in the wider sphere of geopolitics, the U.S. policies with regard to the USSR were circumscribed by the nature of its relationship with West Germany. U.S. power was derived from its military force, sufficient to destroy the world, but all the more unusable for that. Far from being a situation of submission/dominance, the U.S. satellites had become parasitic upon its power.[34]

So what is fixed and what is transitory in the political constellation drawn by Morgenthau? The examples used by Morgenthau are the operation of the balance of power and the primacy of the nation state as the ultimate point of reference in contemporary international affairs. The balance of power, says Morgenthau, is a perennial feature of all "pluralist" societies (which by definition includes the international society), yet the rules of its operation are subject to change. Contrary to later definitions of Realism, there is for Morgenthau no *permanent* logic of international anarchy in IR, as the balance of power could be transformed into a stable and peaceful system for the competing interests of nations, as the competing interests of parties in national politics have been institutionalized in the domestic sphere.[35] The nation state is also a transitory historical phenomenon, "bound to disappear in the course of history." Interest and power, not the system (i.e., the international society of states) or the unit (the state), are permanent features in the intellectual topography of political Realism. Any transformation of the international system that may take place is dependent upon a realization of the centrality of power in the achievement of change: the political Realist must work with the forces that dominate the political world in order to change it.

The vexed question of the relationship between power and morality is the subject of the fourth principle of political Realism. Again, Morgenthau applies his historico-empirical criteria to the selection of a moral course in

IR: political action must be conditioned not by an absolute moral scale, but rather upon the exigencies of the time and place in which an action takes place. Prudence, defined in terms of an ability to recognize the political consequences of a moral action and to act on the basis of political rationality is the foundation for a political ethics that serves the political Realist in his deliberations about the proper relationship between power and morality in international politics (in this Morgenthau would seem to be influenced by Machiavelli). Writing about the nature of political morality in the later work *In Defense of the National Interest*, Morgenthau explicitly rejected the false identification of the incommensurability of Realism and morality:

> The equation of political moralising with morality and of political Realism with immorality is itself untenable. The choice is not between moral principles and the national interest, devoid of moral dignity, but between one set of moral principles divorced from political reality, and another set of moral principles derived from political reality.[36]

With one eye on the quasi-Messianic ideological positions of the USSR (and, in a sly way, of the United States), the fifth principle denies the equation of the individual morality of a state (or actor) in international affairs with universal moral laws.[37] The only true guide to moral action in international politics is an honest awareness of the role played by interest and power in the international arena: by being able to judge our own actions in this light, shorn of ideological or moral pretence, one can begin to appreciate the motives of other actors in the international environment. This instrumentally rationalist approach is typical of Morgenthau's attempt to constrain the moral element of international politics within the political framework of Realism, affording little or no autonomy to morality in the conduct of IR. The sole guide to international conduct in Morgenthau's conception is one of moderation, gained not from a transcendent sense of ethics, but from rational self-interest and an awareness of the political consequences of one's own actions.[38]

The sixth principle of political Realism concerns the distinctiveness of political Realism, the nature of its objectives, and the knowledge that it provides. Although Realism has a "pluralistic" conception of politics, it nonetheless insists on subordinating other aspects of human behavior (the economic, legal, moral) to a place outside the center of analysis—the primacy of the political must be asserted. Again, Morgenthau dispenses with the historico-empirical theory of knowledge when it suits him, and claims that in order to understand one of the natures of man, one must study it in isolation from the others. He describes the necessity of "emancipation from other standards of thought" similar to that in economics (an attitude singularly lambasted by Carr in *The Twenty Years' Crisis*), as the "purpose of political Realism."[39]

Science, Theory, and System in Politics among Nations

Morgenthau's position on scientific endeavor in general is clear: "the natural aim of all scientific undertakings is to discover the forces underlying social phenomena and the mode of their operation." The scientific task of understanding IR is dependent upon recognizing the distinctiveness of the object of inquiry: international politics requires its own logic, divorced from the insights of recent history, international law, and political reform. Embracing a sociology of knowledge, Morgenthau is anxious to stress the contingent and relative nature of political knowledge: "the observer is surrounded by the contemporary scene with its ever shifting emphasis and changing perspectives." Morgenthau's solution to this is not to embrace the uncertainty of knowledge, but rather to ground it in both the historic-empirical bedrock of historical precedent and a belief in the "perennial qualities of human nature."

The primary difficulty in creating theoretical understanding of international politics is the question of the ambiguity of the events analyzed, as these events are both singular and unrepeatable. They can only be understood according to Morgenthau in terms of their similarity to previous events in analogous circumstances. Morgenthau posits social forces not simply as the cause of these events, but also as the reason for their similarity: under his logic similar forces produce similar results. Social forces in turn are the product of human nature, which is revealed as the engine that drives IR.

The primary tool for the explication of foreign policy identified by Morgenthau is that of historical analogy. Morgenthau is aware of the difficulty of using this method, in particular he is perturbed by the condition of knowledge that results from the use of historical analogy. Morgenthau is particularly troubled about whether or not the knowledge gained is specific to individual instances or part of a general pattern. Following the logic of his argument about social forces being the manifestation of human nature, deterministically the latter must be the case, but Morgenthau casts doubt upon this by asserting, "the answer is bound to be tentative and subject to qualifications. The facts from which the answer must derive are essentially ambiguous and subject to continuous change."[40] Prediction and prescription become impossible in the moot zone of "tendencies" of international politics: the imprecision of political knowledge can only be mitigated by knowledge of analogous situations in the past, it cannot be remedied by it as unforeseen consequences may invalidate any attempt to forecast the political future.

Morgenthau seeks to integrate these social forces into his theory of IR. If the units of the system are nations, the balance of power is the system in which these units operate. This, in essence, is a rationalization of irrational (though coherent) behavior—the operation of these monadic social forces reduced to the simple level of the struggle for power, a uni-cause, single-unit modelized system of description, the mirror image of the theory derided by Morgenthau in *Scientific Man versus Power Politics*. Morgenthau's pursuit of the single cause and single end of political behavior has blinded him, at this stage at least, to the possibilities inherent in an emancipatory discourse of politics. He has become the inverse of Marcuse's *One Dimensional Man*, and is equally incapable of seeing beyond the confines of the theoretical space in which he has closed himself by the adoption of a uni-perspective.

Systematizing International Relation: The Balance of Power

The purpose of all political activity is, according to Morgenthau, the pursuit of power. This being the case, the obvious implication of politics among nations is that they pursue power in the international environment. The social force that determines political activity, the basic bio-psychological drive within human nature is the *animus dominandi*, the desire to dominate. For Morgenthau, power is a zero–sum phenomenon, the actors in the international system must deprive one another of their power in order to add it to their own—apart from the temporary expediency of alliances, power cannot be shared. Politics is simply a form of institutionalized and socially acceptable oppression, both domestically and internationally. The example that he uses is the bourgeois revolution of the eighteenth and nineteenth centuries, which merely replaced one system of oppression with another.[41]

The struggle for power then must be based on one of two principles, the preservation of the status quo or imperialism, which has as its ultimate goal the replacement of the balance of power with hegemony. These principles have the effect of polarizing the international system into pro–status quo or anti–status quo powers, thus constituting the primary motor and motive of international politics.[42] In an attempt to present a wider conception, Morgenthau presents a four-point description of the balance of power as:

1. A policy aimed at the achievement of a certain objective, that is, the preservation of the status quo.
2. The description of an actual state of affairs.
3. A description of the international system in which there is an approximately equal distribution of power.
4. Any distribution of power.

These four conceptual parameters create the theoretical identification of the balance of power as the inevitable and stabilizing element of a society of sovereign states.[43] The attendant logic of the balance of power is quite simple: its operation is based upon the desire for domination and the means by which to achieve this domination:

> This balancing of opposing forces will go on, the increase in the power of one nation calling forth an at least proportionate increase in the power of the other . . . until one nation gains or believes it has gained a decisive advantage over the other. Then either the weaker yields to the stronger or war decides the issue.[44]

This *in nuce* is the systemic logic of IR for Hans Morgenthau. The international system is provided with a "precarious stability," always on the edge of disaster. The operation of the balance of power is characterized by certain procedural logics—the divide and rule logic of Realism, the compensation logic of the *quid pro quo*, and the need for armaments, which are essential for the equality necessary for the maintenance of the status quo, but which are in turn inherently destabilizing. This analysis of the balance of power allows for a Realist interpretation of alliances: they are in short based upon a community of shared interests, nations cooperate in order to benefit from the pooling of their resources.[45]

The problem with the balance of power is its instability, which ensures that its operation is less than ideal. The structures of balances of power are important in that their cohesion, both in terms of the units and the aims of the units involved, is central to the operation of the balances. In the eighteenth century (often taken as exemplary by Morgenthau), the balance of power operated according to the amoral pursuit of power without reference to a wider ideological struggle; the balance of power was seen as a game, the purpose of which was advancement of the national interest on the chess board of Europe.[46] The European balance of power, so long the most important, had become in the twentieth century merely a theater of a greater global balance of power between ideological opposites, the United States and the USSR. It is important to note that the operation of a balance of power is maintained in international politics whether or not there is a local, nonideological, agreed system such as the European balance of power metaphor of the eighteenth century and the larger-scale ideological power balancing of the cold war. Systems, regimes, and political cultures may change, but the logic of international conflict expressed in terms of the interests of the powers involved remains the same in Morgenthau's theoretical treatment of these themes.

The balance of power is itself a problematic concept, according to Morgenthau, due to its origins within the rationalistic *zeitgeist* of the late-eighteenth-century Enlightenment. It is simply a serviceable metaphor, derived from the scientific discourse of mechanics. At the heart of the metaphor is a desire to picture the universe as a rationally ordered sphere: society mirroring the observable rules of motion inherent in the physical universe, in short a mechanization of the political world. Evincing his intellectual debt to Nietzsche, this metaphor of the balance of power merely serves to disguise the true nature of international politics, which is the will to power and the need for domination. The power and attraction of the balance of power metaphor is so deeply rooted in the modern mind's conception of the physical world that it results in the balance of power idea assuming "a reality and a function that it actually does not have, and therefore tends to disguise, rationalise, and to justify international politics as it actually is."[47] Such is the fragility of the balance of power as a system of IR; it falls apart in the absence of a common moral commitment to equilibrium and civilizational standards:

> Where such a consensus no longer exists or has become weak and is no longer sure of itself, as in the period starting with the partition of Poland and ending with the Napoleonic Wars, the balance of power is incapable of fulfilling its functions for international stability and national prosperity.[48]

In contemporary theoretical parlance, Morgenthau is aware of the social construction of political reality.[49] He uses the diplomatic culture of Enlightenment Europe as a perfect example of this:

> Everybody took it for granted that the egotistical motives that animated his own actions drove all others to similar actions. It was then a game of skill and luck as to who would come out on top. International politics became indeed an aristocratic pastime, a sport for princes, all recognising the rules of the game and playing for limited stakes.[50]

Moral and political consensus and the awareness of a common civilizational heritage then are unmasked as the silent though essential guarantors of the balance of power. The complex relationship between these elements and the "limitless lust for power" is the central relationship in Morgenthau's theory of IR.

The Reaction against Power: Morality, Law, and Civilization

Morgenthau is anxious to place the balance of power within the wider context of Western philosophy, in doing so he revisits the idea of the "curious dialectic" of power and morality that he first identified in *Scientific Man versus Power Politics*. Power and morality are effectively juxtaposed: "the very threat of a world where power reigns not only supreme, but without rival, engenders that revolt against power which is as universal as the aspiration for power itself." Far from being an aspect of power as in the works of Carr, for Morgenthau, morality is the dualistic counterpart, the means of salvation, from the lust for power. The great normative systems that express themselves through moral statements, mores, and law are designed to keep power politics in check. This is perhaps the most important difference between Morgenthau and Carr and explains the attack on Carr in *World Politics*— Carr's genuinely inductive, pragmatic approach could not allow him to view the world in anything other than relativist terms. Morgenthau, seeking a transcendent ethic, has to erect a morality against the dark force of the *animus dominandi*, has to embrace the moral aspect of human nature as the source of a theoretical corrective to the lust for power.[51] Morgenthau wants to use the language of historical empirical reality, but needs the grand theoretical form of dualism in order to justify his vision of world order.

This battle for hearts and minds plays itself out across the centuries, with the prophets of power Machiavelli and Hobbes counterposed by Augustine and Locke, "potent forces" in the promotion of Western civilization. The failure of Nietzsche, Hitler, and Mussolini demonstrates the strength of the irenistic traditions that seeks to "eliminate, at least to regulate and restrain the power drives that otherwise would either tear society apart or deliver the life and happiness of the weak into the arbitrary will of the powerful."[52] Morality is not a factor in the social world of politics and economics, rather it is to be understood as a form of social logic that underlies their operation, "limiting the choice of ends and means and delineating the legitimate sphere of a particular branch of action altogether."[53]

What we call civilization is in a sense nothing but the automatic reactions of the members of a society to the rules of conduct by which that society endeavors to make its members conform to certain objective standards, "to restrain their aspirations for power, and to domesticate and pacify them in all socially important respects."[54] In the domestic sphere this has led to a more stable society, but the international society (sketchily drawn by Morgenthau) is a much less stable and regulated environment. International morality is an even vaguer concept, which is only intermittently applied and successful: with his entrenched conservatism coming to the fore, Morgenthau locates the breakdown of international society in the dismantling of aristocratic diplomatic culture as a result of the atomization of political order in the eighteenth and nineteenth centuries.

Despite the weaknesses of these concepts, Morgenthau's unmasking of mores and norms of behavior as central to the maintenance of the balance of power system is crucial to an understanding of his emancipatory prophecy of international transformation working with the forces of Realism rather than against them.

Realism and Change in International Relations: The Morgenthau Contribution

Characteristically, the conservative Morgenthau resents the revolutionary forces that he maintains are threatening the overthrow of Western civilization:

> The three great revolutions of our age—the moral, political and technical— have this in common: they support and strengthen each other and move in the same direction—that of global conflagration . . . Their coincidence in time and their parallel development aggravate the threat to the survival of Western civilisation which each of them carries independently.[55]

Unlike Carr, who welcomes revolution as a necessary part of the historical progression of mankind, Morgenthau laments the revolutionary impulse. In many respects his attempt to produce a theory of political change are designed to counteract the revolutionary impulse. This is seen in the international sphere in the conflict between status quo and imperialist powers as the motive force ("the dynamics") of historic processes.[56] The management of this fundamental conflict of interests is the ultimate task of IR. Liberal solutions such as disarmament and collective security are dismissed for ignoring the realities of international politics. Men have arms, Morgenthau points out, because they fight, not the other way around. Collective security is singled out for the flawlessness of its logic, but that logic is dependent upon international politics being conducted in a vacuum and is often contrary to rational self-interest. Collective security, states Morgenthau, far from preventing war merely led to the globalization of localized conflicts, as attempts to use it for peace were either unsuccessful or actually precipitative of war. Law is summarily dealt with as an inappropriate response to political problems: the international legal system is predisposed toward the status quo and is systemically bound to the powers that constitute international legal bodies.[57] Justice cannot be achieved at the international level as there exists no agreement on the common good. Taking the UN as his example, he highlights the disparity between the rhetoric of the UN and the reality of its power distribution. Even the rhetoric of the UN is highly circumscribed by the necessity of not imposing a block on the effective rule of the Security Council—"nowhere in the main body of the Charter is there a definition of, or reference to, a substantive principle of justice." This is explained by Morgenthau in terms of the persistence of the diplomatic system as the primary form of international activity: the system of diplomacy had mutated but the logic of Realism remained intact, with the ideal of the UN and League of Nations being subverted by political necessity. Morgenthau claims that the eclipse of the General Assembly and the secretary general by power politics are proof of the intractability of the problem rather than of its possible solution.[58] The problem is that the range of interests embodied in an international organization are simply too wide to be bridged—"conflict . . . resolves itself into diametrically opposed standards of judgement and action, which virtually incapacitate the international organisation."[59]

Putative solutions to the problem of international order, such as the world state and the world community, are also dismissed as unachievable chimera. The world state is described as contrary to the will of the nations that it would replace; the world community, a prerequisite for the world state, is in turn an unlikely scenario with bodies such as UNESCO described as having the wrong analysis of the situation: cultural awareness in itself could contribute nothing to world order, as it ignored the fact that the history of the West was littered with wars between likeminded nations. While recognizing the novelty of the European political bodies and NATO, Morgenthau wondered to what extent they were merely aspects of a modified traditional alliance and the possible success of the eradication of the national interest within Europe and in particular the experiment of attempting to control German hegemony by absorption.[60]

In opposition to these attempts to recast world order, Morgenthau posits the alternative: the retention and reinvigoration of the diplomatic system as the means to achieve international harmony. Diplomacy is described as "the instrument of peace through accommodation." Diplomacy as the art of international governance requires awareness of how and when to use the three means of threat of force, compromise, and persuasion. The conduct of diplomacy, it would seem, is governed by rational self-interest (the absence of which was highlighted as the major failing of the liberal approaches to the question of world order). The diplomat must achieve four tasks: determine objectives according to the capabilities of power; must be able to take into account the aims of other powers; the power must create policy based on the extent of the competing aims of its own objectives and other powers; finally, diplomacy must establish the correct means for the achievement of policy objectives.[61] There are, states Morgenthau, two varieties of diplomacy, one public and crusading, the other private and business like. The operation of diplomacy in the public sphere, in this case in a parliamentary context, is ultimately counterproductive as it merely serves to poison the atmosphere in which diplomats work. Progress toward a peaceful world cannot be achieved, argues Morgenthau, until the traditional model of private diplomatic practice is restored.[62]

The Redundancy of Simple Power Politics

In the first chapter of the book, I examined ways in which Morgenthau challenged the primacy of the nation state as the ultimate actor in international politics. As the cold war progressed and the nature of post–World War Two *International Relations* became clearer, Morgenthau began to recast Realism in such a way as to embrace, rather than resist change. Morgenthau still considered the direction in which international politics were heading in a pessimistic fashion, but undaunted by this, remained committed to a social science based on the principle of engaging with real problems as they occurred in the social reality of the international arena.

The cold war forced Morgenthau to engage with more radical notions such as the prospect of political organization in the aftermath of a nuclear war. Nuclear weapons had effected a new reality in IR as the relationship between the use of violence and the attainment of rational foreign policy objectives had been removed by the introduction of weapons of total destruction, the use of which would be a "suicidal absurdity."[63] The three revolutions, in morality, politics, and technology, had effected a major change in the superstructure of the international society. The ultimate casualties of this revolution were the notion of sovereignty and the nation state itself. Interpreting the technological innovation of the atom bomb as a new phase of history, Morgenthau stated that political theory was lagging behind existence in "a dream world" that failed to take account of the new dispensation in IR.[64]

This lag between theory and technological and political experience of reality was a recurrent theme in Morgenthau's later works, especially those of the 1970s. By this stage Morgenthau was convinced that one of the prerequisites of the survival of Man was being conscious of the fact that our modes of thought and action belong to an age that has been left behind by technological development.[65] From evidence provided by his former student, David Fromkin, it would appear that he suspected that his own thought, at least that of *Politics among Nations*, should be placed in this category of redundancy. The world and the philosophy that underpinned *Politics among Nations* must have seemed to him to be fading into another age by the end of his life: the system it described of diplomats working in a system still dominated by the primacy of the political relationship between nation states had been eclipsed by the prospect of nuclear war and the reality of energy crises undermining the international political system. The failure of the American policy elites to respond rationally to the Communist threat, and to neglect the national interest by pursuing war in Vietnam made him question the nature of politics.[66] If the rational outline of politics was incapable of providing an ideal type from which to analyze "deficient" reality, then the style of theorization that Morgenthau had employed in *Politics among Nations* was inadequate.

According to Fromkin, the influence of the "brilliant, mad" Gustav Ichheiser's attempted development of an irrational theory of politics, in which paranoia, misunderstanding, and the irrational pervade the political sphere forced Morgenthau to reconsider the assumption of rationality in politics. This combination of an epistemological alternative at least as compelling as his own, and the close approximation of the U.S. foreign policy to irrational modes of action in the 1970s resulted in a dejected Morgenthau concluding that he should discard his model of IR.[67]

The closing statement on the first phase of his intellectual development in Weimar Germany seems apt as an epitaph for Morgenthau's career as a whole: "[T]he experience of disillusionment . . . is virtually coterminous with life itself, consciously lived . . . empirical reality endlessly denies the validity of our aspirations and our expectations."[68]

But despite this disillusionment, Morgenthau eschewed fatalism and clings to the possibility of the mind illuminating Plato's cave, eventually leading toward the truth of a transcendent reality.

What we get is an enigma compounding the riddle. What remains is a searching mind, conscious of itself and of the world, seeing, hearing, feeling, thinking, and speaking—seeking ultimate reality beyond illusion.[69]

CHAPTER 5

Nuancing Realism: Martin Wight, Power Politics, and International Society

The purpose of this chapter is to examine the international theory of Martin Wight. The depictions of Wight as a Grotian (Bull and Dunne) or as a Christian moralist (Epp) are contrasted with an alternative reading of Wight's works. I suggest that the basis of Wight's theory of international society is essentially Realist. This chapter does not claim that Wight was a Realist *tout court*, as in the paradigmatic representation, but that his theory of an international society rests on a Realist foundation. As Wight was anxious to stress, the three traditions that he used to navigate the international were distinct but interweaving; nonetheless, it is possible to look at the play of ideas in Wight's theory scheme, and to argue that Realist thought predominates within the three traditions, at least in how they apply to the balance of power and the nature of international society. Similar to Carr, there is an asymmetrical dialogue in which other theories interact with Realism, but it is the case that Realism dominates as the primary source of understanding the nature of international society.

This is not to say that Wight was exclusively a Realist in the way that Morgenthau deliberately proposed a theory of international politics that was intended to present a solely Realist position (albeit in contrast to a largely underrepresented idealism). Wight's technique was to create a hermeneutic circle (or perhaps spiral) in which the three traditions represented various attitudes to international politics. Yet this representation of three traditions does not necessarily imply that the three traditions were of equal importance: the current generation of English School theorists largely share the opinion that rationalism is the key theory of the three traditions—a *via media* between the cynicism of Realism and the impracticalities of revolutionism.[1] I believe that this approach is mistaken in that Martin Wight's professed personal "prejudices" toward the rationalist stream within the IR theory do not determine the relationship among Realism, rationalism, and revolutionism. Rather I propose that there is an internal logic in the relationship that is predominantly Realist, albeit a Realist logic penetrated and contextualized by its coexistence with the other traditions.

The first task of the chapter therefore is to reassess the role of Realism within the three traditions. I argue that the centrality of Realism in the three traditions is due to Wight's Christianity—by tapping into 2,000 years worth of Christian/Augustinian notions of sin and imperfection as the inheritance of Man, Wight could not but favor Realism as a political philosophy of IR. The second task is to assess the Realist nature of modern international society, an international society that owes its origins and its operation to the balance of power that was created in order to allow the contest for power within an agreed framework in preference to the untrammeled anarchy of pure power politics. This does not mean that international society is not an arena of power politics, merely that international society is a more complex arena than the Hobbesian war of all against all. The balance of power in Wight's theory again displays aspects of the different traditions, but again the predominant role is accorded to the Realist interpretation. The presence of both rationalist and Realist elements within his analysis of the balance of power provides further evidence of the intentionally unresolved nature of Wight's theory of international politics as a dialogue between the Machiavellian and Grotian standpoints (with the Kantians standing outside as occasional conversational partners). The asymmetry of the relationship is also clear in that it is the pursuit of power that creates anarchy but ultimately the development of order is seen as in the perceived interest of all powers concerned—Grotian institutions such as law and diplomacy owe their origins to Realist maneuvering, and can be, when perceived as necessary or desirable, disregarded in the Realist impulse toward power.

Wight's Realism

That Wight does not fit textbook definitions of Realism is beyond question—his theory scheme is far too complex to fit the various tripartite descriptions of Realism often proffered as a definition.[2] His system is one of the critical historical evaluation of attitudes to IR and employs separate categories in order to place the study of IR within a tripartite, genealogical interpretation—the Machiavellian/Realist, the Grotian/Rationalist, and the Kantian/Revolutionist.

Wight's system is dialogical, not axiomatic, and is described in his own words as follows:

> all I am saying is that I find these traditions of thought in international history dynamically interweaving, but always distinct, and I think they can be seen in mutual tension and conflict underneath the formalized ideological postures.[3]

It is important to note that the idea of cyclical progress and transformation typical of the dialectical form is absent from Wight's self-diagnostic appreciation of his work, all three traditions are distinct despite their interaction, and each remains distinct—there is no progressive synthesis here, nor any real evocation of a *via media*.

It is this potential for dialogue that distinguishes Wight's theory from the closed Realists, and in particular the attempts at creating a discrete science of IR associated with the "behavioral revolution" in American IR. Wight's system is a dialogue of three conversational poles, but that is not to say that one of the poles is not more dominant than the other. It is my contention that Wight recognized the predominance of the Machiavellian interpretation over the other two, and thus, in terms of his own theory set, he was indeed a Realist.

Representing Wight as Anything but Realist: Bull, Epp, and Dunne

The most important figure in our appreciation of Wight is Hedley Bull, a close colleague at the LSE, he wrote a number of pieces on Wight, including a memorial lecture and introductions to *Systems of States* and the revised edition of *Power Politics*. Bull's most well-known exposition of Wight's theoretical orientation was delivered at the second Martin Wight memorial lecture, claiming that if forced, he would place Wight in the Grotian or liberal tradition of IR.[4] According to Bull, Wight was drawn to the moderate nature of the Grotians, but Bull admits that Wight was also deeply influenced by the other two traditions, and that Wight's Grotianist tendencies were tempered by "partaking of the Realism of the Machiavellians, without cynicism, and of the idealism of the Kantians, without their fanaticism . . . a *via media*."[5] Bull then changes his position and states, "it would be wrong to force Martin Wight into the Grotian pigeonhole. It is truer to view him as standing outside the three traditions, feeling the attraction of each of them but unable to come to rest within any one of them."[6] This is in contradiction to an earlier statement in 1969 that Wight, singled out by Bull as "learned and profound," was, along with Morgenthau and Carr, a representative of the first generation of Realists.[7] Bull's detection of a shift in emphasis in Wight's work from 1946 onward has been attributed to his own Pauline conversion in the 1970s from the Realist to the rationalist wing of international theory: as Kenneth Thompson states—"the reader wonders whether the student occasionally introduces ideas of his own into interpretations of the master."[8]

Roger Epp also recognizes that Wight was different from the state-centric Realists of the American School because Wight was conscious of the important role played by ideology in determining IR. He claims that this was as a result of Wight's reading of international theory, which was top heavy with "a kind of philosophical idealism."[9] Epp points out that Wight, a conscientious objector during World War Two, never identified himself as a Realist in print.[10] Perhaps Epp's most important contribution to our understanding of Wight is his emphasis on the Christian element of Wight's thought. According to Epp, Wight was opposed to the neo-paganism of modernity and the idea of an accommodation between Christianity and "post-Christian civilization."[11] Epp then quotes a speech of Wight, regarding the moral shortcomings of the modern system of power politics, which is characterized by "the emancipation of power from moral restraints," in which the superpowers had carved up the world in an "inverted and terrifying fulfillment" of the biblical command to "go forth, multiply, fill the Earth and conquer it." Wight further condemns modernity by reference to four "demonic perversions," war, the state, nationalism, and revolution.[12]

Epp goes on to state that though *Power Politics* was a statement of "classical" Realism, this Realism was not at the expense of the "juridicial and cosmopolitan" opinions expressed in *Diplomatic Investigations* and *Systems of States*, and that in fact Realism was "denied a commanding position," in the dialogue envisioned by Wight. Wight, according to Epp, is not concerned with IR as "the realm of repetition and recurrence, but as the realm of persuasion."[13]

Within the current incarnation of the English School, Tim Dunne has emerged as a leading historian and a significant theorist in his own right, in the grouping that is coalescing around the many initiatives of Barry Buzan to present the English School as a "third way" in IR theory. Dunne's *Inventing International Society* presents Wight as a predominantly rationalist thinker and this representation is increasingly becoming canonical in IR. Although recognizing the Realism of a "thwarted pacifist" in Wight, it is Dunne's conviction that the later Wight became increasingly rationalist.[14]

There is of course a certain amount of evidence in support of this contention that Wight was a rationalist—a category apparently wide enough to accommodate Burke, Hamilton, Jefferson, Kant, and even Morgenthau.

Dunne also quotes Wight on his preference for rationalist thought: "I find my own position shifting round the circle. You will have guessed that my prejudices are Rationalist, but I find I have become more Rationalist and less Realist during the course of these lectures." Dunne also states that Wight's British Committee for the Study of International Politics paper, "Western Values in International Relations," indicates a "growing alignment with rationalism."[15]

Together, the contributions of Bull, Epp, and Dunne present a powerful *prima facie* case for the proposition that Wight was not a Realist, or that he experienced a conversion to rationalism in later life. While this may be true of Wight's personal beliefs (a result of the softening of his Christian pessimism perhaps), it does not affect the primacy of Realism with respect to rationalism and revolutionism in the context of the three traditions, and most importantly in relation to the nature of international society. In the same paragraph where he proclaims his personal rationalist "prejudice," Wight states that while rationalism was a civilizing factor, and revolutionism a vitalizing factor, Realism is a *"controlling disciplinary factor"* in international politics" (italics added).[16] In the three traditions, as in IR, the primary component, the controlling factor, is Realism. This is the mature Wight reiterating in a more contextualized form the position of the young Wight. The reason Realism is the controlling disciplinary factor lies in the problem of conflict and war: a phenomenon that Wight placed at the center of his lectures—"War is the central feature of International Relations, although in academic study this is sometimes forgotten." Wight goes on apologetically—"If this is too Realist a statement, one can say instead that war is the ultimate feature of International Relations."[17]

In a telling statement Wight defines IR as predominantly amoral or immoral, at the same time recognizing that morality plays a secondary role in the decision-making process:

> It would be foolish to suppose that statesmen are not moved by considerations of right and justice . . . But it is wisest to start from the recognition that power politics [understood as politics among powers] . . . are always inexorably approximating to power politics in the immoral sense, *and to analyse them in this light.*[18] (Italics added)

Thus, according to Wight himself, the Machiavellian conception of IR is usually correct and is the foundation for the correct study of IR. The desire for power, which in Wightian terms may be described as the ability of a state to engage in the activities of the world stage without the necessity of recourse to the involvement or mediation of another political entity (whether it be a state or a non-state actor) is the fundamental social reality of IR.[19]

As further evidence of Wight's Realist leanings (as he understood Realism—the Machiavellian attitude), we can compare his treatment of the three strands of international thought in *Diplomatic Investigations*, in the chapter entitled "Why Is There No International Theory?" Wight denounces the legalistic tradition, or *irenists*, as "hard to consider . . . as other than the curiosities of political literature."[20] Whereas he also dismisses the Realist tradition of the prehistory of the discipline, he isolates Machiavelli as the "tutelary hero of International Relations." Were Grotianism or Kantianism Wight's preferred "theoretical" positions, he would hardly cite Machiavelli's amoral political theory of power as the starting point of genuine IR.[21] In the same chapter, Wight provides the most telling example of his essentially Realist attitude; contrasting the progress of the domestic sphere with the international, he states that if Sir Thomas More and Henry IV were to examine the international politics of the twentieth century, they would recognize that "the stage would have become much wider, the actors fewer, their weapons more alarming, but the play would be the same old melodrama."[22] A key influence upon his thought he states is Burke: international politics *is* the "realm of recurrence and repetition," because it is the most "necessitous."[23] Progressive, Kantian theories in turn are treated as the natural, but ultimately flawed, response to the tyranny of Realism's use of historical analogy as a description and prescription in IR—"it is surely not a good idea for a theory of international politics that we shall be driven to despair if we do not accept it."[24] Both principles of natural and positivistic law are derided in the chapter for ascending "into altitudes of fiction through the multiplication of worthless agreements in the age of Mussolini and Hitler."[25] Wight concludes the chapter by isolating the distinguishing feature of international theory: "international theory is the theory of survival . . . (it) involves the ultimate experience of life and death, national existence and national extinction."[26] In so far as existing theory was appreciable to the truly objective observer, de Maistre's pessimism that *[l]a terre entière, continuellement imbibée de sang . . . sans mesure, sans relâche, jusqu'à la consommation des choses*, at least "deserved a mark over some other candidates for not misrepresenting the historical world."[27]

Free Will and Original Sin: A Christian Logic of Realism

Wight made reference to the depressing picture of international politics that he had drawn, but concluded, "we must start from the situation as it is, not the situation as we should dearly like it to be," before concluding that human history has been catastrophic, and that we have been forced back to a position where we have to accept the Christian interpretation of history, which has the "further, not inconsiderable, advantage of being in accordance with our historical experience."[28] The identification of the role of Christian pessimism to the theory scheme of Martin Wight is of crucial importance in understanding the complex Realism that issues from the fusion of politics and Christianity. One of his critics, Michael Nicholson, identifies the basic element of Wight's Christianity as it relates to political life: "[t]hrough folly, original sin, basic animal aggressive instincts or some other cause inherent in the human condition, mankind is doomed to misery."[29] In addition to the role of immoral man is the key role played by God in IR; for Wight, at the level of the divine, what matters is not the occasion of war, but rather to understand it as a consequence of God's Justice (if the war occurs) or of His mercy (if the war is averted). Free will is granted by God to man, but conditioned by man's natural propensity to immorality as a consequence of original sin, and acts as a paradoxical tool of God in the divinely ordered universe. Thus men are free to choose, but the results of their actions are in fact determined as a result of God's judgment—punitive or merciful.[30] As Milton's God described the revolting angels in *Paradise Lost*:

I formed them free, and free they must remain
Till they enthrall themselves: I else must change
Their nature, and revoke the high decree
Unchangeable, eternal, which ordained
Their freedom; they themselves ordained their fall.

The doctrine of original sin gave Wight a perfect starting point for the study of human motivation in international politics. Given the strictness of his religious beliefs, it would have been impossible for Wight to adopt anything but the most pessimistic attitude toward human nature; although as a responsible teacher he presented rationalist and revolutionist theories as to the nature of Man, as a Christian he could not ignore biblical pronouncements on Man as a corrupt entity.

Wight's Christian pessimism is the ultimate source of his Realist attitude and explains why the nature of IR is always approximating toward the immoral. For Wight, the immorality of man is the ultimate cause of international anarchy, the flawed system of flawed creators. In an article entitled "The Church, Russia and the West," Wight expands on this theme. The removal of any moral input in Western society in the last three centuries has created the conditions for the logical outcome of the anarchic balance of power system, in which the strength of powers increases as their number decreases, rendering the Earth into two mutually opposed camps. Wight expresses the logic of Realism in IR as a consequence of the nature of states: "Leviathan is a simple beast: his law is self-preservation, his appetite is for power." If left to themselves humans will inevitably bring about a third world war as the balance of power, for the means by which Mankind has, according to its own reason, ordered IR is "inherently unstable."[31]

Immorality, rooted in original sin, is ontologically prior to all other conditions in IR. Original sin links the two positions of Christianity and Realism. The role of the Christian thinker is to embrace Realism, not to disown it:

> It is the duty of Christians to analyse the secular situation with ruthless Realism, and without the timidity, distaste and self-deception that Communists attribute to bourgeois culture in decline. The Church was enjoined to cultivate the wisdom of the serpent as well as the simplicity of the dove . . . Ruthlessly Realistic analysis is not incompatible with hope, for hope is a theological, not a political virtue.[32]

Liberal notions of progress and advance in human affairs are described as unscriptural and contrary to the knowledge of the future revealed by Jesus at the Sermon on the Mount:

> [t]he notion that the Christian Era should be a period of the gradual perfection of men and society is the opposite of what we find in the New Testament . . . (Jesus) described the remainder of history in terms which suggested that it would be even more full of tumult and confusion, of wars and famines than what had gone before.[33]

Even in his theological writings, Wight recognized the importance of recognizing the existence and primacy of evil in human IR: he states that secular pacifists underestimate "the wickedness of men" and also that "[t]he amount of evil in the world remains pretty constant: and my refusal to fight will not obliterate the doctrines of *Mein Kampf* nor change the state of mind of its author.[34]

The doctrine of original sin is central to Wight's worldview as the ultimate source of the necessity of Realism. In order to account for this we have to make reference to the issue of Augustine's influence on Wight. Following Augustine, Wight differentiated between the City of God, which was perfect, and the City of Man, which was imperfect. Wight as a Christian believed in the eventual victory of the City of God, but this was after the end of history: Wight the political theorist recognized that the *saeculum* was of a very different order, and operated according to the rule of Man, not God, and thus had a different logic underpinning its relationships, one that was best understood as conceiving Man as a sinful and corrupted being and a slave to his passions, chief among them Greed and Anger. This conception of Man has important consequences for the IR system that he creates—the system is the flawed product of flawed creators. The best means to understand the international environment is to assume that it is, in Wight's words, "approximating towards the immoral," and the tradition associated with this assumption is Machiavellianism or (in Wight's conception at least) Realism.

Wight's understanding of international society is highly developed, and is dependent upon the interaction of ideas and politics in the transition from the medieval world to the modern: the development of a structure of international society from the Council of Constance to the cold war. This development is a result of three attitudes in conflict: the Machiavellian, the Grotian, and the Kantian. Truth is therefore perspective dependent rather than the conceptual reflection of an unchanging reality, as in Morgenthau's *Politics among Nations*. The attitudes merely serve to illuminate the dominant reasoning of a specific time and place, the political *zeitgeist* of a given era. Ideas and reality are linked by historical experience, hence Machiavelli produced the most insight into the relations between the city states of the Italian wars of the Renaissance, Grotius best expressed the political philosophy of the legalist peace movement of the period dominated by the Thirty Years' War, and Kant best expressed the notions of universalism and systemic transformation in the era of the French Revolution. All of these theoretical positions have had periods of dominance within the thought world of international society, but it is Realism that provides the key to understanding the underlying logic of this international society.

This is a very contextual Realism: a historically contextualized Realism, in the sense that Realist practices beg the emergence of Realist discourses, discourses that are themselves placed into theoretical context by the rationalists and revolutionists. Machiavelli is the "tutelary hero" of IR because in *The Prince* he recognized politics as a secular activity rather than a duty for an ideal archetype:

[I]t appears to me more proper to go to the real truth of the matter than to its imagination . . . for how we live is so far removed from how we ought to live, that he who abandons what is done for what ought to be done, will rather learn to bring about his own ruin than his preservation.[35]

Machiavelli's determination to create a *speculum princeps* that was based on the real, in turn provoked a series of responses, rationalist and revolutionist. Wight's invocation that "we must start from the situation as it is, not the situation as we should dearly like it to be," is a reiteration of Machiavelli's position and a statement of intent by Wight of the correct starting point of theory.

The Realism of International Society

Typically, Wight was unwilling to engage fully with the ramifications of his identification of the theory sets. Although allowing the reader to identify the Grotian subtext in his writings through the concept of international society in addition to the Realist analyses based upon the idea of international anarchy, neither *Anatomy of International Thought* nor *International Theory: The Three Traditions* attempts to come to grips with the social logic of what appears to be the paradoxical situation of a Grotian international structure based upon the institution of diplomacy and alliances operating a Realist logic based upon the principle of competition in international anarchy. The key to understanding the implicit relationship between the international society (which embodies Order, and to a degree, Justice) and international anarchy (which is created by the desire for Power and the potential for acquiring it) lies in an awareness of the importance of the role of the balance of power within international society.

The current English School is determined to downplay the Realist element of Wight's analysis of international society, but this does not seem to tally with Wight's emphasis upon international anarchy and the struggle for power as the foundation of international society. He recognizes in *Power Politics* that "[q]ualifications are necessary: there is a system of international law and there are international institutions to modify or complicate the workings of power politics. But it is roughly the case that . . . in international politics law and institutions are governed and circumscribed by the struggle for power. This indeed is the justification for calling international politics 'power politics' *par excellence*."[36] In this statement, Wight approximates Carr's position on the derivation of law from politics—politics understood as the pursuit of power. When Wight argues in *International Theory: The Three Traditions* that Realists do not believe in international society, he is arguing that Realists do not believe in a natural predisposition toward the social, he does however credit Hobbes with the discovery of a contracted and minimal international society based on the accommodation of interests. Wight's analysis of the UN as a Hobbesian IR system demonstrates that it is possible to speak of a Realist international society—albeit of a minimalist variety.[37] The problem of the existence of different truths about international society is resolved by Wight by stressing the "complementary" nature of Realist and rationalist truths about international society:

> it is possible that these truths, Realist and Rationalist, are complementary, not contradictory. On the Rationalist view, the role of force would then be simply to remedy the insufficiencies of custom; where the Realist says that custom gives a coating to acts of force, the Rationalist says that force steps in where custom breaks down.[38]

This amounts to an accommodation of Realism within the international society idea, not a repudiation of Realism. What Wight has achieved is a fusion of two "realities" of international society: the Realist and the rationalist. The operation of the balance of power as a Grotian institution and a Machiavellian impulse in international society further explores this idea of Realist/rationalist coexistent duality. In the supposedly Grotian repudiation of Realism, *Western Values in International Relations*, Wight demonstrates the secondary, epiphenomenal nature of the rationalist position in relation to the Machiavellian by the identification of a paradox in Burke's writings against the French Revolution:

> Is it fair to say that Burke's writings against the French Revolution illustrate a central paradox of the view of international society that he propounded, that its principles of legitimacy have been modified instead of being dissolved, only because men have been ready to fight that they should undergo no change at all? It is those who have died to prevent modification who have made possible a modification within limits that posterity can accept.[39]

The maintenance and continuance of international society, therefore, is dependent not upon the continuity of ideas that constitute it, but rather upon the power struggle between satiated and revisionist powers, for whom the ideas are part of the conflict. In any case, Wight's intention in *Western Values in International Relations* is to account for the emergence of modern Western notions of a positive ethicality in politics, rather than the identification of international society as a rationalist principle per se.

Moreover it should be pointed out that the category of Grotian is not reserved for those committed to a legal or formulistic understanding of international politics, for example, Hans Morgenthau, an archetypal Realist, is placed in the Grotian category in *International Theory: The Three Traditions*.[40] Grotianism is not simply a "Third Way" (although certainly there are thinkers who fall unambiguously into this category) of international thought, it is closer to a zone of ideational interaction and interlocution, where Realist, rationalist, and revolutionist ideas merge and diverge.

The Balance of Power: The Realist Foundation of International Society

The key to understanding this Heraclitean tension between the competing truth claims of Realist and rationalist theories of international society lies in the balance of power. Power lies at the center of both international society and international anarchy: Wight conceived of both conditions as aspects of political existence. The balance of power plays a key role in demonstrating the logic of Wight's theory scheme, with each of the traditions viewing it from a different angle. In the Grotian tradition, the balance of power is the rational pursuit of equilibrium in IR, stability is guaranteed by plurality of power within a system.[41] The Machiavellian approach emphasizes political analysis of the relationships inherent in a balance of power: in any balance of power there are those powers satisfied with the status quo and others who are dissatisfied. For the revolutionists, the term balance of power only reaffirms the authority of the satiated powers. By extension, those revolutionary powers that find their situation "irksome" are forced into an antagonistic stance by the reiteration of the correctness of the balance of power.[42]

The Realist understanding of the balance of power is more concerned with the distribution of power in an anarchical society, their analysis of the system is one in which nations are stratified in relation to their power: great powers, lesser powers, and superpowers. Wight termed this the pattern of powers and the ordering logic of this pattern "the balance of power."[43] For Wight the Realist concept of the balance of power "leads to considerations of military potential, diplomatic initiative and economic strength."[44] Yet the concept itself is amorphous, with the meaning of the metaphor changing over time: discovering timeless laws or concrete principles (à la Morgenthau), therefore, is difficult (if not impossible) to achieve—the truth about the effect and the nature of the balance of power, like that of international society, is contested. The dualism of Realism and rationalism is evident in Wight's attribution of both descriptive/analytical Realist aspects of the balance of power as well as its rationalist prescriptive characteristics to a rational system of IR—the foundation of international society.[45]

For the Grotians, according to Wight, "the balance of power had been a system of keeping international order." The balance of power therefore is at the core of international society, that system which Wight identified as most typical of the international political sphere based around nation states. International society as opposed to international anarchy is the embodiment of Wight's "second pattern" of international cooperation between states; for example, he cites the League of Nations as an attempt to create an international society based around a legal, institutionalized balance of power in an effort to make it "more rational, more reliable, and therefore more effectively preventive."[46] The alliance system, which organizes the powers of varying sizes into groups with shared interests (strategic, economic), creates an impulse toward order, which in turn creates the structures of the international society—diplomacy, international bodies, conferences, and so on, as an alternative to conflict, or an alternative arena for power contestation. The Italian wars of the Renaissance and the attendant development of the diplomatic system are classic examples of this development of an international society through the interaction of a Realist struggle for power creating the conditions for the emergence of systems of mediation of power.

In the Realist understanding of the balance of power, the defining concept is that of the hierarchy of power. This hierarchy has a determining effect upon the conduct of IR in that the position occupied by a power or state in the hierarchy determines whether it is a great, minor, or world power. It is also the primary determinant of how powers relate to one another: the failure of the League of Nations was that it did not recognize the primacy of power politics over the institutions of normative international society:

> An attempt had been made in 1919 to restrain the collective authority of the Great Powers within the forms of permanent membership of the Council of the League of Nations. The Great Powers soon threw off these constitutional trappings. Some did not join the League, some resigned from it and those who retained their membership found a greater common interest with the Great Powers outside than with the other members inside the League.[47]

Although the effect of the balance of power can be to create and preserve international society—the logic of its operation is derived from the struggle for power. In his historical analysis of the balance of power in *Diplomatic Investigations*, Wight examines the balance of power in terms of the systemic logic of anarchy. From this perspective, the balance of power, which is the precondition for the foundation of Grotian order in an international society, in its operation obeys a Realist logic; this logic is revealed in the successive interpretation of the balance of power, for example:

4. The principle of aggrandisement of the great powers at the expense of the weak.
5. The principle that our side ought to have a margin of strength in order to avert the danger of power becoming unevenly distributed.
6. (When governed by the verb "to hold") A special role in the maintaining of an even distribution of power.
7. (Ditto) A special advantage in the existing balance of power.
8. Predominance.

Each of these definitions points to the Realist logic of the balance of power as the pursuit of a national interest expressed in terms of power. "Aggrandisement," "margin of strength," "special advantage," and "predominance" within the balance of power and the international society all demand

Machiavellian policies in order to achieve these goals. To be sure, the balance of power was unstable, and could not achieve the goal of guaranteeing security; it could result in universal tyranny, but it is the ordering principle within anarchy, as Wight stated in one of his lectures:

> Hobbes saw so deeply into the nature of political life that now after three centuries, when the whirligig of time has brought round conditions similar to those he constructed in the logic of abstract fantasy, things happen much as he said they would.[48]

Conclusion: The Persistent Logic of Realism. Systemic Change, Realist Consistency

There is then a tension in the system of international society between the structural effect of cooperation and the anarchical logic of the units that compose this system. International society becomes ever more sophisticated in nature, with international bodies such as the EU, NAFTA, and MercoSur beginning to transcend the sovereignty *problematique* of the nation state system. But has the systemic logic of the balance of power, in which actors compete, been replaced by a balance of interests, in which actors cooperate? For Wight, though the players could change the motives of power remain the same, from the relationship of Greek city states to the modern European international society. Proponents of a rationalist conversion in Wight's international theory neglect the fact that in one of the chapters in his latest work *Systems of States* he describes as characteristic within a "triangle" international society an attitude of "unremitting suspicion, tension, hostility."[49]

In *Systems of States*, Wight examines two main categories of state systems based on the operation of the balance of power: "open" and "closed." The open system is characterized by continual expansion and is therefore in a state of flux, in the more rigid closed system, expansion ends, facilitating the creation of "triangles" and "duels." Each of these is a form of conflict based upon the balance of power.[50] A triangle is a system in which three sides predominate: in this system group A, B, and C are in a two against one system in which C defeats A and ultimately B to become the system hegemon, thus the initial triangle becomes a duel, with ultimately one power dominating—this Wight called the Endgame scenario. In the Semi-Final scenario, A and B combine to beat C; if the system is open, A and B can be joined and superseded by another power D creating a new triangle system. If the system is closed, after a period of uneasy cooperation a duel ensues between powers A and B that should proceed to an Endgame. In the final scenario, Wight examines the possibility of the Hobbesian war of all against all, *A* vs. *B* vs. *C* vs. *A*, the ultimate result of which is the monopoly of power by *X*, either the victor in the struggle or the successor power from outside the initial conflict. In each case the predominant logic is not cooperation but conflict.[51] In terms of the logic of IR as the sphere of Realism, there is little difference between Wight's analysis of the role of the balance of power and Morgenthau's theory that systems based upon the balance of power were inherently unstable "as a result of the dynamics of the struggle for power."[52]

It is a difficult task to state with any conviction the intention of Wight's theory of international society, as he did not codify his theory in any one text. Contemporaries attribute this lack of codification to an overly perfectionist approach to preparing his written work.[53] However, I think it fair to say that his consistent aim, from the first edition of *Power Politics* to the posthumous publications, was to engage with the power politics of his time and previous times to attempt to provide a series of answers pertaining to the logic of the system and IR mechanisms. From his unpublished works were constructed the much expanded second edition of *Power Politics, Systems of States*, and *The Three Traditions*: in none of these posthumous publications is there any evidence of a totalizing principle in the fashion of the positivist school. This absence of "totality" provides Wight a connection with postmodernism, in that neither supports an IR theory that would put an end to disagreement and uncertainty. There is an awareness that the role of the commentator is not to make claims to understand an objective reality in the international environment but to concern himself with the debate among the contending theories and doctrines of theorists without an expectation of ultimate resolution. Wight expressed his awareness of the distance between theory and practice in a paper tellingly entitled "Why Is there no International Theory?": "What I have been trying to express is the sense of a kind of disharmony between international theory and diplomatic practice, a kind of recalcitrance of international politics to being theorized about."[54]

Ultimately, Wight's position is in fact antitheoretical in the sense that Neorealists understand the term. There is no IR model in his work, nor is there a commitment to the discovery of timeless principles. Wight's purpose is to uncover the shifting logic of international society. The logic of power and the "order" of power are reconciled through the structural imperative of the balance of power resulting in the creation of international society and the logic of the operation of the balance of power. In terms of the equations outlined by Wight in *Anatomy of International Thought*, the unspoken corollary of his thought system is that anarchy creates order creates anarchy. International order and international anarchy act as mutually reinforcing mechanisms that ensure the continuance of both patterns within international society. Realist logic and Grotian structure instead of being understood as antinomian worldviews, or in dialectical terms, can be seen as conversational partners in the academic sense and as effective partners in the sphere of political evolution in IR. Lying outside the primary relationship is the systemic corrective of the third pattern of "Revolutionism," a species of catalytic thought that according to Wight is "a series of waves, that have an effect upon the timestream of international politics. Based on principle of supersession, an attempt to accelerate or step out of history."[55] The ultimate effect of this third pattern is of "transposing the melody of power politics to a new key."[56] Wight qualifies the importance of revolution by emphasizing the corrective power of the logic of international power systems on revolutionary enthusiasm, citing numerous examples of revolutionary regimes allying with doctrinal or ideological opposites in accordance with *raison d'etat*.[57] Thus, although the system may take on important new characteristics, the quotidian procedures of the system (and fundamentally the structures and institutions of international order) are not usually affected outside the general systemic effect of the new ideology—thoughts, once expressed and disputed, cannot be unthought, but can be assimilated into the mainstream of international political reference. The last 200 years have been characterized by the huge ideological impact of the French and Russian Revolutions, yet in each case the pariah revolutionary state was reintegrated into both international society and into the logic of Realism.

Wight's IR system is a complicated attempt to resolve the apparent paradox in the relationship between rationalist structural order and the Realist anarchic logic of the operation of power in IR. Composed of mutually opposed structure and imperative action, the system nonetheless makes sense. A key component of Wight's theory set is his religious background: the primacy of Realism in his thought, while he expresses both pacifistic and liberal attitudes in his works can be explained by the doctrine of original sin, which forms the bridge between his individual convictions and his analysis of international politics. In this analysis of international politics, Wight played out a dualistic drama based upon the relationship between a morally informed "Order" represented by international society and the immoral (at least from the point of view of his personal morality) anarchic logic of power.

CHAPTER 6

The Retreat from the Real: Kenneth Waltz and the International System

This chapter examines the emergence of Neorealist theory and demonstrates the transvaluation of the Realist tradition in the development of Neorealism. I investigate the origins of the concepts and the theoretical assumptions that underlay Neorealist thought and how Waltz has responded to the various challenges that have been made since the publication of the seminal text *Theory of International Politics*. The first part of the chapter focuses on the relanguaging and relocation to a structural framework of previous "Realist" concepts, the constitutive acts that separate Neorealism from "classical" Realism. The second part concentrates on the various attempts to challenge Neorealism's position as a general IR theory. The third part examines the attempts of Waltz to counter these criticisms and the attempt to reorient Neorealism for the post–cold war world. The chapter concludes with a critical assessment of the theoretical power of Neorealist theory.

The Development of Neorealism in Waltz's *Theory of International Politics*

Neorealism has two origins, one may be referred to as the conceptual origin: the series of concepts that are employed throughout *Theory of International Politics*, especially the anarchy principle, the balance of power, and states as the primary (if not sole) actors in IR. The second lies in the realm of the construction of theory itself—Waltz seeks to reorient the very nature of international theory into a more "rigorous" and scientific form, one that more adequately conforms to the standards of the philosophy of science. The means by which Waltz seeks to achieve this task is through the use of structural and systemic theory.[1]

The nature of theory in IR is most important in the formulation of Neorealism. As *Theory of International Politics* claims to institute a new style of theory in international politics, Waltz is careful to lay the epistemological groundwork in advance of the presentation of the substance of the theory in the latter half of the book. It is for this reason that both Waltz and I begin our investigations with a consideration of the epistemology of international theory.

In a sense, *Theory of International Politics* is one of the last great entries in the so-called Second Great Debate of IR—that between the scientific and classical wings of international theory. It is in this text that Realism gets its definitive makeover into a rationalist, structural theory of international politics, an inversion of the epistemological position taken by two of its most important founders as a theory of international politics, E.H. Carr and Hans Morgenthau. As referred to in the introduction, the importance of language is crucial in understanding the successful transformation of Realism from a multiplicity of various approaches (critical, dialogical, and historical in the case of Carr and Wight; philosophical and theoretical in the case of Morgenthau) toward the political philosophy of power in IR to a streamlined social science.

Waltz achieves his aim of creating a science of international politics by eliding the difficulties of an application of the methodologies of the physical to the social sciences. The distinction in Morgenthau's work between human sciences and natural sciences (which lies at the heart of Morgenthau's first major work in English *Scientific Man versus Power Politics*) is ignored by Waltz, who attempts to subsume the social under the scientific method associated with disciplines such as physics and the poster boy of such attempts microeconomics. The major problem with IR theory for Waltz is that it seldom refers to work that meets philosophy of science standards.[2] This is a clear epistemological signposting of intent by Waltz that he intends to create a theory of international politics based on these principles.

In order to achieve philosophy of science standards, Waltz first creates a theoretical taxonomy of necessary mental apparatus for the construction of theory—ideas, laws, theory, and science. By doing so he creates the possibility of defining the nature of theory: "theories are collections or sets of laws pertaining to a particular behavior or phenomenon."[3] Waltz refines this later to a position where, "rather than being mere collections of laws, theories are statements that explain them." The act of distancing his work from his progenitors, and the seizure of theory to the rationalist wing of IR is revealed in the distinction Waltz makes in his juxtaposition of philosophy and theory:

> This meaning [of theory as a means of explaining laws] does not accord with usage in much of traditional political theory, which is concerned more with philosophical interpretation than with theoretical explanation.[4]

This quote is significant in that we see the appropriation of "theory" to the rationalists' cause and the relegation of previous forms of theory to the subordinate realms of tradition and philosophy. But what is the nature of this new form of theory?

"A theory, though related to the world about which explanations are worked, always remains distinct from that world. Reality will be congruent neither with a theory nor with a model that may represent it."[5]

There is then a dislocation of theory from the historical to the ideal, from the practice of politics to a mirror of politics in an abstracted universe. The model is not to be confused with the reality, it is its own creation, with its own laws that condition behavior within its theoretical boundaries. Waltz's model is built upon the related ideas of system and structure. In contrast to reductionist theories of international politics, which concentrate on the activities at the unit level, Waltz suggests that the most important variable in international politics is the system of states. It is the structural nature of this system that allows one to think of international politics as taking place within a distinct form rather than as a simple collection of states. Waltz here is attempting to create an explanatory theory of state behavior in the context of an existing system that both constrains and gives meaning to the conduct of states. This is the rationalized model of international politics replete with a structural over-logic of systemic behavior that he later relates to the problem of anarchy that Waltz promised in the first chapter of *Theory of International Politics*.

In his discussion of Hoffman's attempt to create a systemic approach, Waltz criticizes his efforts by employing an economic rationale. This is a typical theoretical aspect of Waltz—he venerates economic theory as the only social science to approximate to the standards of the philosophy of science and then uses economic theory against IR theorists, claiming that they are not living up to the standards set by economics. The reader is drawn into a complex web of theoretical aesthetics and interdisciplinary polemic, in which Waltz privileges his reading of economics and the philosophy of science. In this aesthetic of theory, Waltz insists on system, elegance, simplicity, and the avoidance of complexity. In this sense, he is the inheritor of Morgenthau's maxim that "reality is deficient." The extent to which these aesthetics determine the validity of a theory is obvious when Waltz describes Hoffman's work as "untheoretical" and "any glimmerings of theory remain crude and confused." Hoffman then is cast into the void of the untheoretical, and Waltz's conformity to the aesthetic form is reaffirmed by the extirpation of the heretics of theory. Even one of the most vociferous of the early scientific theorists, Morton Kaplan, is singled out for his lack of an appropriate theory in that he "failed to develop concepts that would permit him to bend the recalcitrant materials of international politics to fit the precise and demanding framework of a system's approach."[6]

The wholesale adoption of extraneous theoretical forms is justified by Waltz as "borrowing across fields is legitimate if the fields are homologous." At no point in *Theory of International Politics*, however, does Waltz make a clear case for adopting the form of theory that he employs. He does not clearly demonstrate why economic theory and international theory are homologous other than making vague comparisons related to structure. In fact he berates "economists" and "economically minded political scientists" for doing this, so why is his use of economic theory legitimate?[7] Also, the idiosyncratic eclecticism of his approach, which includes economics, biology, physics, and even occasional references to politics, is certainly no more elegant or simple than previous theory and does not match Lakatosian or Popperian standards of the philosophy of science. The closest Waltz comes to a reason for the development of his theory is that of emulation:

> Natural scientists look for simplicities: elemental units and elegant theories about them . . . no matter what the subject, we have to bound the domain of our concern, to organize it, to simplify the materials we deal with, to concentrate on central tendencies, and to single out the strongest propelling forces.[8]

But is emulation enough of a reason to reorient international theory to an epistemological position that Morgenthau had identified as anachronistic and "folkloric" more than 30 years before? Is IR immune from developments in the philosophy of science? Advances in quantum physics, such as the Heisenberg Principle, and the whole nature of contemporary science are ignored by Waltz as it would interfere with the nineteenth-century modernist aesthetic of purity, simplicity, and order. This is evidence of the will to power, the desire to constrain science by reference to an apparatus of meaning that magically invests the author with authority. Deleuze and Guattari effectively contrast the reality of science with the belief in science: "[S]cience would go completely mad if left to its own devices. Look at mathematics: its not a science, it's a monster slang, it's nomadic."[9] Rather than face this challenge, the rationalist attempts to ignore it and contain the radical elements of science, to discipline the subject of IR by reference to a monopoly of legitimacy inherent in the agreed articles of faith, even when that faith has long been surpassed.

The charge could be made that these epistemological criticisms of Waltzian Neorealism are unimportant. The proponent of Neorealist theory could counter that it remains a general theory of international politics despite its somewhat shaky foundations as an act of textual will on behalf of Kenneth Waltz rather than a science per se of international politics. Ironically, given the rationalist wing's devotion to the philosophy of science, this is exactly what Lakatos deplored about Kuhn's sociology of knowledge as a matter of the biggest group making the loudest noise determining what is true. How then to judge a theory that uses the philosophy of science as a totem rather than as a genuine theoretical foundation? I shall return to this problematic question at various points in this chapter but for the moment I intend to concentrate not on the theoretical base, but rather on the conceptual superstructure of Neorealism in order to see if it bears up to critical scrutiny.

Anarchy, Balance of Power, Stability, and Bipolarity: Key Neorealist Concepts

For Waltz, the key feature to be explained in international politics is the persistence of its essential form over the centuries:

> The texture of international politics remains highly constant, patterns recur, and events repeat themselves endlessly . . . a dismaying persistence, a persistence that one must expect so long as none of the competing units is able to convert the anarchic international realm into a hierarchic one.[10]

Waltz sets out to account for this persistence and to account for the political logic of its continuance in international politics and to provide a theory that explains the regularity of behavior. The key concept is that of structure, which provides an elegant and general model for understanding the international system, it also has the benefit of explaining continuity within the international system.[11] The problem of modelizing a structure of IR that does not include a theory of the state is surmounted by Waltz by use of an analogy to microeconomic theory. Just as microeconomic theory can operate without a theory of the firm, so can international theory operate without necessarily investigating the nature of the state. States then become functionally similar in the model of international politics, but with the important proviso that a general theory of IR "is necessarily based on the great powers."[12]

The horizontal relationship of structuralism across boundaries is evidenced in a positive fashion by Waltz in another episode of theory emulation:

A political structure is akin to a field of forces in physics: interactions within a field have properties different from those they would have if they occurred outside of it, and as the field affects the objects, so the objects affect the field.[13]

This is crucial to understanding the synergistic dual action of unit and structure in international politics. Structure becomes a means of bounding the IR discipline, a means by which order is produced from a chaos of competing pieces of information. Thus structure is a prerequisite for theory as it is structure that enables students of international politics to determine the nature of international politics, in that structure emerges from the interaction of states, but in turn it constrains them from taking certain actions and encourages them toward others.[14]

But the IR structure requires ordering principles: for Waltz the two most important are the condition of anarchy and the distribution of power across the structure. Anarchy is the means by which Waltz suggests that the order of international politics may be understood in the absence of an "orderer." From the point of view of Waltz's brand of theory, it is necessary to engage in a radical simplification of reality to account for the operation of this anarchy principle. He does this by means of an extended analogy to microeconomics and the theory of the market. This condition of state coexistence is equivalent to the coexistence of firms and it is from this coexistence that structure emerges. Intentionality is not an issue as it is the self-interested nature of states that gives rise to international anarchy. Self-help can give rise to a large series of policy decisions ranging from amalgamation with other states to the conduct of war—but the overarching logic of IR remains the same.[15]

This emphasis on the role of the state, its logic of preservation through self-help, and the nature of politics led Waltz to conclude that the state was set to be the ultimate standard of IR for the foreseeable future. Following Hobbes, Waltz insists that the international system is "governed" by the condition that contact leads inevitably to conflict and occasionally to violence.[16] According to Waltz, balance of power theory is perfectly suited to the explanation of the international arena and has the further benefit of being analogous to economic theory. The reason for this is its general level of applicability over a period of time that is coterminous with the Westphalian system itself. In a rational, self-help environment, balancing against the most powerful is the best long-term means of preserving autonomy.

In his consideration of the various balances of power conceivable in IR, Waltz argues that the most beneficial to the preservation of order in international politics is that of bipolarity. As the balance is one of simple antagonism, there is no need or possibility to court the support of another bloc in order to tip the balance in one's own favor. Bipolarity then is the ultimate in the effective management of international affairs because it is the most effective form of mitigating the effects of anarchy.

Challenges to Neorealism: Theory and Practice

Waltz's reformulation of Realism to Neorealism had a tremendous impact on IR theory in the 1980s. Structuralism had come late to IR but it had arrived with a vengeance. The debate around Neorealism culminated in the publication of a volume of works that allowed Waltz to restate his case and also allowed both explicit and implicit criticisms of the Neorealist enterprise. This volume was entitled *Neorealism and Its Critics*; but the debate has not ended with Neorealism coming under attack from all angles. The extent to which Neorealism is a contested theory is evident from its critics, who span the spectrum of international theory from the philosophy of science (John A. Vasquez) to the postmodern wing of International Relations (Jim George).

Perhaps more significant than the theoretical critiques of IR is the fact that Neorealism did not provide any foreshadowing of the collapse of the bipolar international order, which was the result of the collapse of the Soviet Union, and the existing system of bipolarity; quite the contrary.

In the following section, I intend to examine how Neorealist theory, and Kenneth Waltz as its primary proponent, has weathered these two storms of theoretical and practical upheaval.

Neorealism and Its Critics: The Location of an Intellectual Debate

Neorealism and Its Critics is almost unique in IR history as it contains in one place perhaps the only true "debate" in international politics between opposing positions. Neorealism is criticized by a number of authors and Waltz is then given the opportunity to respond to his critics on the specific charges that they bring against his particular brand of theory.

These critiques of Neorealism range from Ruggie's perceptive identification of Neorealism's inability to explain the nature of international systemic origins and transformation, to the epistemological critiques of Richard K. Ashley, who maintains that far from being a structuralist theory per se, Neorealism is instead a confusion of structuralist terminology with statist, utilitarian, and positivist concerns. For Ashley, Neorealism is a mongrel theory that has no right to masquerade as a structural theory of international politics—the isomorphic advantages highlighted by Waltz as the major attraction of Neorealism therefore is incorrect. Neorealism is unmasked as an "orrery of errors" every bit as eclectic and uncoordinated at the most basic theoretical level as classical Realism, but without what R.W. Cox identifies as the historical critical theory capabilities of theorists such as Carr.

In his replies to these criticisms Waltz simply reiterates his original position regarding the structural nature of his IR theory. In response to Ruggie's accusation that he cannot account for the transition from medieval to modern European international systems, Waltz states that in the context of his theory the transfer of power across classes is simply unimportant at the structural level. He does not deny that unit-level phenomena may have an important effect, but stresses that his theory should be understood as the interaction of unit and structure: the international system is the product of these forces. Revealingly, Waltz does not seriously engage with Ashley's critique of his methodology and the epistemological eclecticism that underpins it, preferring to concentrate instead on the impossibility of incorporating history into the rational, deductive IR model proposed in *Theory of International Politics.*[17]

In his conclusion to "Reflections on Theory of International Politics. A Response to My Critics," Waltz draws ever closer to structuralism as the means of constructing a theory of international politics. This is perhaps in response to the criticism by Ashley that his theory was more a thicket of nineteenth-century scientific positivism than a genuine structural theory of international politics. Waltz does make some important qualifications—he states for example that the role of a structural theory of international politics is not all encompassing at all points in time, but rather is a means of isolating important features and patterns of behavior within a systemic framework. His theory, claims Waltz, cannot explain everything in international politics and operates only on the general level: it is not a theory that is designed to cope with the specifics of international politics, but the generalities.

As one of the leading rationalist deductive models of international theory, it is unsurprising that Neorealism came in for a lot of flack during the Third Debate of the discipline in the 1980s and 1990s. The wider effect of the Third Debate was, as Yosef Lapid wrote, a general reconsideration of the metatheoretical bases and shibboleths of positivist theory.[18] Perhaps the most vociferous critic of the Neorealist enterprise is Jim George, who operates at the critical level to undermine the methodology and underlying philosophical assumptions of Realism and Neorealism. According to George, Neorealism is merely the product of a closed modernist discourse that simply reaffirms the status quo of IR that is based on the parable of the market: "the result . . . is an ahistorical, depoliticized scenario replete with vague references to 'spontaneously' generated markets and political structures that mysteriously 'emerge.' "[19] The paradox of Neorealism is that it is a structural theory that does not explain the origin or operation of structure in international politics, he quotes Wendt: "systems structures cannot generate agents if they are defined exclusively in terms of those agents in the first place."[20] As we have already seen from Ashley's criticisms, Neorealism is statist before it is structural, as it relies upon the ontological priority of the state, therefore there can be no structure or system independent of the state.

Vasquez's critique of Waltz's work is interesting in that unlike George or Ashley it operates within the modernist, rationalist theoretical sphere that Waltz inhabits. Perhaps this explains his willingness to engage with Vasquez over matters of theory, when he is patently unwilling to do so when confronted by post-positivist theorists. Vasquez's primary complaint about Realism and Neorealism in particular is that it demonstrates degenerating tendencies according to his reading of Lakatos. The most important of these degenerating tendencies is the continual emendation of Realist and Neorealist theory (in particular the auxiliary hypotheses of the core theory) in an ad hoc fashion in response to theoretical challenges or changes in global politics.[21] According to Vasquez, the theory of the balance of power can give no clear answer to the question of when a war is likely to occur even at the level of generality to which Waltz adheres, therefore Realism has little or no utility.[22]

Waltz's response to this is important in that he stresses the fact that he, unlike Vasquez, is not committed to a positivist framework of analysis. Vasquez, claims Waltz, is misconstruing Lakatos and ignoring the interdependency of fact and theory (although this is in contradiction to Waltz's own statement that theory and reality are separate, although perhaps he means that they are separate but interdependent). Perhaps the most important fact to emerge out of the Vasquez–Waltz debate is that Waltz rejects falsification as a means by which to judge or assess IR theories. This forces Waltz into a more offensive position regarding falsification: "Among natural sciences, falsification is a little used method (Bochenski 1965, 109; cf. Harris 1970). Social scientists should think about why this is so."[23] It is for this reason that Waltz makes "fruitfulness" (a Lakatosian notion) of a research program the means of theory assessment. But how to judge "fruitfulness"? This is one of the silences of Waltz so decried by George. Ultimately, fruitfulness becomes solely an issue of individual choice—a subjective decision informed not by positivism but by rationalism. This somewhat detracts from the projection of scientific purity, which in aspiration at least underpins *Theory of International Politics*. Neorealist theory becomes ever more detached from any objective means of determining its validity, while never making a decisive break with the form whose language gave it its authority. Instead Waltz retreats into a more intersubjective sociology of knowledge approach to theory stating that a theory of explanation is more important than a theory of prediction—and his justification of this is that "[a]t least Steven Weinberg and many others think so."[24] This marks the point where Neorealism exits the Lakatosian and Popperian world of science and enters into a subjective sociology of knowledge, perhaps the one place Waltz did not want to be— one voice among many, a theory of international politics, not the theory of international politics.

Neorealism and the End of the Cold War: The Challenge of Global Political Change

The failure of Neorealism to predict the end of the cold war perhaps explains Waltz's willingness to stress the explanatory rather than the predictive power of Neorealism. But how has Neorealism, now revealed as a rationalist rather than positivist theory of international politics, withstood the test of time, and in particular the end of the cold war?

If the method that Waltz uses is merely a parable, is the parable in itself a useful theory for understanding IR? Since the end of the cold war, Neorealism has had to adapt itself to a world order that is different from the one in which it was created—does it still provide an adequate means of conceiving the international system? Does the theory of Neorealism remain consistent within itself? An examination of Waltz's development of the core Neorealist themes during the 1990s reveals a change in the actors and orientation of the system, but, crucially, not of the theory itself.

The shock of the ending of the cold war was clearly something that Waltz had to address as a major shift in IR. Prior to its conclusion, Waltz himself identified not only the embeddedness but also the transience of the cold war as a specific instance of an international structure: "the Cold War . . . is firmly rooted in the structure of post war international politics, and will last as long as that structure endures."[25] Rather than seeing the collapse of bipolarity as a refutation of the theory of Neorealism, Waltz maintains that the contemporary world is merely in a transitional phase and that the world will revert to the structure of power balancing across an anarchic system dictated by the great powers. The logic of this state of international affairs is quite simple: "Countries that wield overwhelming power will be tempted to misuse it. And even when their use of power is not an abuse, other states will see it as being so . . . [Because] the United States is a mighty country and has become a frightening one . . . the fears and the resentments are easy to understand."[26]

This is the Hobbesian state of nature adapted for the 1990s (and beyond), and as Hobbes predicted that the princes of Europe would be in the state and posture of Gladiators ever poised in continual jealousies, Waltz predicts the same for the New World Order: "we can expect as in the old days a world of five or so great powers, probably by the first decade of the next millennium."[27]

Waltz's first extended attempt to use structural Realism to delineate the current world order was in the article "The Emerging Structure of International Politics." In this article, the demise of the Soviet Union and the emergence of Russia as its successor state led not to the condition of multi-polarity proper, but rather to an intermediary stage in which "bipolarity endures but in an altered state."[28] The reason for the persistence of bipolarity is that no other country has emerged that could rival the United States and the Russian Federation in the various fields of power capabilities outlined by Waltz as the threshold for great power status. The economic realm is singled out by Waltz as the new locus for the pursuit of advantage in IR.[29] The structural logic of IR is reasserted in his analysis of the post–cold war world in which economic competition has supplanted military competition as the primary motivation of relations between states. The anarchy principle is restated as the fundamental reality of IR, with the preservation of a relative balance of economic power between Japan and the United States preferred to an absolute rise in the economic growth of both countries cited as evidence of the logic of competition between great powers.[30] The effect of structural change is not to displace the over-logic of anarchy, but to adapt it to changing international circumstances. Waltz expresses this well in terms of the revival of political economy strategies in which states take the lead in providing their corporations with a dynamic advantage in the international economy: "the distinction between high and low politics, once popular among international political economists, is misplaced. In self-help systems, how one has to help oneself varies as circumstances change."[31] The essential point for Waltz is that countries have always sought power and wealth in a competitive environment. He asks the rhetorical question, "[w]hy should the future be any different from the past?" All that has changed in the current transitional period is that the field of military security has been subordinated to that of economic competition: as the military dimension of IR falls into relative abeyance, the United States is no longer willing to subordinate the economic factor in its approach to IR. Conversely, Japan, once reliant upon American protection militarily, will have to take steps to protect itself as America increasingly sees Japan as an economic threat rather than as a strategic ally. Ultimately, according to Waltz, Japan and Germany will become nuclear powers as the units within the international system seek to emulate each other in terms of their capacities.[32] The final section of the article puts forward the proposition that in the emergent world structure there will be four great powers which will have to find the means to accommodate each other's ambitions and movements in the international arena: "[t]he old and the new great powers will have to relearn old roles, or learn new ones, and figure out how to enact them on a shifting stage." Waltz then remains committed to the use of "structural theory to peer into the future, to ask what seem to be the strong likelihoods among the unknowns that abound. One of them is that over time unbalanced power will be checked by the responses of the weaker who will, rightly or not, feel put upon."[33]

Even important unit-level transformations within the international system, such as the introduction of nuclear weapons, do not have a major effect on the international system, as it remains a "self-help" system and thus have not altered the anarchic system. Changes in weaponry and polarity do not affect the fundamental logic of Neorealism as a theory of international politics, in fact it could be argued that they merely augment its credentials as an explanatory model of the international system.[34]

Instead of being a structural transformation, the end of the cold war is best understood in Neorealist theory as a change in polarity, a change within the system, rather than a change of the system itself. Waltz has spent a great deal of time in the past several years explaining this point and developing the propositions of Neorealist theory in the light of the new global political dispensation. In this endeavor the shifting patterns of the balance of power play an important role. The balance of power remains the fundamental organizing principle within international politics as it is the means by which the distribution of power in an anarchic realm manifests itself. *Theory of International Politics* and earlier works stated that bipolarity was the most stable of the various polarities possible in international politics, but that others were possible. Of all the possible polarities, the most unstable is that of unipolarity, which by the Summer of 2000 Waltz recognized as the polarity that best represented the current condition of world politics. Waltz predicts (which is odd given the disdain for prediction that he mentions in the controversy with Vasquez) that unipolarity will fade and be replaced by a more typical multipolarity. The only limitation that Waltz is willing to admit for Neorealism is that it cannot say when the operation of the balance of power will result in the restoration of a multipolar or bipolar world—a limitation that he insists is "common to [all] social science theories."[35]

Neorealism: A Persistent but Compromised Simulacrum

Given the terms in which Neorealism was expressed in *Theory of International Politics*, it is unsurprising that it remains a consistent and coherent theory of IR.

The structural organization of the theory around a series of taxonomical categories (laws, theories, structure, system) and the emergence of a series of concepts within these taxonomical spaces (states, anarchy, balance of power, stability, order) leads to a rational model of international politics that works well in its own theoretical space. As Waltz has demonstrated throughout the 1990s, the changes that accompanied the end of the cold war are perfectly consistent with his IR theory.

This very consistency begs a question of Neorealism—with what kind of international system would it not be compatible? Is Neorealism successful as George believes simply because it is so "slight," because it says so little of anything that it cannot be incorrect? Other than the statement that structure impacts upon state behavior in IR there is very little analytical power in Neorealism—it is instead a descriptive IR theory, nothing more and perhaps a little less.[36] In a descriptive theory one would expect the theory to be able to explicate the nature of the international system involved. Yet, as Mouritzen has pointed out, Waltz makes little or no attempt to work out the details of the theory's "salient local environment."[37] In concentrating almost exclusively on the structural level he loses sight of the interaction of unit and structure— the very interaction that is supposed to constitute the system according to Waltz in *Theory of International Politics*. This is perhaps accounted for by the fact that Waltz does not want to get bogged down in developing an accommodation between foreign policy analysis and international theory, which is understandable, but it brings up the problem of the state's primary ontological status that was highlighted by Richard Ashley. Ultimately, a major element of the structure of Neorealist theory is left unaccounted for and unexplained in its presentation—state preferences are basically assumed out of existence, when according to the two-way system pointedly explained by Waltz to Vasquez, they should be at the core of the structure rather than a metaphysical constant.

This leads to the problem of Neorealist theory itself—Waltz makes a major distinction between theory and reality—arguing that reality must be greatly distorted by theory. In perhaps his oddest statement on the nature of international theory, Waltz argues that "the assumptions on which theories are built are radical simplifications of the world and are useful only because they are such. Any radical simplification conveys a false impression of the world."[38] It seems an odd defense of a theory to assert that its utility is bound up with the *problematique* of its methodology and a rather bizarre exculpation of its epistemology that if its radical simplification is false then Neorealism has no real use.

This epistemology would seem to be another odd feature, and certainly not the rigorous science of international politics promised by Waltz in *Theory of International Politics*. The philosophy of science is not a mix and match pot pourri from which one may pick and choose as one wishes—but this is exactly what Waltz does. Waltz admires the language of the philosophy of science, but refuses to adopt its principles—Kuhnian, Lakatosian, or Popperian (to which he prescribed at the time of *Theory of International Politics*). To his credit, Waltz admits that he may have given a false impression in the first chapter of *Theory of International Politics*:

> In my simple, and perhaps simplistic, recipe for the testing of theories, given in Chapter One of *Theory of International Politics*, I may have sounded like a "naïve falsificationist." I should like to correct the impression . . . I do indeed part company with Karl Popper, who insists that only efforts to falsify theories count as legitimate tests . . . Because of the interdependence of theory and fact we can find no Popperian critical experiment, the negative result of which would send a theory crashing to the ground.[39]

Waltz makes no attempt to solve this particular problem by reference to anything other than a vague commitment to test theories *ad infinitum*. In light of his later admission that his theory is assumptive and therefore false, what are we to make of its utility? By denying falsificationism and questioning the testability of theories, Waltz is basically trying to make his theory immune to criticism. This in itself would be acceptable if he permitted the same privilege to other theories, but he does not. As we saw in the first section of this essay, he has employed the language of the philosophy of science against other theorists to deny that theirs are genuine theories of international politics—a charge that given the extent to which he has distanced himself from the rigors of the philosophy of science may be equally applied to Neorealism. The best justification that Waltz can provide for this peculiar position is to state that science is not built on solid foundations, but rather on evolutionary foundations.[40] The implication is that rather than being a general theory of international politics, Neorealism is merely a specific theory bounded in place and time.

How then to understand Neorealism? By its author's admission it gives a distorted picture of the world in which its assumptions act according to the logic of the model only and not the logic of the "reality" it is supposed to mirror. The most accurate description and analysis of this sort of theory is that of the simulacra. The negative effect of the simulacra on how we construct knowledge is a good reflection of Neorealism:

> It is no longer a question of imitation, nor duplication, nor even parody. It is a question of substituting the signs of the real for the real, that is to

say of an operation of deterring every real process via its operational double, a programmatic, metastable, perfectly descriptive machine that offers all the signs of the real and short circuits all its vicissitudes.[41]

Waltz's problematic relationship with his own episto-mythology of the philosophy of science speaks to the "implosion of meaning" that Baudrillard identifies as the consequence of a terminal confusion over truth claims in a world that values simulation over the real.[42] In the final analysis, Neorealism is not a Realist theory of IR but the clever operation of a series of signs, allegories, and metaphors that relate almost solely to themselves.

Conclusion: A Counter-Memory
of Realism

Only as creators!—This has caused me the greatest trouble and still does always cause me the greatest trouble: to realize that *what things are called* is unspeakably more important than what they are. The reputation, name, and appearance, the worth, the usual measure and weight of a thing—originally almost always something mistaken and arbitrary, thrown over things like a dress and quite foreign to their nature and even their skin—has, through the belief in it and its growth from generation to generation, slowly grown onto and into the thing and has become its very body: what started as appearance nearly always becomes essence and *effectively acts* as its essence! What kind of a fool would believe that it is enough to point to this origin and this misty shroud of delusion in order to *destroy* the world that counts as "real," so called "reality"! Only as creators can we destroy!—But let us also not forget that in the long run it is enough to create new names and valuations and appearances of truth in order to create new "things."

Friedrich Nietzsche, *The Gay Science*, Book II, No. 58.

The question or questions that have to be asked are: "what types of knowledge are you trying to disqualify when you say you are a science? What speaking subject, what discursive subject, what subject of experience and knowledge are you trying to minorize when you begin to say: "I speak this discourse, I am speaking a scientific discourse, and I am a scientist." What theoretical-political vanguard are you trying to put on the throne in order to detach it from all the massive, circulating, and discontinuous forms that knowledge can take?"

Michel Foucault, *Society Must Be Defended*, p. 25.

Throughout this book two concurrent processes have been at work. The first of these processes was to challenge, problematize, and undermine the orthodox representation of Realism. The second process was, through detailed interpretation and historical recovery, to present another, alternative perspective on the emergence of Realist concepts in the works of Carr, Morgenthau, Wight, and Waltz. The first process concerns the question of the "name" of Realism, and the meanings inherent in names. The genealogy of Realism presented here has demonstrated that our present meaning of Realism is different, perhaps, even an inversion of Realism as it was proposed by Carr and Morgenthau. There may have emerged a difference between "offensive" and "defensive" Realism, but this difference is strictly contained within a paradigmatic framework.[1] The vice-like grip of pseudo-structuralism— a theoretical approach that employs the language of structuralism without applying its concepts thoroughly, but rather according to expediency—has had the effect of squeezing Realist discourse into suspended animation. This conceptual squeeze has resulted in Realists such as Mearsheimer putting forward a redefinition of the Realist tradition that possesses the language of classical Realism but is still dependent upon Neorealist categories for "theoretical" validation, thus rendering blunt the cutting edge of Realism. This can be seen in his reduction of Realism to a tripartite definition of a type that has become standard within Realist thought, at least in the United States:

> First, Realists, like liberals, treat states as the principal actors in world politics . . . Second, Realists believe that the behavior of great powers is influenced mainly by their external environment, not by their internal characteristics. The structure of the international system, which all states must deal with, largely shapes their foreign policies. . . . Third, Realists hold that calculations about power dominate states' thinking and that states compete for power among themselves.[2]

This quotation illustrates the extent to which Neorealist concerns have become embedded in Realist thought, leading to the freezing of the Realist tradition. Where Waltz is keen to stress the separation of theory and reality, Mearsheimer is anxious to build a "sound" theory of political reality. Mearsheimer's approach is illustrative, in that his "theory" is based on "bedrock assumptions" derived from rationalist approaches to IR. But the tyranny of pseudo-structuralism in IR, an epistemological position that has severe difficulty recognizing the validity of other approaches, runs deep: Mearsheimer declares that his "offensive Realism" (so called to differentiate it from Waltz's defensive Realism) is a structural theory of international politics that departs from defensive Realism only in respect to their attitudes to power, offensive Realism being more concerned with the extension of power than defensive Realism, the primary concern of which is the preservation of power. The foundations of Mearsheimer's and Waltz's theories therefore remain the same: they are essentially rooted in a theory of politics as a structuralist enterprise.[3] Rationalism and structuralism, then, are the two grand *shibboleths* of the contemporary Realist enterprise. Realism therefore remains conceptually stuck in the period 1979–1986, the period of the first flowering of neo or structural Realism. In his attempt to defend the Realist paradigm against John Vasquez, Stephen M. Walt defines Realism as characterized by general assumptions "such as states are the key actors, the international system is anarchic, power is central to political life" (1997, 932).[4] Richard Rosecrance's review essay of Lloyd Gruber's *Ruling the World: Power Politics and the Rise of Supranational Institutions* (Gruber 2000) puts forward the idea that twentieth-century Realists such as Carr and Morgenthau "believed that International Relations were a kind of state of nature in which the rule of the stronger prevailed . . . [and] independence and territorial integrity depended on self-help."[5] This idea that Morgenthau and Carr were committed to the territorial integrity and independence of states is simply incorrect, and it also ignores the moral or ethical elements that both authors were determined to integrate into their theoretical approaches. To say that power is at the center of Realism is not very revealing, what is necessary is to examine what the Realists say about power, to analyze the role it plays in their theories of world politics.

What is becoming increasingly evident is that the differences between Realists are growing smaller, what is more disturbing still is that the differences already existent in Realism are being forgotten due to the uniperspectivism of paradigmatic approaches.[6] Despite the historical trappings, Mearsheimer's work, for example, depends on an understanding of theory that is remarkably similar to that of Kenneth Waltz. Where before Waltz's epistemology was revolutionary and overt, Mearsheimer's decision to leave it in the background is testimony to the extent to which this position has become the default position, an unchallenged given in IR theory, for Realism. As we saw earlier in chapter 6, this is a theorization based on the exclusion of anything other than that which is inside the defined space of theory. That which is outside is no longer theory, no longer a part of the core and relegated to the ephemera and apocrypha of the "true" understanding of things.[7]

How this happened is described in Stanley Hoffman's "An American Social Science: International Relations," which is his identification of the emergence of American approaches to hegemony within IR. The social context of this intellectual revolution should not be overlooked, and Hoffman provides a convincing case on the social origins of the intellectual revolution that was necessary for the emergence of the concept of both a paradigmatic reading of Realism in the 1960s and a Realism conceived and constructed according to the principles of the American social science discourse:

> There is, first, the profound conviction, in a nation which Ralf Dahrendorf has called the Applied Enlightenment, that all problems can be resolved, that the way to resolve them is to apply the scientific method—assumed to be value free, and to combine empirical investigation, hypothesis formation, and testing—and that the resort to science will yield practical applications that will bring progress. What is specifically American is the scope of these beliefs, or the depth of this faith: they encompass the social world as well as the natural world, and they go beyond the concern for problem-solving (after all, there are trial-and-error, piece-meal ways of solving problems): they entail a conviction that there is, in each area, a kind of masterkey—not merely an intellectual, but an operational paradigm. Without this paradigm, there can be muddling through, but no continuous progress; once one has it, the practical recipes will follow. We are in the presence of a fascinating sort of national ideology: it magnifies and expands eighteenth-century postulates . . . the national experience of economic development, social integration, and external success has kept reinforcing this set of beliefs.[8]

The spread of consensus on the ideology of how to perform theory in the United States was guaranteed by the identification of rationalism in Economics as a model to be followed by other social sciences, especially Political Science and its subdiscipline, International Relations. What emerges then is an *episteme*, a common way of looking at the world across disciplines, a mode of knowledge that made the practice of theory homologous, and its foundations, its grammar, and its logic were to be found in science— "something like a worldview, a slice of history common to all branches of knowledge, which imposes on each one the same norms and postulates. A general stage of reason, a certain structure of thought that the men of a particular period cannot escape—a great body of legislation written once and for all by some anonymous hand."[9]

Nietzsche, Realism, and Science

One of Nietzsche's first statements on science is telling in relation to his attitude toward it as a species of thought: "Might the scientific approach be nothing but fear, flight from pessimism? A subtle form of self-defence against—the truth?"[10] This fear is related to the Socratic–Platonic orientation of knowledge away from "apparent" existence toward the "real" world of ideal forms, another flight from pessimism, to a perfect reality. When Nietzsche attacks Realists, it is those who believe in some "other" more perfectly real reality other than the one in which we live. As we have seen throughout this book, this attitude is shared by the Realists in IR (with the exception of Waltz) who are committed to confronting the ugly truths experienced in "our" reality. Just as an ideal world is challenged, so also is the concept of a pure rationality, Kant's noumenal sphere. Only in a condition of absolute knowledge would human behavior appear calculable on the basis of pure rationality:

> [I]n the case of human action; if one were all-knowing, one would be able to calculate every individual action, like-wise every advance in knowledge, every error, every piece of wickedness . . . if for one moment the wheel of the world were to stand still, and there were an all-knowing, calculating intelligence there to make use of this pause, it could narrate the future of every creature to the remotest ages and describe every track along which this wheel had yet to roll.[11]

Nietzsche's objection to this is that no such "all-knowing, calculating intelligence" exists, nor is it ever likely to exist. Human consciousness exists in a state of becoming, but it is not oriented toward the goal of noumenal reason, or the approximation of noumenal reason—we remain human, all too human. For Nietzsche, scientific man was situated in relation to Art, a "further evolution of the artistic." This scientific knowledge is merely another attempt at making sense of the world, it should not be understood as the ultimate form of reason, a precondition for intellectual and moral advancement.[12] Yet Nietzsche is aware that "science presses for the absolute dominance of its methods, and if this pressure is not relaxed there arises the other danger of a feeble vacillation back and forth between different drives."[13] In the careers of Morgenthau and Waltz, we see exactly this impact of the claims of science to totality, Morgenthau vacillating between skepticism and rationalism, whereas Waltz embraces the scientific discourse completely.

Scientific discourse in IR theory has had the effect of severely limiting the condition of knowledge of the discipline. Resting on a uniperspectival epistemological metatheory, it inherently insists that its mode of thinking about IR is correct, and the content of IR must be made to fit the perspective of "science." IR theory as a practice then has two groups: the "fettered and firm intellects" who accept the metatheory of "science" and those who adhere to a "spiritual nomadism."[14] The relationship between the two is not equal, however, as "science" has defined what it is to be scholarly—"All of our educational methods take their bearings from this ideal: any other form of existence has a hard struggle to survive alongside it, and is in the end tolerated rather than encouraged."[15] Science is a special case of the will to truth, an exercise of power over the IR discipline, determining and directing the "correct" form of theorization. Because of its power as a hegemonic metatheoretical tradition, it possesses an authority "which one obeys, not because it commands what is *useful* to us, but because it *commands* . . . It is fear in the presence of a higher intellect which here commands, of an incomprehensible, indefinite power, of something more than personal—there is *superstition* in this fear."[16] The effect of this metatheoretical tradition is, ultimately, to systematize IR to such an extent that it rounds off the horizon of thought.[17] The "metaphysical faith" upon which science is based ("I will not deceive or be deceived") rests upon the assumption that truth is divine.[18] What Nietzsche poses as a challenge to this is that instead of being a relationship of revelation to real or imagined worlds, truth was something that came from the practice of power. As he puts it, what if the belief in God, in Truth, was "to turn out to be our longest lie?"[19] A lie we have told ourselves about the construction of our knowledges of the world, in order to escape the metaphysical shock of our existence, that is, that no metaphysical or transcendent meaning is attendant on our being—a conclusion reiterated by Morgenthau and to an extent by Carr, though rejected by the Christian Wight, he nonetheless denied the ability of Man to know any transcendent category independent of the revelation of God. Waltz avoids such existential questions by abstracting IR to as simple ("parsimonious") a model as possible.

It is the fear of the unfamiliar and strange that reinforces the power of "science" as a dominant discourse: it seeks to control what is unknown through comparison with what is known, homogenizing the strange and domesticating it by reference to the familiar.[20] It is precisely this process that has led to the production of a paradigm of Realism: the determination to make the strange, diverse writings of Carr, Morgenthau, Wight, Waltz, and others fit into a familiar "shape" through the application of a paradigm. This shaping and systematization of knowledge into "scientific," formal theory is itself an aspect of the "tyrannical drive" of "the most spiritual will to power, to 'creation of the world' to *causa prima*."[21] Where Carr, Wight, and, to a lesser extent, Morgenthau, were willing to place their perspectives on IR in the context of other IR theories, it is Waltz who insists on a Realism, insulated against the context of intellectual debate and insistent upon *causa prima* and the notion of a single truth of IR/ir.

With the advantage of a powerful set of ideas, a seductive epistemological stance, and its emergence to dominance from within the hegemonic power in global politics, the scientific approach redefined the language of IR. Through the exercise of a will to truth (e.g., Kaplan's call for science as opposed to "wisdom literature"), it established its dominance over IR theories: "out of multiplicity it has the will to simplicity, a will which binds together and tames, which is imperious and domineering."[22] As argued in chapter 1, the greatest casualty of this epistemic shift was Realism, as it was swamped by efforts to turn it into a paradigm. This will to simplicity is important to recognize as it leads to the reconfiguration of Realism through its determination to order theory according to its principles as it seeks "to simplify the complex, to overlook or repel what is wholly contradictory: just as it arbitrarily emphasizes, extracts and falsifies to suit itself certain traits and lines in what is foreign to it."[23] Nietzsche's finding on the role of science was to state, "It is not the victory of science that distinguishes our nineteenth century, but the victory of scientific method over science."[24] The "entire apparatus of knowledge" has become a process in the possession of those professing "scientific method."[25]

Royal and Nomad Science: Desubjugating Realism I

> Will to truth is a making firm, a making true and durable, an abolition of the false character of things, a reinterpretation of it into beings. "Truth" is therefore not something there, that might be found or discovered—but something that must be created and that gives a name to a process, or rather to a will to overcome that has in itself no end—introducing truth, as a *processus infinitum*, an active determining—not a becoming-conscious of something that is in itself firm and determined. It is a word for the "will to power."[26]

The will to power in knowledge, the will to truth, is not just about the imposition of order onto any given discourse through a determining process. Taking their cue from Nietzsche's identification of "firm, fettered intellects" and nomads of spiritualism, Gilles Deleuze and Felix Guattari examined the relationship between what they characterized as Royal Science and Nomad Science. The interpenetration of language and power is of central importance to Deleuze and Guattari and sheds light on the development of Realist theory. There are essentially two languages in any discourse—the language of power and the language of resistance. In theoretical terms, the language of power is the language of "science," an idiom of domination. Opposed to this is the "minority" language, which poses a direct threat to the monolithic language of "science."[27] The language of Royal Science operates under the assumption of its own superiority as the means for assessing theoretical validity—despite the tenuous claims to science that this "language" of science possesses. The effect of this is to leave theory in a state where it possesses "a deliberate will to halt or stabilize the diagram [or theory], to take its place by lodging itself on a level of coagulated abstraction too large for the concrete but too small for the real."[28]

Royal science attempts to territorialize knowledge and to make itself sovereign of that domain, with the theorist as a priest-king, the possessor/creator/guardian of a knowledge that both gives him his authority and confirms his wisdom. In IR, this phenomenon reached its peak with the domination of the discipline by "scientific" approaches emanating from America in the 1960s and 1970s, when a power/language coup occurred, resulting in the plethora of neos, cybernetics, rational choice, game theory, and mathematical modeling. The irony of all this scientization, as Morgenthau was acutely aware, was that these axiomatics were far from the cutting edge of science and deliberately ignored new developments in the philosophy of science.

Nomadic science is the term that Deleuze and Guattari use to designate science that conflicts with the monolithic, hierarchic royal science. The basis of nomad science lies in pragmatics, an approach that puts the emphasis on the radical rather than the normal practice of science and the revolutionary thinker rather than the guardian.[29] Pragmatics may be understood as an attempt to keep theory plural and multiperspectival—to maintain the multiple entryways essential for the manufacture of different Realist theories. Realism emerged as a nomad science of IR in that it attempted in the works of Carr and Morgenthau to repudiate the royal science of IR as a modern liberal enterprise. By making power its lodestar, Realism made itself relevant as an approach to IR. By adopting the discourse of royal science and instituting a retreat to the ideal, Neorealism formalizes the end of Realism as a critiquing minor or nomad science, the role it played in the 1930s and its entrenchment as a royal science of IR. By colonizing and paradigmizing Realism, the dominant episteme of scientism confirmed the formalization of IR into positivist, behavioralist, or rationalist straitjackets. Theory became the power to order truth and knowledge about IR theory. Realizing that this is the condition of knowledge in IR is the first step to changing it.

Desubjugating Realism II: Counter-Memory

Intrinsic to the project of genealogy is the process of creating a counter-memory of the practices and discourses that have achieved dominance, and the established histories of these practices or discourses. The epic history of Realism that stresses the continuity of a tradition that stretches back from Waltz to Thucydides is just such an established history. This is in effect an act of "reordering and new assessment of the earlier masters and their works, that in them which is attuned and related to him, which constitutes a fore-taste and annunciation of him, henceforth counts as that which is really significant in them and their works—a fruit in which there is usually concealed a great worm of error."[30] Thus Carr, Morgenthau, and Wight are now significant not in terms of their texts, their works, but to the extent that they are precursors to the present "paradigmatic" reading of Realism.[31] The nature of their theory is distorted in order to fit within a single perspective, the will to truth of scientism as a will to unity under the sign of Realism as paradigm, in which the nuance of their works is sacrificed for conformity. This, in effect, is typical of what Nietzsche called the "worst readers," those whose reading is determined in advance and insisting on this as the only genuine perspective, readers who in Nietzsche's words "behave like plundering troops: they take away a few things they can use, dirty and confound the remainder, and revile the whole.[32]

What is necessary therefore in order to counter the power of the paradigmatic representation of Realism, and the inscription of science into Realism in Neorealism, is a counter-memory of Realism, which stresses individual knowledge, the differences between Realists, and their repudiation of scientific theorization as understood by those professing a paradigmatic approach. A counter-memory is an act of genealogical diagnosis, seeking to assist the recovery of "other voices which have remained silent for so long, 'naturalized' as they were through the language of reason."[33] It achieves its task by dissociating the plurality of concepts within the Realist tradition from the paradigmatic definitions of Realism, opposing the legitimacy of this definition (or definitions, there is a surprising number of Realist paradigms), by recourse to the excluded past. What follows is a reiteration of the findings of the genealogy of Realism conducted throughout this book.

Realism, the State, and State Centrism

[M]odern democracy is the historical form of the decay of the state.—The prospect presented by this certain decay is, however, not in every respect an unhappy one: the prudence and self-interest of men are of all their qualities the best developed; if the state is no longer equal to the demands of these forces then the last thing that will ensue is chaos: an invention more suited to their purpose than the state was will gain victory over the state . . . a later generation will see the state too shrink to insignificance in various parts of the earth—a notion many people of the present can hardly contemplate without fear and revulsion.

Friedrich Nietzsche, *Human, All Too Human,* No. 472.

The role played by the state and state centrism in Realist IR theory is complex and varied, especially in comparison to the supposed content of the Realist paradigm. That the state is a major player in global politics for Realism is correct, but to state, as those wedded to the uniperspectival reading of Realism do, that Realism is concerned solely or almost exclusively with the state is incorrect. For Realism the state is a locus of political power and nothing more. Given that modern Realism emerged in the twentieth century, in which the state reached the apogee of its power capabilities, it is unsurprising that they should concentrate on state behavior as a major element of IR theory. What is surprising, given the paradigmatic representation of the state's role as key, principal, or central actor in IR, is their skepticism in relation to the future of the state.

At various points in the book, selected passages in the writings of Carr and Morgenthau are quoted that demonstrate an unambiguous rejection of the state as the central feature of IR. To argue, as Carr does, that the state is an anachronism is to flag the importance of the historical impermanence of the state. The state is not defined tautologically by reference to a theory to which it is necessary, but rather as a temporary institution the purpose of which was to contain or manifest popular sovereignty in the transition to bourgeois and mass democratic societies. Necessity is not just the mother of the invention of the state, but is also the author of its destruction. The modern state, a product of the transfer of sovereignty, had outlived its function, indeed had begun to jeopardize its function, the provision of security. Far from its preservation being the solution to political problems, the state had become an element of these problems—with nationalism and imperialism, the dominant ideologies of the European state, being in effect the cause of both world wars. Either the state was to assume an existential totality of meaning in the manner of Nazi Germany or Soviet Union, a meaning entirely alien to its functions of embodying popular sovereignty and providing security, or the state would have to be replaced.

Morgenthau also appreciated this changing context of the state. Morgenthau, like Carr, argued the necessity of transforming international politics, but couched his argument in the concept of interest, which for him was the "perennial standard by which political action must be judged and directed," not the state. Again, he stressed the historical transience of the connection between interest and state, which he stresses is a "product of history, and therefore bound to disappear in the course of history." The temporal factor, a blind spot in the paradigmatic representation of Realism, reduces the state to a mere vessel for interests. Other factors outside the remit of the "scientific" perspective such as technology ("technical potentialities") and intriguingly the "moral requirements" of political life also impinge upon the centrality of the state. Modern technology, and, in particular, the nuclear bomb, invalidated the state as a means of social organization as the state was now incapable of providing a means of protecting its citizens—its *raison d'etre*. Rather than insist on the conduct of international politics as "fixed and uniformly conflictual interests," which he should as a paradigmatic Realist (*the* paradigmatic Realist), Morgenthau argues instead for "amalgamation of nation-states," an instance in which interests demand cooperation (if not the transcendence of the state) not conflict. For Morgenthau, like Carr, the importance of the state was in its role as a mediator of power, rather than as a possessor of power in itself. The state as an entity is eclipsed by the practice of power.

Wight's attitude to the role of the state is similarly complex. At one level he recognizes that International Society, the means by which he analyzes IR, is "a unique society composed of the other, more fully organized societies which we call states." Yet in the next sentence he states that "there is a sense in which its ultimate members are men."[34] Again, the state system is referred to in terms of its historically anomalous nature: "it will help us to understand this state of affairs if we recall that it is by no means the rule in history . . . we have the illusion that it is normal."[35] The modern sovereign state is based upon a redefinition of loyalties, transitioning from the medieval system of a multiplicity of loyalties to "a narrower and at the same time a stronger unit of loyalty."[36] Loyalty as a facet of identity is malleable, as Wight demonstrates by reference to the transition from medieval to modern international society, and it is his treatment of history in international politics that demonstrates that the state is not a guaranteed feature of the international system—he identifies the medieval multiplicity of "kingdoms, fiefs and cities," of medieval Christendom, the anarchy of the "confusions and migrations" of the Dark Ages and the Roman Empire as different media for the practice of power. The modern, sovereign state is again merely a medium of power, not the essence of an international system. Rather than identify his theory as concerned with states per se, Wight takes the trouble to identify it with "powers": "A power is simply a collection of human beings following certain traditional ways of action, and it is possible that if enough of them chose to alter their collective behavior they might succeed in doing so." Powers therefore may be defined as other than the state. Thus the way is open for a redefinition of political space that Wight recognizes is the aim of several collections of human beings, particularly the Revolutionists who offer a different vision of world politics. International Society does not necessarily require a system of states in the modern, paradigmatic sense, as Hedley Bull correctly identifies in *The Anarchical Society*; other options, such as his "neo-medieval" configuration of interlocking loyalties exist. Despite the reconfiguration of political space, however, the logic of political existence shall remain Realist; as Robert Gilpin writes, "It may very well be the case, as many observers have come to believe, that under contemporary conditions the nation-state has become an anachronism and in time will be displaced . . . If these developments were to occur, the result would not be the end of political affairs as understood by realists; it would still be a jungle out there."[37]

When we talk about a Realist paradigm in which the state is an unchanging entity that comprises the unit of an international system, we are really talking about Neorealism's version of the state in its conception of how theory should be performed. Waltz's theory rests on a fundamental break with previous modes of Realist thought. Realism is a theory that is characterized by a commitment to studying political events as they occur in the empirical realm from a variety of competing perspectives. The historical evolution of the state and the state system is a vital part of the Realist attitude toward the state as a historico-philosophical entity: Realism could be described in terms of the state system in Nietzschean terms as the analysis of the becoming and transcending of the state system. By rendering the state analogous to the firm in microeconomic theory, instead of treating it as a political entity, Waltz removes the state and state system from IR and places them instead into a new category, that of a model that does not exist in our world (the real) but rather in the space of a model one step away from our already "compromised" linguistically dependent rendering of the world. Neorealism, in its search for a "pure" theoretical space, sacrifices engagement with the real for an idealized image of the real, thus inverting Realism's concept of the state as a social construction of limited value and the state system as a temporary organization of power (albeit one characteristic of modernity), and created in Neorealism a "pallid mental picture" of the state, and the state system, divorced from and eschewing historical reality in favor of a projection. In this "pallid mental picture" of the state and state system, the possibility of change is minute, due to the dependency of the theory on a permanent relationship between unit and system. Prudence and self-interest, unfixed to a particular form of social organization are human and Realist species, or qualities of thought. They are sacrificed to the hypostatized model of unit and system, beyond which little is significant in Neorealism, where prudence and self-interest are tied to the state under the rubric of "self-help," but with no prospect of those in charge of the state ever thinking beyond the survival of the state. Thus the Realist calculations of the Czechoslovak government in 1938 in capitulating to the Germans, or the decision to disintegrate the USSR in 1991, based squarely on the principles of prudence and self-interest make little sense in the context of Neorealist theory, because it is a theory based solely on states as entities with a "life" of their own, not social constructions of, by, and for people. The decision to capitulate being in essence a bad calculation of the state's "fundamental" interest, that is, its survival as an individual unit in the system.

Realism then, despite its depiction in the paradigmatic reading, has social transformation of an international society in continual flux at its core. Carr and Morgenthau both argued for more functional approaches to international politics stressing the benefits to be gained from a transition from the nation state to conditions more adapted to the security and economy needs of humanity. Although Wight did not foresee any major advance on the system of states in international society, he did not state that any change would be improbable, merely that it was in the hands of the individuals who comprise the ultimate membership of international society. Neorealism may stress the continuation of the states system, and may be correct in that emphasis, but it does so on the basis of an inverted idealism rather than on a Realist basis.

Realism, Politics, Morality

The relationship between politics and morality in Realism is also a complicated one. No one strand connects the approach of the Realist texts examined in the current work. What we can say, though, is that the representation of Realism as amoral or immoral is incorrect, there are several attitudes to morality in Realism, ranging from Carr's relativist position, to Morgenthau's morality of the lesser evil, to Wight's Augustinianism, to Waltz's deliberate decision to remove it from view as an epiphenomenal aspect of state behavior.[38]

One thing that does unite all four writers is the agreement that power supersedes morality in the conduct of international politics. Although subordinate to the demands of power, however, morality played a lesser but prominent role in international politics for Carr. Power may be prior to morality, but morality was able to have an influence on the conduct of power, not in the sense of providing dictates through international law, but in the sense of providing a loose ethical framework for international conduct, a sensibility between states. As he argues, the pugnacious morality of states is bound up with survival, not with absolute moral codes. The best that may be achieved for Carr is a pragmatic morality, one that is based on a shifting consensus about the right thing to do in the circumstances. His location of international morality within the international society is significant in that he attributes ideological shifts in international society as conditioning changes in international morality. The primary example of this that he provides is the difference between the norm of balance, typical of the concert system and the Versailles settlement, which was based on the survival of the fittest. Both the last third of the *Twenty Years' Crisis* and his later works, *Future of Nations: Independence or Interdependence, Conditions of Peace*, and *Nationalism and After*, attest to his determination to infuse the Realist practice of power with at least a measure of morality.

For Morgenthau the issue of morality was dealt with in a manner similar to that of Carr. Although his primary focus was on the practice of power according to its own logic, or illogic, Morgenthau emphasized the presence and importance of norms in the international community. Given the anarchic nature of IR, these norms could not be enforced in all times and in all places, but they were present, at least in the background of events, as a template for behavior. The decline of moral certainty, or at least of a diplomatic community subscribing to the same norms, accompanying the political, scientific, and moral upheavals of the Revolutionary Age was a tragic phase in human history, as humanity drifted toward the extremes of rationality and irrationality. The extreme of rationality producing an indefatigable belief in the power of science and law to remedy international politics, and the extreme of irrationality culminating in Fascism and the denial of any morality except that of the strong. Surprisingly, given his condemnation of Carr as a Machiavellian for his shifting moral pragmatism and relativism, Morgenthau in *Scientific Man versus Power Politics* endorses Carr's standpoint of indeterminate morality in that absolute ethical standards and human action are incompatible. Both also share a political morality of the lesser evil—moral behavior in politics lies not in the conscious decision to "do good" but in the decision to do as little harm as possible.

Martin Wight, as a stern High Anglican, expected little from Man as a moral being, and even less of Man in the practice of international politics. In many ways he is more pessimistic than Carr and Morgenthau in relation to the possibility of a moral input into the practice of power. Man's tendency to use freewill in a manner approximating toward the immoral is a constant, however, another constant exists in Reason and natural law. The natural law tradition has informed the practice of power in international politics, perhaps not to the degree which its adherents would like to believe that it has or should, but the Grotian tempering of Machiavellian impulse is undeniable. Always recognizing the primacy of power politics, Wight nonetheless took pains to distinguish the practice of power from the law of the jungle.[39] International politics is not quite a war of all against all, or if it is, it has at least developed a normative *ius in bello* to moderate and codify the behavior of the combatants.

Again it is Kenneth Waltz's reformulation of Realism in the abstract that removes the moral element from Realism. By abstracting the behavior of states to a level that emphasizes solely their power relative to each other, Waltz strips away the epiphenomena of the moral heritage of humanity. Instead a more "rational" morality emerges in the concept of balancing. There is a utilitarianism to Neorealism that few have acknowledged. Implicit in Waltz's argument is that power balances, and in doing so creates the political condition of stability. Stability in turn produces peace, which is a moral good. In terms of its Waltzian formulation, Neorealism is oriented to a moral end, stability, and peace.[40] In its more instrumentalist variation of "offensive" Realism, however, the drift to the extreme of rational thought is apparent as Mearsheimer argues for the extension of power to the achievement of hegemony as the only certain way to achieve security. This is the peace of domination, not balance, and can only be good for those who exercise domination, unless they do so in such a way as to earn the respect and love of those they dominate, which is unlikely, but essentially unimportant in the offensive Realist worldview.

There is then a range of moral positions in the Realist family, not an absence. From the minimalist positions of Carr and Morgenthau to the Augustinian moral theory of Martin Wight, through to the unheralded utilitarian morality of Waltzian Neorealism, Realism has been concerned with ethical questions of international conduct. That it has not done so in the dominant traditions of the concepts of morality and rights in terms of Christian and Enlightenment discourses is not to state that it is amoral or immoral, but rather to state that it has taken these issues significantly seriously to devote considerable effort to develop a workable framework for behavior in an anarchic realm.

Realism and Power

That states are motivated to gain power, either in absolute or relative terms, is one of the aspects of Realism that the paradigmatic perspective has correctly identified. All the Realists agree that the pursuit of power is a key element of political life. Carr's Realism stresses the relationship between satiated powers and revisionist powers, Morgenthau the impulse to power of the *animus dominandi*, Wight the simple lust for power of the Leviathan, and Waltz the determination of powerful states not to lose power relative to their rivals. All four of the Realists agree on the motivation of states to gain power.

This is only the surface of the Realist attitude to power in IR and a concentration of it to the exclusion of all other elements of the varieties of Realism. The question of power obscures the valuable contribution that Realism makes to theorizing power as more than a simple commodity the exchange of which determines the relative standings of various states in the international system.

Carr's treatment of power, for example, does not rest content with the idea of states merely seeking to gain or secure their power. Power is more than a simple commodity, it is the very stuff of international politics, something that permeates not simply the state and the state system, but how we perceive the world itself. Power encompasses more than the practice of statecraft, it is the "living structure of domination" that determines life itself. Morality, law, ideology, public opinion, all supposedly part of the Utopian project against the excesses of power politics in international politics are revealed to be elements of the power of modern elites in the Western world to project values based on the protection not of universal, but of particular interests. For Carr there can be no escape from power by instituting a liberal utopian agenda, as this agenda was itself an aspect of power that would necessarily deprive someone of power in its expression and instrumentalization, copper-fastening structurally the existing advantage of the satiated in the international community. It is only by being aware of this wider dimension of power that politics can begin to operate effectively at the international level. Carr's prescriptions, generously described as accommodation (less generously as appeasement) in *The Twenty Years' Crisis* and integration in *Conditions of Peace*, recognize that power capabilities and the demands of power are forcing a reconsideration of the established practices of statecraft.

Morgenthau's interpretation of power was similarly wide-ranging. Civilization is merely a means of dominating individuals' "aspiration for power" through habituation in the state, while the international society lacks an alternative to the *animus dominandi* to an even greater extent. All systems of politics are for Morgenthau systems of oppression, with a change in the superficialities of the systems being the only genuine change. The primary system of power in international politics was the balance of power imported from mechanics in the eighteenth century. This system was inherently unstable and perched on the brink of collapse. It required the cooperation of the great powers in order to maintain efficiency. The balance of power then is a sort of presocial contract based on a tacit understanding of how power should be employed. At a deeper level, power's universality is attributed to the impossibility of achieving universal love—the lust for power being the only element of human behavior observable at all times. Power as a pathology of mankind, a determination to dominate is not akin to the rational deployment of power in order to achieve limited aims of security. It is, in fact, akin to Nietzsche's concept of power as the will to power, but if anything is even more extreme as Morgenthau's deeply pessimistic attitude toward humanity does not allow for anything other than a continuous cycle of domination, revolution, and domination. It is therefore rooted in the concept of the tragic as opposed to a rational understanding of Man's relationship to power.

Wight's concept of power is multifarious, incorporating elements of the three traditions, and the later addition of the inverted revolutionists. As demonstrated in chapter 5, Wight attempts to contextualize his Realism by reference to other traditions of thought in international politics while still recognizing that it is the controlling disciplinary factor. Power considerations dictate the logic of international society, but also and in a manner similar to Carr's analysis of international law and international norms of moral behavior. Wight attributes their operation to the power of the states who established them in the first place. The institutions of international law, diplomacy, war, and so on all rely either on an initial investment of power political capital, from which they have achieved a very limited (if important) autonomy, or are dependent upon their operation upon the powers of states to ensure this operation, generally on the basis of the interest of the safeguarding power. Again, similar to Carr, the international society is revealed as a product of power and the institutionalization of the interests of the powerful, status quo powers. International society may not quite be red in tooth and claw, but its ultimate feature remains war, and its secondary feature is the maintenance of international society that favors the great powers, who are accorded a special role in its upkeep and development.

Waltz also promotes the role of the great powers in his concept of power as it operates in the international system. For Waltz though the international system and the units that constitute the system are not constrained by the idea of an international society. The extent to which extraneous elements exercise an effect on the operation of the international system is excluded as to introduce it would interfere in the parsimony of the theory. Therefore no autonomy can be granted to the institutions of the international society, whether they be operational institutions such as diplomatic culture, international law, or formal institutions such as the United Nations or other international bodies. Relative power between states, treating power as analogous to money, is the Neorealist concept par excellence. It leads to the concept of balance, as if State A perceives that State B has more power than it does, it is likely to align itself with state C in order to counterbalance this relative advantage of State B. There is an elegant, almost ballet like quality of this notion of units agglomerating, an aesthetic understanding that correctly identified the politics of alignment during the cold war, but in its very effort to achieve timelessness as a theory of politics, Nerorealism could not escape the time in which it was formulated, or the idea of science from which it was derived.

Realism, Rationalism, Science

Perhaps the most peculiar inversion of Realism in both Neorealism and the paradigmatic reading of Realism is the assumption that it is a rationalist theory of international politics. There is no doubt that Neorealism rests on these foundations, but it is certainly not the case for Realism as a whole, if indeed it can be seen as a whole. The transition from a form of theory based upon the study of history and politics to a scientific theory of IR is perhaps the most significant of all the inversions of Realism, given the earlier Realists' antipathy to this form of theory.

The antipathy of Realism to Rationalism unites Carr, Morgenthau, and Wight. Carr considered Rationalism "an orderly blight" on thought, and the pretensions to scientific theory in IR a particularly unproductive example of the inapplicability of the universal claims of modern reason to provide answers to international politics.[41] Carr, like Nietzsche, opposed the uniperspectival character of scientific method, which could only provide a lopsided view of the world. Science, in the Greek sense of "knowing" could only be achieved through creating competing perspectives on international politics. The dialectic of Utopia and Reality was necessary to break the chains tying IR theory to modern science and liberalism. Carr refused to be tied to any one tradition and his critiques and analyses are derived from numerous sources. Pragmatic and inductive in his approach, Carr juxtaposed his form of theorization against abstraction and theory for theory's sake. Instead, Carr offered a purpose-driven approach that was dedicated to a problemsolving human science.

Given his conceptual confusion, it is understandable that people have read Morgenthau as either a precursor to, or the first, Realist to offer a "scientific" IR theory. Particularly in the early chapters, *Politics among Nations* presents itself as offering a science of international politics. Yet this is not necessarily a science based on either the natural sciences or the philosophy of science or modern rationalism. Morgenthau's understanding of theory as a scientific endeavor is in the sense of the *geisteswissenschaften* of the German academy. The distinction is important. In *Scientific Man versus Power Politics* and in *Science: Servant or Master?*, Morgenthau deliberately attacks the use of methodologies and philosophies of natural science as they are applied to questions of international politics. Rationalism is described as a mode of thinking that is historically situated in the Enlightenment and in the rise of the bourgeoisie, hence it is not a sufficient basis for creating answers to what are essentially political questions, which Morgenthau doubts Rationalism can provide. The science that Morgenthau offers is one that incorporates history, political theory, philosophy, economics, and sociology. His work is therefore as eclectic as that of Carr and organized in a similarly creative fashion.

Martin Wight's quiet disposition ensured that he did not, like his colleague Hedley Bull, engage in a confrontation with the scientific approach that was gaining ground in the 1960s. Wight regarded the Enlightenment as a "false dawn" and an *aurora borealis*, so the scientific approach, rooted in the Enlightenment tradition of confidence in human reason in identifying and solving problems according to rational analysis, did not hold much appeal. Wight, as a committed Christian, considered Man to be an inherently fallen creature, whose mind was quite insufficient to the task of providing the means of salvation, which was in the hands of God alone. Human reason has produced traditions of thought, the interplay of which provides some insight on the nature of international politics, but this insight is of a limited nature.

Neorealism evades the problem of meaning by removing Realism from deficient reality and providing it with a new abstract locale in which rational behavior can be expected of the units in the system. Where Morgenthau was at least concerned with attempting to draw some relationship between Realism and reality, even though he was never quite sure how best to do this, Waltz simply dispatched with reality altogether, except when it intruded on the purity of the theory as in the period after the cold war, which has seen Waltz put up a spirited defense of Neorealism despite, not because of, reality.

Where the earlier Realists were determined to engage with empirical reality, Waltz has been equally determined in his theoretical work on IR to avoid it whenever possible. In this sense he has, like the Rationalists before him, fled from our imperfect reality, to the perfect Reality of the ideal. It is significant that Waltz in *Theory of International Politics* does not refer to it as a Realist work, and it is not until later that it is described as a Neorealist work. By engaging in this flight from reality, Waltz effectively burned his bridges with the Realist tradition and ensured the emergence of Neorealism as a species of inverted idealism based on a notion of science that reduces reality to an abstract model rather than facing the ugly truths gained through an engagement with the practice of power. All IR theories are essentially narratives, what is necessary is to recognize that the richness of Realism offers advantages that have been lost in the flight from reality represented by Neorealism.

Conclusion

The proliferation of Realisms noted by James Der Derian in his introduction to *Critical Investigations*, which listed no less than 49 varieties of Realism, some belonging to and others outside (insofar as anything can be outside) the purview of IR theory, has continued apace.[42] Tempting as it is to engage on the relationship between magical Realism and IR theory, the range of Realisms discussed herein was kept to an IR-related minimum, although that in itself provides enough evidence of the impressive growth of Realisms: in addition to the Der Derian 49 we can add (among others) Offensive, Defensive, Romantic, Constructivist, American, Historical, Grotesque,

Subaltern, and my particular favorite—Realistic Realism. In addition, Realism has been cast in roles as varied as science, tragedy, and ideology.

Clearly Realism is breaking through the paradigmatic barriers and engaging with both theoretical challenges and the realities of international politics. In a sense, this is a return to the understanding of Realism professed by Carr as an eclectic *esprit de contradiction* determined to prick the balloon of utopianism, but also to gain some of utopianism's exuberant energy in facing global issues. Carr's disregard for barriers could serve as the template for a more critical engagement with contemporary politics, and there is also much to be gained from the insights of Morgenthau and Wight on the nature of power politics in the contemporary international society. Kenneth Waltz's embattled Neorealism remains the most convincing of the rationalist formulations of IR, and certainly is the most prevalent form of Realism in the American academy. Although it inverts many of the earlier positions of the Realists, Neorealism remains a part of the Realist family—it retains a lot of the concepts and logic of Realism, and as such there are resemblances as well as important differences.

The version of Realism presented here is one presented from the perspective of a genealogy of Realism, one of many possible historical reconstructions of the Realist tradition. It does not insist that it is the only way of understanding Realism, but would argue that it provides a more historically nuanced account of the emergence and descent of Realism in the twentieth century and the extent of the differences between, and sometimes within, the major texts of Realism. The purpose was to highlight the inconstancy, the argument, and the discord that has typified this tradition of thought.[43] The counter-memory related here allows each of the Realists presented a distinct voice in the flow of Realist ideas. If nothing else, the genealogy of Realism herein should deepen and broaden our perception of Realism. The counter-memory of Realism portrayed here should restore a certain vitality to Realism that has been lost in the transition to its paradigmatic form. IR can only benefit from efforts to restore Realism to its stance of being a theoretical critique and exposure of the ugly truth of our political existence at the international level.

Notes

Introduction: A Genealogical Reading of Realism

1. Nietzsche, *Beyond Good and Evil*, p. 53.
2. Nietzsche, *The Gay Science*, pp. 53–54.
3. See, e.g., Fozouni, "Confutation of Political Realism," which concludes, "A good starting point for critical reflection would be to explore why for the past several decades the discipline of international politics remained mesmerized by a false theory," p. 508. The nature of this "critical reflection" does not, however, extend outside the conceptual toolbox of the philosophy of science as used by Fozouni. A similar dedication to the philosophy of science, albeit different interpretations of the philosophy of science, characterizes the debate between John Vasquez and Kenneth Waltz in the pages of *The American Political Science Review* (see chapter 6 of the present study), see also Stephen Walt's denial of the inapplicability of Lakatosian evaluation and more pluralist conception of Realism and IR theory in general in "The Progressive Power of Realism," pp. 931–935.
4. For an excellent discussion of Realism as a political theory of IR, and a good identification of the problem of seeing Realism as a single tradition, see Walker, "Realism, Change, and International Political Theory," pp. 65–86. See also Steven Brooks's description of Realism as a house divided, this time between Neorealism and Postclassical Realism in, "Duelling Realisms"; and Waltz, "Realist Thought and Neorealist Theory."
5. Schmidt, *The Political Discourse of Anarchy*; Spegele, *Political Realism in International Theory*; George, *Discourses of Global Politics*. See also Haslam's *The Virtue of Necessity*.
6. Donnelly, *Realism and International Relations*; Vasquez, *The Power of Power Politics*.
7. For an analysis of epistemes see Foucault, *The Archaeology of Knowledge*.
8. Nietzsche, *The Gay Science: With a Prelude in German Rhymes and an Appendix of Songs*, pp. 239–240. On the issue of doing justice to Realism (and Morgenthau in particular), Jaap Nobel warns against taking for granted popularizations "that may serve the standard bearers of the new paradigm, but which do not do justice to Realism"; Nobel, "Realism versus Interdependence," p. 171.

9. Walker, *Inside/Outside*, p. 29.
10. Gadamer, *Truth and Method*, p. xii. Although I agree with Gadamer about the need for recognition that the human sciences are qualitatively different from "science" per se, I do not agree with his insistence that a "correct" method of hermeneutics should serve as its base. To do so seems to substitute an ideal practice for an ideal content.
11. Der Derian, "The Boundaries of Knowledge and Power in International Relations," p. 4.
12. Brian C. Schmidt, "The Historiography of Academic International Relations," p. 353.
13. Nietzsche, "On Truth and Falsity in Their Ultramoral Sense," p. 176.
14. For a fuller discussion of these themes, see chapter 1 in this book.
15. Waltz, "Realist Thought and Neorealist Theory," pp. 21–38.
16. "Nothing is rarer . . . than intellectual integrity . . . only certain truths are admitted; they know what they have to prove; that they are at one over their truths is virtually their means of recognizing one another," Nietzsche, *The Will to Power*, p. 246.
17. Heidegger, *Nietzsche, Vol. I, The Will to Power as Art*, p. 59 ff. See also in this tradition the Heidegger-inflected Ted Sandler, *Nietzsche: Truth and Redemption*.
18. Derrida states that any reading of Nietzsche that insists on a "single" or "true" reading of Nietzsche in a hermeneutic approach uncovering meaning, such as that of Heidegger is mistaken: "The hermeneutic project which postulates a true sense of the text is disqualified under this regime. Reading is freed from the horizon of meaning or truth of being, liberated from the values of the product's production or the present's presence," *Spurs*, p. 107. Insisting on a *sache*-based reading of Nietzsche, which insists that only a select band of interpreters can understand the nature of Nietzsche's truth, Sandler insists that there is a way of knowing "How to Read Nietzsche," which stresses the limited rather than the limitless nature of interpretation: Sandler, *Nietzsche*, pp. 209–215.
19. Vattimo, *The Adventure of Difference*, p. 92.
20. Nietzsche, *Gay Science*, pp. 239–240. See also Nietzsche, *The Will to Power*, "there are many kinds of eyes. Even the sphinx has eyes—and consequently there are many kinds of truths, and consequently there is no truth," p. 291. See also Williams, *Nietzsche's Mirror*, p. 94.
21. See Blondel, *Nietzsche. The Body and Culture*. "Perspectivism implies, not the negation of meaning, but more insistence on speech than on the body and the impossibility of a totalization of meaning. Every interpretation is *in fact* limited," p. 241. For Blondel, truths are singular to the interpreter and dependent upon the interpreter's perspective. In IR theory, Mohammed Ayoob bases his theory on perspectivism: "A perspective by definition does not exclude other perspectives because unlike 'theory,' it does not claim to be the sole repository of 'truth.' 'Perspective' thrives by building upon earlier insights, while modifying and adapting earlier perspectives to fit contemporary situations"; Ayoob, "Inequaity and Theorizing in International Relations," p. 28.
22. Nietzsche, *Human, All Too Human*, pp. 12–13.

23. Ibid., pp. 21–22. See also Nietzsche, *Daybreak*, p. 73: "there is absolutely no escape, no backway or bypath into the *real world*! We sit within our net, we spiders, and whatever we may catch in it, we catch nothing at all except that which allows itself to be caught in precisely *our* net."

24. Nietzsche, *Human, All Too Human*, p. 85. For his dismissal of utilitarianism as merely a partisan position, p. 109.

25. Although compare with his early, Schopenhauer-influenced notion of truth as gained/experienced through suffering in the third of the untimely meditations, Nietzsche, *Untimely Meditations*, p. 140 ff. By the time of the *Gay Science*, Nietzsche was even more skeptical regarding the notion of "truth": "What then are men's truths ultimately? They are the irrefutable errors of man," p. 151. Nietzsche's final statement on truth in *Ecce Homo* posits the idea of "truthfulness as the supreme virtue, that is to say the opposite of the cowardice of the 'idealist' who takes flight in the face of reality," Nietzsche, *Ecce Homo*, p. 98. This would seem to indicate that we cannot state what truth is, but we can state what it is not.

26. Nietzsche, *Twilight of the Idols and the Antichrist*, p. 45.

27. Nietzsche, *Beyond Good and Evil*, p. 51.

28. See, e.g., his identification of the role played by grammatical structures in determining the course of philosophy in the Indo-European language groups: Nietzsche, *Beyond Good and Evil*, pp. 49–50. Indeed, the power of language is such that Nietzsche states in *Twilight of the Idols*—"I fear that we are not getting rid of God because we still believe in grammar," p. 48.

29. Nietzsche, *Daybreak*, p. 1.

30. Nietzsche, *Daybreak*, p. 9.

31. Nietzsche, *Human, All Too Human*, p. 248.

32. Nietzsche, *Daybreak*, p. 54; see also Section 318, p. 158.

33. Foucault, *Society Must Be Defended*, p. 7.

34. Nietzsche, *Daybreak*, p. 206.

35. For one of his more concise expositions of the will to truth, see *The Will to Power*, p. 298, and for a short statement of the will to truth as "an art of interpretation," *The Will to Power*, p. 317.

36. Nietzsche, *Gay Science*, pp. 200–201. Nietzsche goes so far as to say that the will to truth is perhaps a kind of self-deception, but a valuable one. In *Human, All Too Human*, Nietzsche describes the "belief in having found truth" as responsible for the emergence of reason, logic, and mathematics, luckily before people realized "that they propagated a colossal error with their belief in language," p. 21.

37. See *Daybreak*, sections 168: *A Model* on Thucydides, pp. 169 and 448; *Honouring Reality*, p. 188 for Plato's flight from reality.

38. *Daybreak*, section 550, p. 221. See also, *Gay Science*, section 25, p. 50.

39. Nietzsche, *On the Genealogy of Morals*, p. 12.

40. "The apparent world is the only one: the real world has only been lyingly added," *Twilight of the Idols*, p. 46.

41. *Gay Science*, pp. 69–70. See also section 409 of the *Will to Power*: "What is needed above all is an absolute scepticism toward all inherited concepts," p. 221.

42. Deleuze and Guattari, *A Thousand Plateaus*, p. 7.
43. *Gay Science*, p. 168.
44. Nietzsche clearly sets up his genealogy as the inverse of that of the "English" "origins" of morality school rooted in Darwin and utilitarianism, that he found in his friend Paul Reé's *The Origin of Moral Sensation*: "There for the first time I clearly encountered an inverted and perverted kind of genealogical hypothesis, the genuinely English kind, and found myself drawn to it—as opposites attract one another." Preface to *Genealogy of Morals*, p. 5.
45. Nietzsche, Preface to *Genealogy of Morals*, p. 9. Foucault's reiteration of this sentiment is found in "Nietzsche, Genealogy, History," p. 369: "Genealogy is gray, meticulous, and patiently documentary. It operates on a field of entangled and confused parchments, on documents that have been scratched over and recopied many times."
46. Foucault, *Society Must Be Defended*, p. 9.
47. Ibid.
48. Ricouer, e.g., expresses the act of interpretation as the conflict of apparent and hidden meanings: "*Interpretation . . . is the work of thought which consists in deciphering the hidden meaning in the apparent meaning, in unfolding the levels of meaning implied in the literal meaning,*" Ricouer, "Existence and Hermeneutics," p. 13. The effect of interpretation is, in Ricouer's analysis, that "each interpretation, by definition, reduces this richness, this multivocity, and 'translates' the symbol according to its own frame of reference," p. 14. The advantage of a genealogy is that it recognizes that the multivocity exists, and is not insisting on univocity as a condition of truth. In the contest of ideas the worst thing that can happen is that ideas are "calmly laid on ice, the ideal is not refuted, it freezes." *Ecce Homo*, p. 60.
49. Nietzsche, *Ecce Homo*, p. 60.
50. See Bernauer and Mahon, "The Ethics of Michel Foucault." They isolate two moments in (Foucaultian) genealogy: "The first critical moment is a historical questioning of our existence . . . Second, genealogy separates out, from the contingent circumstances that have made us what we are, the possibility of no longer being, doing or thinking what we are, do, or think," p. 144.
51. *Human, All Too Human*, II. 126, p. 242.
52. Nietzsche, "On the Uses and Disadvantages of History for Life," p. 75.
53. Even one of the more intelligent and perceptive of those committed to understanding Realism as a paradigm, Stefano Guzzini, falls into this trap of insisting on "a more narrow definition . . . it is a game Realism cannot avoid engaging in—it must find a distinct and logically consistent definition of itself," Stefano Guzzini, "The Enduring Dilemmas of Realism," p. 537.
54. Nietzsche, "On the Uses and Disadvantages of History for Life," p. 86. See also his dismissal of the mask of objectivity as a history without philosophy in the person of St-Beuve in *Twilight of the Idols*, pp. 79–80.
55. As Nietzsche states in "On Truth and Falsity in their Ultramoral Sense," "Every word becomes at once an idea . . . by having simultaneously to fit innumerable, more or less similar (which really means never equal, therefore altogether

unequal) cases. Every idea originates through equating the unequal. As certainly as no one leaf is exactly similar to any other, so certain is it that the idea 'leaf' has been formed through an arbitrary omission of these individual differences, through a forgetting of the differentiating qualities." It is the act of forgetting therefore that enables the emergence of a Realist paradigm and the notion of Neorealism as its final embodiment.

56. Nietzsche, *Daybreak*, p. 205.
57. Foucault, "Nietzsche, Marx, Freud," p. 275.
58. Nietzsche, *Human, All Too Human*, p. 17.
59. Foucault, "Nietzsche, Marx, Freud," p. 278.
60. Preface to *Human, All Too Human*, p. 11.
61. Nietzsche, "On the Uses and Disadvantages of History for Life," p. 76.
62. On the perils and delights of genealogy see Der Derian, *On Diplomacy*, pp. 3–4.
63. Nietzsche, *Will to Power*, section 556, pp. 301–302.
64. Foucault opposed genealogy to "History" in much the same way: "Genealogy does not oppose itself to history as the lofty and profound gaze of the philosopher might compare to the molelike perspective of the scholar; on the contrary, it rejects the metahistorical deployment of ideal significations and indefinite teleologies. It opposes itself to the search for 'origins,' " Foucault, "Nietzsche, Genealogy, History," p. 81.
65. Buzan, "The Timeless Wisdom of Realism?" pp. 47–65.
66. Foucault, "Nietzsche, Genealogy, History," p. 81.
67. Flynn: "As genealogist, Foucault thus joins Marx, Nietzsche, and Freud as a 'master of suspicion,' uncovering the unsavory provenance (*pudenda origo*) of ostensibly noble enterprises," in "Foucault's Mapping of History," p. 36.
68. Mahon, *Foucault's Nietzschean Genealogy*, p. 9.
69. Nietzsche states something similar, "There is no struggle for existence between ideas and perceptions, but a struggle for dominion: the idea that is overcome is not annihilated, only driven back or subordinated," *Will to Power*, p. 323. It is the very capacity of Realism to reorient itself that is its greatest strength, particularly by reference to its own "history": Daniel H. Deudney writes, "[t]he strength of the Realist tradition lies in the great number and diversity of its arguments. As some decline in value, others emerge as more important. Old insights are forgotten, rediscovered, reformulated, refined, relabeled, and even occasionally improved upon," "Regrounding Realism," p. 6.
70. See Derrida, *Spurs*, p. 99.
71. Foucault, *Society Must Be Defended*, p. 10.

Chapter 1   Square Pegs and Round Holes

1. See the preface and first essay of Nietzsche, *On the Genealogy of Morals*.
2. Der Derian, *On Diplomacy*, p. 3.
3. Morgenthau, *Scientific Man versus Power Politics*, pp. 2–3.
4. Ibid., p. 10.

5. Hoffman, "International Relations," pp. 356–357.
6. Ibid., p. 357.
7. Kaplan claimed that Bull was too reliant upon Hoffman's reading of *System and Process*, see Kaplan, "The New Great Debate," p. 7n.
8. Bull, "International Relations: The Case for A Classical Approach," p. 370.
9. Ibid., p. 371.
10. Ibid., p. 376.
11. Carr, *The Twenty Years' Crisis*. However, see chapters 2 and 3 of this book for the specific understanding of science in Carr's work.
12. Kaplan "The New Great Debate," p. 3.
13. Ibid., p. 17.
14. Hoffman, "An American Social Science."
15. See also Krippendorf, "The Dominance of American Approaches in International Relations," pp. 28–40.
16. Young, "Aron and the Whale: A Jonah in Theory."
17. Keohane, "Theory of World Politics," p. 159.
18. Ibid., pp. 164–165.
19. Mansbach and Vasquez, *In Search of Theory*, p. xv.
20. Vasquez, *The Power of Power Politics*, p. 23. See also *In Search of Theory*, p. 4.
21. Mansbach and Vasquez, *In Search of Theory*, pp. 5–6n.
22. Vasquez, *The Power of Power Politics*, p. 31.
23. Mansbach and Vasquez, *In Search of Theory*, p. 3.
24. Vasquez, *The Power of Power Politics*, p. 37.
25. Ibid.
26. Ibid., p. 37.
27. Ibid., pp. 65–66. It should be noted that the questions are related to IR and not solely to Realism.
28. Ibid., p. 122.
29. Ibid., 130–153.
30. Ibid., p. 286.
31. Legro and Moravcsik, "Is Anybody Still a Realist?" p. 9n.
32. Ibid.
33. Ibid., p. 11.
34. Ibid., pp. 11–22.
35. Ibid., p. 53. As a corrective to the arguments put forward by Moravcsik and Legro, see the response to this article by Feaver et al., "Brother Can You Spare a Paradigm," pp. 165–193.
36. Bull, "International Theory the Case for a Classical Approach."
37. Kuhn, "A Response to my Critics," p. 245.
38. Kuhn, *The Structure of Scientific Revolutions*, p. 175.
39. Kuhn, *The Structure of Scientific Revolutions*, p. 208. As Friedrich Kratochwil writes, "It hardly augurs well for the practitioners of political science when they apply Kuhnian criteria in a field in which most of the preconditions for a scientific community are not met," Friedrich Kratochwil, "The Embarrassment of Changes: Neo-Realism as the Science of Realpolitik Without Politics," p. 68.

40. I have noted in the text above where the "paradigmists" admit deviating from the original Kuhninan notion in terms of theoretical advances. For a critique of positivism from the "scientific realism" wing of the philosophy of science, see Lane, "Positivism, Scientific Realism and Political Science. Recent Developments in the Philosophy of Science," pp. 361–382. Scientific Realism, currently the most influential school within the philosophy of science is more accepting of a wider array of methods than positivism, "Approaches that were largely outlawed by positivism's insistence upon universal laws, axiomatic theory structures and vigorous falsificationism would be acceptable under the alternative scientific roof of realism," p. 378. Lane adds the proviso "realists see their position as *more rather than less rigorous* than positivism."

41. It is worth noting that Vasquez does not mention *Scientific Man versus Power Politics* in his bibliography and also seems unaware that Morgenthau wrote a positive introduction to David Mitrany's *A Working Peace System*. Mitrany is one of the authors that Vasquez sets up in opposition to Morgenthau.

42. Barkin has made a similar point about the misidentification of Realism with Neorealism due to conceptual and theoretical confusion in relation to epistemology and ontology in the discipline of IR, see Barkin, "Realist Constructivism," pp. 325–332.

43. Popper, *The Logic of Scientific Discovery*, p. 33.

44. Ibid., p. 87n.

45. In a critique of Realism that became typical in the 1990s, Bertrand Badie argues that Realism's state centrism has led to its "death": "due to the intolerable requirement that obliges states to compromise with ordinary actors . . . The international non-state actors may be considered the 'new bourgeoisie' of international politics, challenging the monopolistic and absolutist role of the state," Badie, "Realism Under Praise, or Requiem?" p. 258.

46. Marxist interpretations of Realist thought are similarly concerned with representing Realism as state-centric, see, e.g., Lacher, "Putting the State in Its Place: The Critique of State-Centrism and Its Limits," pp. 521–541.

47. E.H. Carr, *Twenty Years' Crisis*, p. 3. Some authors deny the validity of the term first great debate, as the "debate" was not so much a debate in theoretical terms, it was rather the supersession of utopian international theory by events in contemporary politics, especially the outbreak of World War Two and the cold war, cf. Ashworth, *Creating International Studies*. See also Wilson, "The Myth of the 'First Great Debate,' " pp. 1–17.

48. E.H. Carr, *International Relations between the Two World Wars*, p. 4.

49. Ibid., p. 25.

50. Ibid., pp. 26–27.

51. Ibid.

52. Ibid., pp. 31–38.

53. Ibid., p. 44.

54. Ibid., p. 5.

55. Hobbes, *Leviathan*, p. 187.

56. E.H. Carr, *International Relations between the Two World Wars*, p. 181 ff.

57. Carr, *Nationalism and After*, p. 37. See chapter 3 for a fuller discussion of Carr's attitude toward the state.
58. Ibid., p. 44.
59. Ibid., pp. 59, 70.
60. Carr, *The Twenty Years' Crisis*, pp. 158–159.
61. Ibid., p. 162.
62. Ibid., p. 209.
63. See chapter three.
64. Morgenthau, *Politics among Nations*, p. 10. Duncan Bell refutes the suggestion that Realism is necessarily state centric, "In Freeden's terminology, we can argue consequently that the state is a culturally adjacent concept, in other words a concept that has assumed a central role due to external cultural influences . . . not logically necessary to the core structure," Bell, "Anarchy, Power and Death," p. 230.
65. Morgenthau's introduction to David Mitrany's *A Working Peace System*, p. 9. Thanks to Luke Ashworth for bringing this piece to my attention.
66. Ibid., p. 11.
67. Identifying Realism as an ideological project as opposed to a "scientific" project, Duncan Bell isolates the role of the state as a "culturally adjacent concept, in other words a concept that has assumed a central role due to external cultural influences," Bell, "Anarchy, Power and Death," p. 230. Barkin makes the important observation that many "contemporary definitions of realism assume that the state is the central actor in international politics. For early realists, this premise was more a matter of observation than of deduction . . . E.H. Carr (1964, 224–235) concluded that though states were currently the locus in global politics, they need not necessarily remain the central actor." The problem, according to Barkin, is that both Realists and critics of Realism shifted the concept of the state from an observation to a defining element of Realism; Barkin, "Realist Constructivism," pp. 327–328.
68. Morgenthau, *Scientific Man versus Power Politics*, p. 186.
69. Ibid., pp. 176–177.
70. Ibid., p. x.
71. Morgenthau, *Politics among Nations*, p. 225.
72. Ibid., p. 228.
73. Ibid., p. 231 ff. Morgenthau favors the aristocratic international society of the seventeenth and eighteenth century to that of the democratic age. The intrusion of democratic thinking has resulted in the fragmentation and destruction of international morality as the homogeneous group of aristocrats that dominated the conduct of IR in earlier modernity have been replaced by a more heterogeneous grouping with nationalistic emphases upon particular missions of which they are the centre. The aristocratic community was replaced by atomized individuals acting on the basis of "my country, right or wrong." Nothing testifies to the influence of Burke on Morgenthau's thought more than this peculiar position, despite stating on p. 229 that the practice of politics is more civilized in the contemporary age than in ages past.

Chapter 2   Realism as Contramodern Critique

1. Foucault, "What is Enlightenment?" pp. 309–310.
2. Foucault, "What is Enlightenment?" p. 319.
3. To take just two prominent examples from writers active in the mid-twentieth century from both ends of the political spectrum, on the right, Michael Oakeshott, "Rationalism in Politics," and on the left, Theodor W. Adorno and Max Horkheimer, *Dialectic of Enlightenment.*
4. Schmidt, "Anarchy, World Politics and the Birth of a Discipline," p. 9. For an alternative reading of the prehistory of the field and the interwar period see Schmidt, "Lessons from the Past," pp. 333–459. See chapter 3 in this book for an in-depth discussion of the role played by Carr and responses to his criticisms both in terms of the so-called First Great Debate and beyond.
5. See the various essays in the excellent *Thinkers of the Twenty Years' Crisis* for an introduction to the thought world of the pre–World War Two liberal internationalists David Long and Peter Wilson, *Thinkers of the Twenty Years' Crisis: Inter War Idealism Reassessed.* For a useful discussion of "Idealism," and the work of Leonard Woolf in particular, see Wilson, *The International Theory of Leonard Woolf.* See also Ashworth's *Creating International Studies.*
6. Carr's assault on utopianism should not be seen as a "debate," it is after all simply a critique. See Wilson, "The Myth of the First Great Debate"; Ashworth, "Did the Realist-Idealist Great Debate Really Happen?" pp. 33–51.
7. E.H. Carr, *The Twenty Years' Crisis, 1919–1939,* p. 3.
8. Ibid., pp. 5, 13. Mannheim and Niebuhr are identified by Carr as two leading influences on *The Twenty Years' Crisis.*
9. Ibid., p. 60.
10. Ibid., p. 60.
11. It would be interesting to compare Carr's notion of personification and Gramsci's notion of a nation's "soul." There are also interesting echoes of Mazzini, who is condemned by Carr for his idea of division of labor on the international scale. There are also obvious parallels to Nietzsche's power/morality analysis in *On the Genealogy of Morals.*
12. Carr, *Twenty Years' Crisis,* pp. 71–88.
13. Lucian M. Ashworth states that the harmony of interests was a feature of the early Angell's writings, but not the later. Carr, however, was attacking the idea of the harmony of interests as a feature of international and diplomatic discourse, not its location in any given text. In this sense, again, the First Great Debate is exposed as a myth.
14. Carr, *Twenty Years' Crisis,* p. 105.
15. Ibid., pp. 119–120.
16. Ibid., p. 132.
17. Ibid., p. 141.
18. Ibid., p. 146.
19. Ibid., p. 150.
20. Ibid., p. 148.

21. Carr inveighs against traditional Marxist history on a number of occasions, most notably in *What Is History?*
22. E.H. Carr, *The Twenty Years' Crisis*, p. 61.
23. Carr, *Twenty Years' Crisis*, pp. 158–159.
24. This explains Carr's support for the Munich agreement as a model of negotiated change. In an example of the moral relativism that numerous commentators find particularly worrying (especially Morgenthau, see chapter 3) in Carr's work, the considerations of the Czechoslovaks do not enter this power equation.
25. Ibid., p. 180.
26. Ibid., p. 190.
27. Morgenthau, *Scientific Man versus Power Politics*, pp. 2–3.
28. "Morgenthau has in mind positivist science, alongside rationalism, as an example of an extreme will to know which must be avoided. For Morgenthau the dominance of positivist science has contributed to the deterioration of 'the moral condition of mankind.' " Pin-Fat, "The Metaphysics of the National Interest," p. 227.
29. Ibid., p. 3.
30. Ibid., p. 5.
31. Ibid., p. 10.
32. Morgenthau, *Scientific Man versus Power Politics*, p. 27.
33. Ibid., p. 40.
34. Ibid., p. 46.
35. Ibid., p. 51.
36. Ibid., p. 86.
37. Ibid., p. 87.
38. Ibid., p. 101.
39. Ibid.
40. Ibid., p. 107.
41. Ibid., p. 107.
42. Ibid., p. 115.
43. Ibid., p. 124.
44. Ibid., p. 129. Typical of Morgenthau's conflicted leanings, he nonetheless advocates the use of *homo economicus* as a template for his *homo politicus* in *Politics among Nations*.
45. Ibid., p. 132.
46. Ibid., p. 149.
47. For the full range of influences on Morgenthau see Frei, *Hans J. Morgenthau*.
48. Ibid., p. 143.
49. Ibid., p. 145.
50. Ibid., pp. 155–165.
51. Ibid., pp. 176–184.
52. Ibid., p. 183.
53. Ibid., p. 188.
54. See the excellent article by Gismondi, "Tragedy, Realism, and Postmodernity," pp. 453–460.
55. Morgenthau, *Scientific Man versus Power Politics*, p. 190.

56. Ibid., p. 191.
57. Ibid., p. 193.
58. Ibid., p. 201.
59. Ibid., pp. 120–122, 3.

Chapter 3   E.H. Carr and the Complexity of Power Politics

1. Booth, "Security in Anarchy," pp. 527–545; Haslam, *The Vices of Integrity*; Jones, *E.H. Carr and International Relations*; Cox, Booth, and Dunne, "The Eighty Years' Crisis"; Cox, *E.H. Carr*. The iconic status accorded to Carr is ironic, given his later repudiation of the field of IR. See Cox's new introduction to the latest edition of *The Twenty Years' Crisis*; and Dunne's *Inventing International Society*.
2. Carr, "An Autobiography," p. xix.
3. The magpie like nature of Carr's theory has been commented on by Peter Wilson, "E.H. Carr: The Revolutionist's Realist," p. 9 in PDF version.
4. Carr, *The Twenty Years' Crisis*, p. 11.
5. Ibid., 9–7.
6. Numerous commentators have seen Carr's demand for a science of IR in the light of a modern positivist science, e.g., Gilpin, "The Richness of the Tradition of Political Realism," p. 205.
7. Carr, *Twenty Years' Crisis*, pp. 2–3.
8. Ibid.
9. As late as his autobiographical sketch of Tamara Deutscher, Carr was writing against the idea of an objective history: "One can go on investigating the causes of causes of causes in pursuit of a final objective cause. But of course one never reaches it." Carr, "An Autobiography," p. xxi.
10. Dunne, *Inventing International Society*, pp. 26–31. See also Dunne's chapter, "Theories as Weapons," pp. 217–233.
11. Jones, *E.H. Carr and International Relations*, pp. 46–65. See also the ingenious reading of Carr's rhetorical intentions to persuade both Marxist intellectuals and Foreign Office conservatives in Buzan, Jones, and Little, *The Logic of Anarchy*, pp. 206–208. See also Wilson, "Radicalism for a Conservative Purpose," p. 134.
12. Carr, "An Autobiography," p. xviii. *The Twenty Years' Crisis* is described by Carr as "not exactly a Marxist work, but strongly impregnated with Marxist ways of thinking, applied to international affairs." Ibid., p. xx.
13. Carr, *Twenty Years' Crisis*, p. 5.
14. Jones, *E.H. Carr and International Relations*, pp. 56–60.
15. In discussing Andrew Linklater's reading of Carr, Peter Wilson makes a similar point: "Linklater fails to mention that the dialectic between realism and utopianism is, for Carr, an endless one, and it certainly not clear from his IR writings alone whether he conceived this process as progressive." Wilson, "E.H. Carr: The Revolutionist's Realist," p. 5 in the PDF version.
16. Carr, *Twenty Years' Crisis*, p. 10. See Jones' anthropocentric Freudian interpretations in *E.H. Carr and International Relations*, p. 56. See also Jones, "E.H. Carr: Ambivalent Realist," pp. 95–119.

17. Carr, *Twenty Years' Crisis*, p. 11.

18. Carr, *Twenty Years' Crisis*, p. 10. Emphasis added.

19. Guzzini makes the point that Carr's system was almost entirely one of negation: "His synthesis was not based on particular values, but unfolded in the mere negation of the leading ideology of the day: at times it required a critique of Utopianism, as during the interwar period, and at others a critique of the stasis of *Realpolitik*, as during the heyday of the Cold War." Guzzini, *Realism in International Relations*, p. 23.

20. This is the central concept that eluded Whittle Johnston. "E.H. Carr's Theory of International Relations." As Wilson writes, "It was not change *per se* which he branded utopian; nor conscious, progressive change; but large–scale constitutional blue–prints for change: the drawing up of covenants and charters and the signing of pacts. . . . Change in Carr's view, needed to be substructural rather than superstructural, social and economic before legal and political." "The Myth of the 'First Great Debate,' " p. 13.

21. Carr, *Twenty Years' Crisis*, p. 214. Carr develops the point on p. 218 in the context of his summation of the bargaining process as the only real option.

22. Peter Wilson maintains that Carr commits a "remarkably sudden abandonment of his twin conceptual pillars of his science of International Relations—'utopia' and 'reality'—in all his subsequent works." "The Myth of the First Great Debate," p. 7. I argue that Carr puts the same concepts to work, but in less explicit form, in *Conditions of Peace* and *The Future of Nations*. Wilson revises his position somewhat in his "E.H. Carr: The Revolutionist's Realist," where he states: "it can be argued that, given his range of interests and concerns, and the eclecticism of his approach, Carr was a remarkably consistent thinker," p. 9 in the PDF version.

23. Carr, *Britain*, p. 16.

24. Carr, *The Future of Nations*, p. 9. See Linklater, "The Transformation of Political Community," p. 331. See also Wilson's reading of Carr's theory of self-determination, and reaction to this theory in "The New Europe Debate in Wartime Britain," pp. 41–47.

25. Ibid., pp. 17–20. Carr almost certainly is overstating his case, despite plebiscite evidence in favor of his position.

26. Ibid., p. 41.

27. Ibid., p. 37.

28. Ibid., p. 48.

29. Ibid., pp. 49–51. Whereas *The Twenty Years' Crisis* is a key text in IR, and *Conditions of Peace* has, at least to some extent, been rediscovered by historians of IR (Peter Wilson in particular), *The Future of Nations: Independence or Interdependence?* has not received the same amount of attention. This is understandable as its core is reproduced in the larger *Conditions of Peace*. The separation of cultural and state nation, as promoted in *Future of Nations*, however, deserves recognition in that it addresses the need for a commitment to develop super-state bodies in the international political economy more in keeping with the pressures of the day, while also retaining the cultural nation as a means by which populaces may retain an attachment to their culture.

30. Peter Wilson argues that *Conditions of Peace* can be seen "as a response, at least in part, to those critics who skilfully revealed the fragility of Carr's Utopia vs Realism dialectic." Peter Wilson, "The Myth of the First Great Debate," p. 7. I contend that *Conditions of Peace* is in fact the location in which the synthesis of utopia and Realism is played out to its logical conclusion: systemic transformation through power to achieve a moral end. Carr, *Conditions of Peace*.

31. I argue contrary to Whittle Johnston, who underestimates the importance of *Conditions of Peace*, describing it as a transitional work between *The Twenty Years' Crisis* and *Nationalism and After*. Johnston's accusation that Carr's theory is inconsistent ignores the continued dialectic of power and morality formulated in *The Twenty Years' Crisis* and explored in *Conditions of Peace* and *Nationalism and After*. Johnston, "Carr's Theory of International Relations."

32. Carr, *Conditions of Peace*, p. 10.

33. Ibid., pp. 26–36.

34. Ibid., p. 108.

35. Ibid., pp. 106–107.

36. For a discussion of Carr's approach in the context of a wider discussion of the fate of Europe in the postwar age, see Peter Wilson's "The New Europe Debate in Wartime Britain," pp. 39–62.

37. Carr, *Conditions of Peace*, p. 254.

38. Ibid., p. 257.

39. Ibid., p. 275.

40. Ibid., p. 255.

41. Carr, *Twenty Years' Crisis*, p. 90.

42. Carr, *Nationalism and After*, p. 37. Peter Wilson writes, "So despite his reputation as one of the main figures of post-war realism—a doctrine which emphasises the inevitable struggle for power between sovereign states—Carr was clearly a proponent of European unity . . . like David Mitrany the high-priest of functionalism, he was of the firm opinion that nationalism had reached its apogee and would henceforth fall into decline." "The New Europe Debate in Wartime Britain," p. 45.

43. Carr, *Democracy in International Affairs*, pp. 1–19.

44. Ibid., p. 19.

45. Peter Wilson has examined the full range of reactions to Carr in three pieces of bibliographical importance, see Wilson, "The Myth of the First Great Debate," pp. 1–16; Wilson, "Carr and His Early Critics"; Cox and the review article "Radicalism for a Conservative Purpose." Many thanks to Luke Ashworth for pointing me in the direction of and giving me copies of, many of the pieces discussed hereafter, and valuable discussion of their contents.

46. Howe, "The Utopian Realism of E.H. Carr," p. 277.

47. For a full description of Woolf's reaction to Carr see Wilson, *The International Theory of Leonard Woolf*, especially Chapter 8.

48. Woolf, "Utopia and Reality."

49. Carr, *Britain*, pp. 172, 195 ff.

50. Wilson writes, "it would be wrong to identify *in toto* Carr's support for *a* policy of appeasement with *the* policy of appeasement pursued by Chamberlain and

Halifax between March 1936 and March 1990." Wilson, "Carr and His Early Critics," p. 184.
51. Woolf, "Utopia and Reality," p. 175.
52. Coventry, "The Illusions of Power," p. 762. Wilson identifies Coventry as Crossman in "Carr and His Early Critics," p. 165, and discusses his criticism of Carr's prescription of appeasement on p. 174.
53. Zimmern, "A Realist in Search of a Utopia."
54. Morgenthau, "The Political Science of E.H. Carr," p. 128.
55. Ibid., pp. 129–130.
56. Ibid., p. 134.
57. Ibid. See also Kenneth Thompson's Morgenthau-inspired, "E.H. Carr: The Immanence of Power as the Standard," pp. 77–78.
58. Hayek, *The Road to Serfdom*, p.146.
59. Angell, "Who Are the Utopians? And Who the Realists?" pp. 4–5.
60. Stebbing, *Ideals and Illusions*, p. 6.
61. Ibid., p. 7. Peter Wilson has detected a strong resemblance between the critiques of Stebbing and Woolf, arguing that, though Stebbing better expressed reservations about Carr, these were nonetheless derived from Woolf's original position. Wilson, "Carr and His Early Critics," p. 195, n. 26.
62. Peter Wilson maintains that "Carr was not 'running away from the notion of good' so much as pointing out that 'good' was a good deal more complicated than many people made it out to be." Wilson, "Carr and His Early Critics," p. 187.
63. Ibid., p. 14. Michael Cox argues that it was Carr's desire to avoid a war that accounts for the fact that "he was quite prepared to let Nazi Germany take over most of Eastern Europe. For the same set of pragmatic reasons he was prepared to let Soviet Russia do the same after the war." Cox, "Will the Real E.H. Carr Please Stand Up?" p. 650.
64. Stebbing, *Ideals and Illusions*, p. 15.
65. Ashworth, *Creating International Studies*, pp. 106–129.
66. Johnston, "Carr's Theory of International Relations," p. 861.
67. Ibid., p. 878.
68. Evans, "E.H. Carr," p. 78.
69. Ibid., p. 81. "The urgency and respect that power demands in international politics does not, in Carr's view, rule out the possibility of a moral basis for international politics."
70. Ibid., p. 86.
71. Bull, "The Theory of International Politics, 1919–1969," p. 191.
72. Bull, *"The Twenty Years' Crisis,"* p. 630.
73. Ibid., pp. 628–629. Bull concentrates exclusively on *The Twenty Years' Crisis*, but some of his criticisms, e.g., that Carr does not offer a vision of a new world order, are addressed in *The Future of Nations, Conditions of Peace*, and *Nationalism and After*.
74. Smith, *Realist Thought from Weber to Kissinger*, pp. 71–72.
75. Ibid., p. 95.
76. Ibid., p. 76.

77. Jones, *E.H. Carr and International Relations*, see the chapter on *The Twenty Years' Crisis*. It could also be attributed to the role of Dostoevsky, who reified the Russian people over and against the intelligentsia as a means to determine moral policy.
78. See Paul Hirst's more sympathetic reading of Carr's misinterpretation of Nazism, "The Eighty Years' Crisis," p. 137. Carr writes, "I don't think it was 'til 1938, after the occupation of Austria, that I began to think of Hitler as serious danger. No doubt I was very blind." Carr, "An Autobiography," p. xix.
79. Smith, *Realist Thought*, pp. 96–98. In an alternative interpretation, Paul Howe argues that Carr was not in fact a relativist or a determinist. Howe, "Utopian Realism," pp. 282–286.
80. E.H. Carr, "Karl Mannheim," p. 180.
81. Ibid., p. 182.
82. Ibid., p. 182.
83. Jones, *E.H. Carr and International Relations*, p. 122.
84. Ibid., p. 10.
85. Cox, "Social Forces, States, and World Orders," p. 207.
86. Ibid., p. 211.
87. Ibid., p. 221.
88. George, *Discourses of Global Politics*, p. 21.
89. Ibid., p. 35.
90. Haslam, *Vices of Integrity*, pp. 44–46.
91. Carr, *Dostoevsky*, p. 198.
92. Ibid., p. 205.
93. Ibid., pp. 289, 300–301. On Rozanov, Carr says, "Modern writers have thought themselves daring and original for saying the same thing more than thirty years later."
94. Carr, *Twenty Years' Crisis*, p. 9.
95. Andrew Linklater, e.g., says, "one of my intentions is to release Carr from the grip of the Realists and to highlight certain affinities between his writings on the state and critical theories of international relations." Linklater, "The Transformation of Political Community," p. 324. Peter Wilson attributes Carr's reputation in IR theory to vindictiveness and laziness in IR theory textbooks. See Wilson, "Radicalism for a Conservative Purpose," pp. 129–130 and 135, "The real Carr is thus a million miles away from the stereotype Carr of the IR textbook."

Chapter 4   The Realist Truths of Hans Morgenthau

1. For the influence of Weber on Morgenthau, and the lasting significance of his engagement with Carl Schmitt, see Williams, "Why Ideas Matter in International Relations," pp. 633–665. See also Tarak Barkawi, "Strategy as Vocation," pp. 159–184. For the complex issue of the Schmittian inflections on Morgenthau's Weberian aspect, see Pichler, "The Godfathers of 'Truth,'" pp. 185–200. For the influence of Nietzsche on Morgenthau see Frei, *Hans J. Morgenthau*.

2. Morgenthau, "Positivism, Functionalism, and International Law," p. 260.

3. Morgenthau, "The Limitations of Science and the Problem of Social Planning," pp. 174–180.

4. Morgenthau, "Science of Peace: A Rationalist Utopia," pp. 24–21. On the fundamental misalliance of international politics and scientific method, see also Jervis, "Hans Morgenthau, Realism, and the Scientific Study of International Politics," pp. 858–859. Murielle Cozette goes further in her interpretation of Morgenthau's concept of reason: "Reason, far from being the ultimate decision maker, is actually used by passions and interest, and moves whenever these passions and interests want to go . . . Reason therefore intervenes *ex post* to provide men with justifications which give human actions the appearance of rationality or morality." Murielle Cozette, "Realistic Realism?" p. 430.

5. Morgenthau, "The Limitations of Science," p. 184.

6. Ibid., p. 185.

7. Morgenthau, "Another 'Great Debate,' " p. 966. Morgenthau wrote this article in response to criticism of *Politics among Nations*, and in particular the criticisms of Robert Tucker, Frank Tannenbaum, and Arthur Schlesinger Jr. It is particularly useful in that it clarifies some of the more technical issues around the construction of Morgenthau's theoretical position that are glossed over in *Politics among Nations* itself.

8. Morgenthau, "The Perils of Empiricism," p. 352. See Bain's "Deconfusing Morgenthau" for an interesting discussion on the anticipation of social constructivist approaches to international theory in Morgenthau's work.

9. Morgenthau, *Scientific Man versus Power Politics*, p. 3.

10. Ibid., p. 5

11. Ibid.

12. Ibid., p. 107.

13. Morgenthau, "Another 'Great Debate': The National Interest of the United States," p. 977. Compare this approach with Carr's rejection of economistic logic in *The Twenty Years' Crisis*.

14. Morgenthau, "Common Sense and Theories of International Relations," pp. 208–209. Morgenthau stresses the difference between the natural and social sciences in numerous places, e.g., "the social scientist is not a detached observer of social events as the natural scientist is a detached observer of the phenomenon of nature." Morgenthau, "The Escape from Power," p. 4.

15. Morgenthau, *Science: Servant or Master?* pp. 12–20.

16. Morgenthau, *The Decline of Democratic Politics*, p. 4.

17. Ibid., pp. 2–3.

18. Ibid., p. 36.

19. Ibid., p. 131.

20. Morgenthau, "Thought and Action in Politics," pp. 617–624.

21. Morgenthau, "The Machiavellian Utopia," pp. 145–147.

22. Morgenthau, *Politics among Nations*, pp. 3–4.

23. Ibid., p. 4. In the prefaces to the second and third editions of *Politics among Nations*, Morgenthau complains of being criticized for expressing beliefs that he

did not hold: "it is not pleasant for an author to be blamed for ideas he has not only never expressed, but which he has explicitly and repeatedly refuted and which are rejected by him," Preface to the Third Edition, *Politics among Nations*, p. xv.

24. Ibid., p. 4.

25. Morgenthau, "International Relations," p. 359.

26. This also contradicts Morgenthau's theory of "social facts," if in the final analysis empirical reality is rooted in the mind of the observer (see note 7), then this historico-empirical reality is also reduced to the level of a subjective, rather than objective category.

27. Michael Smith argues that Morgenthau's approach to history is derived from the perception of a rational pattern of politics inherent in the pursuit of the national interest. Smith, *Realist Thought*, p. 155. He concludes that this principle of the national interest is simply to subjectivize history to a passive content necessary as the basis for the rational theory that Morgenthau is trying to create.

28. Morgenthau, "Love and Power," pp. 189–196.

29. Morgenthau, *Politics among Nations*, p. 5.

30. Morgenthau was anxious to stress that the national interest was the sole means of understanding IR, and that "moral abstractions" were responsible for the decline of American diplomacy and statecraft. See, e.g., Morgenthau, *In Defense of the National Interest*, pp. 3–4.

31. Morgenthau, *Politics among Nations*, p. 7. The significance of this counter theory of irrationalism would grow to have an enormous impact on Morgenthau's thinking in the latter part of his life.

32. Ibid., p. 8.

33. See, e.g., Morgenthau's formulation of this in "The Escape from Power": "Any Realistic conception of politics . . . must assume that man is born and lives in chains. He is the object of political domination . . . man living in chains not only wants to be free but also wants to be master." The Freudian aspect of Morgenthau's interpretation of power is best expressed in his essay, "Love and Power." Both of these essays are to be found in Morgenthau, *Politics in the Twentieth Century*. Morgenthau claimed to have been influenced by Freudian psychoanalysis, but ultimately rejected it because like Marxism it was unable to account for the "complexities and varieties of political experience." Morgenthau, "An Intellectual Autobiography," p. 67.

34. Morgenthau, "The Impotence of American Power" and "The Problem of Germany," pp. 315–325, 332–340.

35. Morgenthau, *Politics among Nations*, p. 9.

36. Morgenthau, *In Defense of the National Interest*, p. 33.

37. The "contemporary phenomenon of the moral crusade" the "ultimate degeneration of international moralism" is found in both Wilsonian and Soviet universalism, *In Defense of the National Interest*, pp. 36–37.

38. That is not to say that a country cannot act in a fashion beneficial to others, just that the benefit should originate in sound principles of enlightened self-interest—it is reasonable for a country to seek another's support by giving it aid.

According to Morgenthau, foreign aid should be allocated according to a political logic, rather than an economic logic. Thus the Soviet paving of the streets of Kabul was more effective in gaining Afghan support than an American dam in a remote part of the country. Morgenthau, "A Political Theory of Foreign Aid," p. 308.

39. This is also in contradiction of his earlier statement on the interdependence of ethics an politics as a result of the "curious dialectic" of ethics and politics, "which prevents the latter, in spite of itself, from escaping the former's judgement and normative direction." Morgenthau, "The Evil of Politics and the Ethics of Evil," p. 5.

40. Morgenthau, *Politics among Nations*, p. 20.

41. Morgenthau, *Politics among Nations*, 6th ed., p. 41. This is a posthumous edition edited by Morgenthau's colleague Kenneth Thompson.

42. Ibid., pp. 52–53.

43. Morgenthau, *Politics among Nations*, 5th ed., p. 167.

44. Ibid., p. 173.

45. Ibid., pp. 184–185.

46. Ibid., p. 193.

47. Ibid., p. 213.

48. Ibid., pp. 219–220.

49. See, e.g., his treatment of the idea of just behavior being dependent upon the social construction of the idea of the "just" of a particular political community, and the absence of an agreed definition of just behavior in the international community: "No man could give answers to these questions which would be more than reflections of his own national preconceptions, for there are no standards at once concrete and universal enough to provide more than *ex parte* answers to such questions." Morgenthau, "National Interest and Moral Principles in Foreign Policy," p. 211.

50. *Politics among Nations*, p. 220.

51. See, e.g., his appeal to a transcendent ethics of human behavior outside of history in the symposium *Human Rights and Foreign Policy* (New York: Council on Religion and International Affairs, 1979), pp. 1–10.

52. Morgenthau, *Politics among Nations*, p. 226.

53. Morgenthau, "The Moral Dilemma of Political Action," p. 17.

54. Morgenthau, *Politics among Nations*, p. 228.

55. Ibid., p. 375.

56. Ibid., p. 406.

57. Ibid., pp. 417–420.

58. Ibid., pp. 465–470.

59. Ibid., p. 475.

60. Ibid., pp. 489–511.

61. Ibid., pp. 517–518.

62. Ibid., p. 538.

63. Morgenthau describes the use of nuclear weapons as a suicidal absurdity in "The Impotence of American Power," p. 327. Morgenthau, *Science: Servant or*

Master? pp. 115 ff. for his analysis of the policies of deterrence, counterforce, arms limitation, and control and alliances see the final chapter of *A New Foreign Policy for the United States*, pp. 207–240.

64. Morgenthau, *Human Rights and Foreign Policy*, pp. 42–43. Elsewhere, Morgenthau described the contemporary world as confronted with novel problems, "the breakdown of the state system . . . and the development of a technology which makes war an instrument of total destruction." The change in the nature of war, and the powers involved in the post WW2 world were such that the balance of power had ceased to be an effective means of conceiving the international environment. Morgenthau, "The Nature of Contemporary World Politics." Morgenthau and Thompson, pp. 293–294.

65. Morgenthau, *Science: Servant or Master?* p. 153.

66. On Morgenthau's opposition to the Vietnam War see Ellen Glaser Rafshoon, "A Realist's Opposition to War: Hans J. Morgenthau and Vietnam," Peace & Change (2001), Vol. 26, No. 1.

67. Fromkin, "Remembering Hans Morgenthau," pp. 87–88.

68. Morgenthau, "An Intellectual Autobiography," p. 68.

69. Ibid. For the influence of Weber on Morgenthau, and the lasting significance of his engagement with Carl Schmitt, see Williams, "Why Ideas Matter in International Relations." See also Barkawi, "Strategy as Vocation," pp. 159–184. For the complex issue of the Schmittian inflections on Morgenthau's Weberian aspect, see Pichler, "The Godfathers of 'Truth,' " pp. 185–200 and Huysman, "Know Your Schmitt." For the influence of Nietzsche on Morgenthau see Frei, *Hans J. Morgenthau.*

Chapter 5   Nuancing Realism

1. Bull, "Martin Wight and the Theory of International Relations," pp. ix–xxiii. Dunne, *Inventing International Society.*

2. Keohane, "Theory of World Politics," pp. 164–165; Vasquez, *The Power of Power Politics*, p. 37.

3. Wight, "An Anatomy of International Thought," p. 227.

4. Bull, "Martin Wight and the Theory of International Relations," p. xiv. For a restatement of the Grotian Wight as opposed to a pluralist Wight, see Suganami, "The International Society Perspective on World Politics Reconsidered," p. 2 n.

5. Bull, "Martin Wight and the Theory of International Relations," p. xiv.

6. Ibid.

7. Bull, "The Theory of International Politics, 1919–1969," p. 191.

8. Thompson, *Masters of International Thought*, p. 51.

9. Epp, "Martin Wight: International Relations as Realm of Persuasion," p. 125. Roger Epp, along with Tim Dunne and Ian Hall, must be credited with the uncovering of many of Wight's lost work, which has added enormously to our understanding of Wight.

10. Ibid., p. 102.

11. Ibid., p. 127.

12. Epp, "Martin Wight: International Relations as Realm of Persuasion."
13. Ibid., p. 135.
14. For a critique of the tendency to describe the English School and Wight in terms of a *via media*, see Little, "The English School's Contributions to the Study of International Relations," pp. 398, 405. Little argues that the English School must be seen from a pluralist perspective, where all aspects of the three traditions are accorded a distinct place.
15. Dunne, *Inventing International Society*, pp. 60–61.
16. Wight, *International Theory: The Three Traditions*, p. 268.
17. Ibid., p. 206.
18. Wight, *Power Politics*, 2nd ed, p. 29.
19. Ibid., p. 46.
20. Wight, "Why Is There No International Theory?" p. 19.
21. Ibid., p. 20.
22. Ibid., p. 26.
23. Ibid., p. 20.
24. Ibid., p. 28.
25. Ibid., p. 30.
26. Ibid., p. 33.
27. Ibid., p. 34.
28. Wight, *Christian Commentary*, pp. 2–5.
29. Nicholson, "The Enigma of Martin Wight," p. 17. Scholars have increasingly become aware of the influence of Christianity on Wight's particular brand of international theory. Thomas, "Faith, History and Martin Wight," pp. 905–929 is a comprehensive historical account of the role of Christianity (and especially the influence of Dick Sheppard) in Wight's life and in his formulation of his theories of international society. Ian Hall investigates the impact of religion on perhaps Wight's most important professional relationship, that with Arnold Toynbee, in Hall, "Challenge and Response," pp. 389–404. Roger Epp places Wight in a wider "Augustinian" framework in "The 'Augustinian Moment' in International Politics."
30. Wight, *Christian Commentary*, p. 5. I am grateful to Ian Hall for providing me with a copy of this and other rare archival material relating to Wight.
31. Wight, "The Church Russia and the West," pp. 30–31.
32. Ibid., p. 33.
33. Ibid., p. 41.
34. Wight, "Christian Pacifism," p. 21.
35. Machiavelli, *The Prince and the Discourses*, pp. 55–56.
36. Wight, *Power Politics*, 2nd ed., p. 102.
37. Wight, *International Theory*, pp. 30–37.
38. Ibid., p. 29.
39. Wight, "Western Values in International Relations," p. 101.
40. Wight, *International Theory*, p. 160.
41. Ibid., pp. 164–168.
42. Ibid., pp. 168–172.

43. Wight, "The Balance of Power," pp. 157–185.
44. Ibid., p. 149.
45. Ibid., p. 150.
46. Wight, "The Balance of Power and International Order," p. 110.
47. Wight, "The Balance of Power," p. 509.
48. Wight, *International Theory*, p. 36.
49. Wight, *Systems of States*, p. 174.
50. Ibid., p. 175.
51. Ibid., pp. 174–200.
52. Morgenthau, *Politics among Nations*, p. 355.
53. Bull, "Martin Wight and the Study of International Relations," p. 15; Roberts, "Foreword" in *International Theory: The Three Traditions*, p. 24.
54. Wight, "Why Is There No International Theory?" p. 34.
55. Wight, *International Theory*, p. 12.
56. Wight, *Power Politics*, 2nd ed., p. 88.
57. Ibid., p. 91.

Chapter 6   The Retreat from the Real

1. A fairly sympathetic reading of Waltz's theory, which stresses the sociological strengths of *Theory of International Politics*, is provided in Goddard and Nexon, "Paradigm Lost?" pp. 9–1. For a criticism of the structuralist underpinnings of Neorealism see R.B.J. Walker, "Realism, Change and International Political Theory," pp. 65–86.
2. Waltz, *Theory of International Politics*, p. 1.
3. Waltz, *Theory of International Politics*, p. 2.
4. Ibid., p. 6.
5. Ibid., pp. 6–7.
6. Ibid., pp. 45–53.
7. Ibid., pp. 92–93.
8. Ibid., p. 68.
9. Deleuze and Guattari, *A Thousand Plateaus*, p. 24.
10. Waltz, *Theory of International Politics*, p. 66.
11. Ibid., pp. 69–70.
12. Ibid., pp. 70–73. It is important to bear in mind, however, that Waltz is not talking about states, or the state system in a "real" sense: "There may be a 'real' international system with a concrete existence, but Waltz's theory is not, strictly speaking, about it . . . Waltz's international system is neither a descriptive reality nor are his units concrete realities." Goddard and Nexon, "Paradigm Lost?" pp. 23–24. Criticisms of Neorealism that do not take this into account somewhat miss the point of Neorealism, thus Duffield's "Political Culture and State Behavior: Why Germany Confounds Neorealism," pp. 765–803, while being correct about the impact of cultural factors on the conduct of German foreign policy invalidating Neorealism's insistence on systemic primacy, Neorealism does not attempt to engage with the "real" world at all.

13. Ibid., p. 73. For a good (and brief) explanation of the appeal of structuralism across disciplines see Foucault, "Truth and Power."
14. Waltz, "Realist Thought and Neorealist Theory," p. 29.
15. Waltz, *Theory of International Politics*, pp. 89–93.
16. Ibid., p. 104.
17. Waltz, "Reflections on *Theory of International Politics*."
18. Lapid, "The Third Debate," p. 236.
19. George, *Discourses of Global Politics*, pp. 118–126.
20. Ibid., p. 127.
21. This is the essential point of John A. Vasquez's criticism of what he considers to be the Realist paradigm, see chapter 1.
22. Vasquez, "The Realist Paradigm and Degenerative Vs Progressive Research Programs," p. 907.
23. Waltz, "Evaluating Theories," p. 914.
24. Ibid., p. 916.
25. Waltz, "The Origins of War in Neorealist Theory," p. 628.
26. Waltz, "The New World Order," p. 189.
27. Ibid., p. 194.
28. Waltz, "The Emerging Structure of International Relations," p. 52.
29. Ibid., p. 59.
30. Ibid., pp. 59–61.
31. Ibid., p. 63.
32. Ibid., pp. 64–67.
33. Ibid., p. 79.
34. Waltz, "Structural Realism after the Cold War," p. 5.
35. Waltz, "Structural Realism," p. 27.
36. As Friedrich Kratochwil asks, "What if the preoccupation with *the* scientific method served neither the advance of science nor our understanding of politics whose illumination, after all, presumably is the goal of the discipline?" Kratochwil, "The Embarrassment of Changes," p. 69.
37. Mouritzen, "Kenneth Waltz," pp. 80–81.
38. Waltz, "Realist Thought and Neorealist Theory," p. 27.
39. Waltz, "Reflections on *Theory of International Politics*," p. 334.
40. Ibid, p. 335.
41. Jean Baudrillard, *Simulacra and Simulation*, p. 2.
42. Ibid., p. 31.

Conclusion: A Counter-Memory of Realism

1. For a description of the offensive versus defensive Realism debate see Taliaferro, "Security Seeking Under Anarchy," pp. 128–161.
2. Mearsheimer, *The Tragedy of Great Power Politics*, pp. 17–18.
3. For example, their attitude to security pressures is almost identical, see Brooks, "Duelling Realisms," p. 447 ff. For an account that stresses the differences

between the two positions see Schmidt, "Realism as Tragedy," pp. 427–441, see also Snyder, "Mearsheimer's World."

4. Walt, "The Progressive Power of Realism," p. 932.
5. Rosecrance, "Review: Has Realism become Cost-Benefit Analysis?" pp. 132–154.
6. Richard Little expresses this very well, "There would be no problem with this . . . provided they had self-consciously decided to make a break with the classical realists. But members of this school often associate themselves with the classical realist tradition without apparently being aware of what they have left behind." Little, "The English School *vs* American Realism," p. 444.
7. See Ashley, "Political Realism and Human Interests," pp. 204–236. This very interesting essay focuses on the relationship between "practical realism" and "technical realism" as opposed aspects of a Realism "that is very far from being an internally harmonious tradition," p. 207.
8. Hoffman, "An American Social Science: International Relations," p. 219. See also Waever's analysis of the impact of American IR on the study of international politics in Waever, "The Sociology of a Not So International Discipline," pp. 687–727. Waever argues that although dominant globally the American influence has reached its peak, and that Europe is increasingly seeking its own means of understanding IR independent of American influence.
9. Foucault, *Archaeology of Knowledge*, p. 191.
10. Nietzsche, *Birth of Tragedy*, p. 4. See also *Thus Spoke Zarathustra*, pp. 312–314.
11. Nietzsche, *Human, All Too Human*, p. 57.
12. Ibid., p. 105.
13. Ibid., pp. 130–131.
14. Ibid., p. 263.
15. Nietzsche, *Birth of Tragedy*, p. 86. Deleuze and Guattari refer to the relationship as one of "a long history of suspicion and even repression," *A Thousand Plateaus*, p. 109.
16. Nietzsche, *Daybreak*, p.11. See also, *Gay Science*, p. 50.
17. Nietzsche, *Daybreak*, p. 158.
18. For Neorealists, truth resides in "objectivity," as Michael C. Williams has stated of Neorealism, "its analysis claims to be founded not on the vicissitudes of opinion and subjective interpretation, but rather on the secure tenets of science which provide an objective representation of reality . . . a claim to know: specifically a 'scientific' claim to know, objectively, the reality of international relations." Williams, "Neo-realism and the Future of Strategy," pp. 200–201.
19. Nietzsche, *Gay Science*, pp. 200–201.
20. Ibid., p. 215.
21. Nietzsche, *Beyond Good and Evil*, p. 39.
22. Ibid., p. 160.
23. Ibid., p. 160. "We may even expect that the more complex and intricate the matters being studied are the stronger the urge to be simple-minded would become." Waltz, "Realist Thought and Neorealist Theory," p. 27.
24. Nietzsche, *Will to Power*, p. 262.
25. Ibid., p. 274.
26. Ibid., p. 298.

27. Deleuze and Guattari, *A Thousand Plateaus*, pp. 101–106.
28. Ibid., p. 144.
29. Comparable to Kuhn's investigation of paradigm or gestalt shifts in *The Structure of Scientific Revolutions*.
30. Nietzsche, *Human, All Too Human*, p. 247.
31. Or in the case of Carr and Wight, of the rapidly expanding and homogenizing "English School."
32. Nietzsche, *Human, All Too Human*, p. 245.
33. Rouchard, "Introduction" in Foucault, *Language, Counter-Memory, Practice*, p. 18.
34. Wight, *Power Politics*, p. 106.
35. Ibid., p. 23.
36. Ibid., p. 25.
37. Gilpin, "No One Loves a Political Realist," p. 26. Arguably Gilpin is exaggerating the Realist attitude by describing the international environment as a jungle.
38. Desch states, "Most realists are not satisfied merely to understand the world as it is; they also study world politics in order to make it more humane and just within the limits of what international anarchy allows." Desch, "It Is Kind to Be Cruel," p. 419.
39. This is the central thrust of his "Western Values in International Relations," pp. 89–131.
40. In terms of a role for moral input, Shibley Telhami writes, "Nothing in Neorealism precludes a theory, or an empirical finding, linking moral factors and the external behavior of states, Although this point is misunderstood even by some of the adherents of Neorealism." Telhami, "Kenneth Waltz, Neorealism, And Foreign Policy," p. 164.
41. See Kahler, "Rationality in International Relations," pp. 919–941. Kahler describes a process of Realism being domesticated by American social science.
42. Der Derian, "Introduction" in *International Theory: Critical Investigations*, p. 1.
43. For a more conventional restatement of Realism's plurality and rude health, see Jervis, "Realism in the Study of World Politics," pp. 971–991.

Bibliography

Adorno, Theodor W. and Max Horkheimer. *Dialectic of Enlightenment* (New York: Continuum/Seabury Press, 1972).

Angell, Norman. "Who are the Utopians? And Who the Realists?" *Headway in Wartime*, January 1940.

Ashworth, Lucian M. "Did the Realist-Idealist Great Debate Really Happen? A Revisionist History of International Relations," *International Relations* (2002), Vol. 16, No. 1.

Ashworth, Lucian M. *Creating International Studies* (London: Ashgate, 1998).

Ayoob, Mohammed. "Inequity and Theorizing in International Relations: The Case for Subaltern Realism," *International Studies Review* (2002), Vol. 4, No. 3.

Badie, Bertrand. "Realism Under Praise, or Requiem? The Paradigmatic Debate in International Relations," *International Political Science Review* (2001), Vol. 22, No. 3.

Bain, William. "Deconfusing Morgenthau: Moral Inquiry and Classical Realism Reconsidered," *Review of International Studies* (2000), Vol. 26, No. 3.

Barkawi, Tarak. "Strategy as Vocation: Weber, Morgenthau, and Modern Strategic Studies," *Review of International Studies* (1998), Vol. 24, No. 2.

Barkin, J. Samuel. "Realist Constructivism," *International Studies Review* (2003), Vol. 5, No. 3.

Baudrillard, Jean. *Simulacra and Simulation* (Ann Arbor: University of Michigan Press, 1994).

Bell, Duncan S.A. "Anarchy, Power and Death: Contemporary Political Realism as Ideology," *Journal of Political Ideologies* (2002), Vol. 7, No. 2.

Bernauer, James W. and Michael Mahon. "The Ethics of Michel Foucault," in *The Cambridge Companion to Foucault*, ed. Gary Guting (Cambridge: Cambridge University Press, 1994).

Blondel, Eric. *Nietzsche: The Body and Culture: Philosophy as a Philological Genealogy*, trans. Seán Hand (London: Athlone, 1991).

Booth, Ken. "Security in Anarchy: In Theory and Practice," *International Affairs* (1991), Vol. 67, No. 3.

Brooks, Steven G. "Duelling Realisms," *International Organization* (1997), Vol. 51, No. 3.

Bull, Hedley. "The Theory of International Politics, 1919–1969," in *International Theory: Critical Investigations*, ed. James Der Derian (London: Macmillan, 1995).

Bull, Hedley. "International Relations: The Case for A Classical Approach," *World Politics* (2002), Vol. 18, No. 3.

Bull, Hedley. "Martin Wight and the Theory of International Relations," in *International Theory: The Three Traditions*, ed. Gabriele Wight and Brian Porter (Leicester: Leicester University Press, 1991).

Bull, Hedley. "*The Twenty Years' Crisis* Thirty Years On," *International Journal* (1969), Vol. 24, No. 4.

Bull, Hedley. *The Anarchical Society. A Study of Order in World Politics*, 2nd ed. (Basingstoke: Macmillan, 1995).

Buzan, Barry, Charles Jones, and Richard Little. *The Logic of Anarchy: NeoRealism to Structural Realism* (New York: Columbia University Press, 1993).

Buzan, Barry. "The Timeless Wisdom of Realism?" in *Theorising International Relations: Positivism and After*, ed. Steve Smith, Ken Booth, and Marysia Zalewski (London: Cambridge University Press, 1996).

Carr, E.H. "Karl Mannheim," in *From Napoleon to Stalin and Other Essays* (Basingstoke, U.K.: MacMillan, 1980).

Carr, E.H. "An Autobiography," in *E.H. Carr: A Critical Appraisal,* ed. Michael Cox (Basingstoke, U.K.: Palgrave, 2000).

Carr, E.H. *Britain: A Study in Foreign Policy from the Versailles Treaty to the Outbreak of War* (London: Longman Green, 1939).

Carr, E.H. *Conditions of Peace* (London: MacMillan, 1942).

Carr, E.H. *Democracy in International Affairs*, Cust Foundation Lecture, University College Nottingham, 1945.

Carr, E.H. *Dostoevsky (1821–1881): A New Biography* (London: Allen & Unwin, 1931).

Carr, E.H. *The Future of Nations: Independence or Interdependence?* (London: Kegan Paul, 1941).

Carr, E.H. *International Relations between the Two World Wars* (London: Macmillan, 1947).

Carr, E.H. *Nationalism and After* (London: Macmillan, 1946).

Carr, E.H. *The Twenty Years' Crisis. An Introduction to the Study of International Relations* (New York: Harper & Row 1964).

Cox, Michael, Ken Booth, and Tim Dunne. "The Eighty Years' Crisis," special edition of *Review of International Studies*, reprinted as *The Eighty Years' Crisis: International Relations 1919–1999* (Cambridge: Cambridge University Press, 1998).

Cox, Michael. "Introduction," in E.H. Carr, *The Twenty Years' Crisis* (London: Palgrave, 2001).

Cox, Michael. "Will the Real E.H. Carr Please Stand Up?" *International Affairs* (1999), Vol. 75, No. 3.

Cox, Michael. *E.H. Carr: A Critical Appraisal* (Basingstoke, U.K: Palgrave, 2000).

Cox, R.W. "Social Forces, States, and World Orders," in *Neorealism and Its Critics*, ed. Keohane (New York: Columbia University Press, 1986).

Cozette, Murielle. "Realistic Realism? American Political Realism, Clausewitz and Raymond Aron on the Problem of Means and Ends in International Politics," *The Journal of Strategic Studies* (2004), Vol. 27, No. 3.

Crossman, Richard. "Richard Coventry, 'The Illusions of Power,'" *The New Statesman and Nation*, November 25, 1939.

Deleuze, Gilles and Felix Guattari. *Anti Oedipus Capitalism and Schizophrenia* (London: Athlone, 1984).

Deleuze, Gilles and Felix Guattari. *A Thousand Plateaus: Capitalism and Schizophrenia* (Minneapolis: University of Minnesota Press, 1987).

Deleuze, Gilles. *Foucault*, trans. Seán Hand (London: Athlone, 1988).

Deleuze, Gilles. *Nietzsche and Philosophy* (London: Athlone, 1983).

Der Derian, James. "A Reinterpretation of Realism: Genealogy, Semiology, Dromology," in *International Theory: Critical Investigations*, ed. James Der Derian (Basingstoke: MacMillan, 1995).

Der Derian, James. "The Boundaries of Knowledge and Power in International Relations," in *International/Intertextual Relations. Postmodern Readings of World Politics*, ed. James Der Derian and Michael Shapiro (New York: Lexington, 1989).

Der Derian, James. *Antidiplomacy: Spies, Terror, Speed, and War* (Cambridge, M.A.: Blackwell, 1992).

Der Derian, James. *On Diplomacy: A Genealogy of Western Estrangement* (Oxford: Blackwell, 1987).

Derrida, Jacques. *Spurs: Nietzsche's Styles*, trans. Barbara Harlow (Chicago: University of Chicago Press, 1979).

Deudney, Daniel H. "Regrounding Realism: Anarchy, Security, and Changing Material Contexts," *Security Studies* (2000), Vol. 10, No. 1.

Donnelly, Jack. *Realism and International Relations* (Cambridge: Cambridge University Press, 2000).

Duffield, John S. "Political Culture and State Behavior: Why Germany Confounds Neorealism," *International Organization* (1999), Vol. 53, No. 4.

Dunne, Tim. "Theories as Weapons: E.H. Carr and International Relations," in *E.H. Carr: A Critical Appraisal*, ed. Michael Cox (Basingstoke, U.K.: Palgrave, 2000).

Dunne, Tim. *Inventing International Society: A History of the English School* (Basingstoke, U.K.: MacMillan, 1998).

Evans, Graham. "E.H. Carr and International Relations," *British Journal of International Studies* (1975), Vol. 1, No. 2.

Feaver, Peter D. et al. "Brother Can You Spare a Paradigm," *International Security* (2000), Vol. 24, No. 1.

Flynn, Thomas. "Foucault's Mapping of History," in *The Cambridge Companion to Foucault*, ed. Gary Gutting (Cambridge: Cambridge University Press, 1994).

Foucault, Michel. "Nietzsche, Genealogy, History," in *The Foucault Reader. An Introduction to Foucault's Thought*, ed. Paul Rabinow (London: Penguin, 1991).

Foucault, Michel. "Nietzsche, Marx, Freud," in *Aesthetics, Method, and Epistemology*, ed. James Faubion, trans. Robert Hurley et al. (London: Penguin, 1998).

Foucault, Michel. "Truth and Power," in *Power. Essential Works of Foucault*, Vol. 3, ed. James D. Faubion (New York: The New Press, 2000).

Foucault, Michel. "What is Enlightenment?" in *The Foucault Reader. An Introduction to Foucault's Thought*, ed. Paul Rabinow (London: Penguin, 1991).

Foucault, Michel. *Society Must Be Defended: Lectures at the Collège de France, 1965–76*, ed. Mauro Bertani and Alessandro Fontana, trans. David Macey (London: Penguin, 2003).

Foucault, Michel. *The Archaeology of Knowledge* (London: Tavistock, 1974).

Fozouni, Bahman. "Confutation of Political Realism," *International Studies Quarterly* (1995), Vol. 39, No. 4.

Frei, Christoph. *Hans J. Morgenthau: An Intellectual Biography* (Baton Rouge: Louisiana State University Press, 2001).

Fromkin, David. "Remembering Hans Morgenthau," *World Policy Journal* (1993), Vol. 10, No. 3.

Gadamer, Hans Georg. *Truth and Method*, trans. Joel Weinshemer and Donald G. Marshall (London: Sheed and Ward, 1989).

George, Jim. *Discourses of Global Politics. A Critical (Re)introduction to International Relations* (Boulder, Colo.: Lynne Rienner, 1994).

Gilpin, Robert. "No One Loves a Political Realist," *Security Studies* (1996), Vol. 5, No. 3.

Gilpin, Robert. "The Richness of the Tradition of Political Realism," in *Neo-Realism and Its Critics*, ed. Robert O. Keohane (New York: Columbia University Press).

Gismondi, Mark. "Tragedy, Realism, and Postmodernity: *Kulturpessimus* in the Theories of Max Weber, E.H. Carr, Hans Morgenthau, and Henry Kissinger," *Diplomacy and Statecraft* (2004), Vol. 15, No. 3.

Goddard, Stacie E. and Daniel H. Nexon. "Paradigm Lost? Reassessing Theory of International Politics," *European Journal of International Relations* (2005), Vol. 11, No. 1.

Guzzini, Stefano. "The Enduring Dilemmas of Realism," *European Journal of International Relations* (2004), Vol. 10, No. 4.

Guzzini, Stefano. *Realism in International Relations and International Political Economy: The Continuing Story of a Death Foretold* (London: Routledge, 1998).

Hall, Ian. "Challenge and Response: The Lasting Engagement of Arnold J. Toynbee and Martin Wight," *International Relations* (2003), Vol. 17, No. 3.

Haslam, Jonathan. *The Vices of Integrity: E.H. Carr, 1892–1982* (London: Verso, 1998).

Hayek, F.A. *The Road to Serfdom* (London: Mackays, 1993).

Heidegger, Martin. *Nietzsche. Vol. 1, The Will to Power as Art*, trans. Farrell Krell (London: Routledge & Kegan Paul, 1981).

Hirst, Paul. "The Eighty Years' Crisis, 1919–1989—Power," *Review of International Studies* (1998), Vol. 24, No. 5.

Hobbes, Thomas. *Leviathan* (London: Penguin, 1985).

Hoffman, Stanley. "An American Social Science: International Relations," in *International Theory Critical Investigations*, ed. James Der Derian (London: Macmillan, 1995).

Hoffman, Stanley. "International Relations: The Long Road to Theory," *World Politics* (1959), Vol. 11, No. 3.

Howe, Paul. "The Utopian Realism of E.H. Carr," *Review of International Studies* (1994), Vol. 20, No. 3.

Jackson, Robert. *The Global Covenant, Human Conduct in a World of States* (Oxford: Oxford University Press, 2000).

Jef Huysman. "Know Your Schmitt: A Godfather of Truth and the Spectre of Nazism," *Review of International Studies* (1999), Vol. 25, No. 2.

Jervis, Robert. "Hans Morgenthau, Realism, and the Scientific Study of International Politics," *Social Research* (1994), Vol. 61, No. 4.

Jervis, Robert. "Realism in the Study of World Politics," *International Organization* (1998), Vol. 52, No. 4.

Johnston, Whittle. "E.H. Carr's Theory of International Relations: A Critique," *Journal of Politics* (1967), Vol. 29, No. 4.

Jones, Charles. "E.H. Carr: Ambivalent Realist," in *Post-Realism: The Rhetorical Turn in International Relations*, ed. Francis A. Beer and Robert Hariman (East Lansing: Michigan State University Press, 1996).

Jones, Charles. *E.H. Carr and International Relations: A Duty to Lie* (Cambridge: Cambridge University Press, 1998).

Kahler, Miles. "Rationality in International Relations," *International Organization* (1998), Vol. 52, No. 4.

Kaplan, Morton. "The New Great Debate: Traditionalism versus Science in International Relations," *World Politics* (1966), Vol. 19, No. 1.

Keohane, Robert. "Theory of World Politics," in *Neorealism and Its Critics*, ed. Robert Keohane (New York: Columbia University Press, 1986).

Klein, Bradley. *Strategic Studies and World Order* (Cambridge: Cambridge University Press, 1994).

Kratochwil, Friedrich. "The Embarrassment of Changes: Neo-Realism as the Science of *Realpolitik* without Politics," *Review of International Studies* (1993), Vol. 19, No.1.

Krippendorf, Ekkehart. "The Dominance of American Approaches in International Relations," in *The Study of International Relations: The State of the Art* (London: Macmillan, 1989).

Kuhn, Thomas S. "A Response to my Critics," in *Criticism and the Growth of Knowledge*, ed. Imre Lakatos (London: Cambridge University Press, 1970).

Kuhn, Thomas S. *The Structure of Scientific Revolutions*, 2nd ed. (Chicago: Chicago University Press, 1970).

Lacher, Hannes. "Putting the State in Its Place: The Critique of State-Centrism and Its Limits," *Review of International Studies* (2003), Vol. 29, No. 4.

Lane, Ruth. "Positivism, Scientific Realism and Political Science. Recent Developments in the Philosophy of Science," *Journal of Theoretical Politics* (1996), Vol. 8, No. 3.

Lapid, Yosef. "The Third Debate: On the Prospects of International Theory in a Post-Positivist Era," *International Studies Quarterly* (1989), Vol. 33, p. 236.

Legro, Jeffrey W. and Andrew Moravcsik. "Is Anybody Still a Realist?" *International Security* (1999), Vol. 24, No. 2.

Little, Richard. "The English School's Contributions to the Study of International Relations," *European Journal of International Relations* (2000), Vol. 6, No. 3.

Little, Richard. "The English School vs. American Realism: A Meeting of Minds or Divided by a Common Language?" *Review of International Studies* (2003), Vol. 29, No. 3.

Lyotard, Francois. *The Postmodern Condition: A Report on Knowledge* (Manchester: Manchester University Press, 1986).

Mahon, Michael. *Foucault's Nietzschean Genealogy. Truth, Power, and the Subject* (Albany: SUNY Press, 1992).

Mansbach, Richard and John A. Vasquez. *In Search of Theory. A New Paradigm for Global Politics* (New York: Columbia University Press, 1981).

Mearsheimer, John J. *The Tragedy of Great Power Politics* (New York: Norton, 2001).

Morgenthau, Hans J. "The Limitations of Science and the Problem of Social Planning," *Ethics* (1944), Vol. 54, No. 3.

Morgenthau, Hans J. "A Political Theory of Foreign Aid," *American Political Science Review* (1962), Vol. 56, No. 2.

Morgenthau, Hans J. "An Intellectual Autobiography," *Society* (1978), Vol. XV.

Morgenthau, Hans J. "Another 'Great Debate': The National Interest of the United States," *The American Political Science Review* (December 1952), Vol. 46, No. 4.

Morgenthau, Hans J. "Common Sense and Theories of International Relations," *Journal of International Affairs* (1967), Vol. XXI.

Morgenthau, Hans J. "International Relations," *Encyclopaedia Britannica*, reprinted in *Politics in the Twentieth Century* (Chicago: University of Chicago Press, 1971, abridged edition).

Morgenthau, Hans J. "Introduction" in David Mitrany's *A Working Peace System* (Chicago: Quadrangle, 1966).

Morgenthau, Hans J. "Love and Power," in *Politics in the Twentieth Century* (Chicago: University of Chicago Press, 1971, abridged edition).

Morgenthau, Hans J. "National Interest and Moral Principles in Foreign Policy," *American Scholar* (Spring 1949), Vol. XVIII.

Morgenthau, Hans J. "Positivism, Functionalism, and International Law," *American Journal of International Law* (April 1940), Vol. 34, No. 2.

Morgenthau, Hans J. "Science of Peace: A Rationalist Utopia," *Social Research* (1975), Vol. XLII.

Morgenthau, Hans J. "The Escape from Power," *Politics in the Twentieth Century* (Chicago: University of Chicago Press, 1971, abridged edition).

Morgenthau, Hans J. "The Evil of Politics and the Ethics of Evil," *Ethics* (October 1945), Vol. LVI.

Morgenthau, Hans J. "The Impotence of American Power," in *Truth and Power. Essays of a Decade, 1960–1970* (New York and London: Praeger, 1970).

Morgenthau, Hans J. "The Limitations of Science and the Problem of Social Planning," *Ethics* (April 1944), Vol. 54, No. 3.

Morgenthau, Hans J. "The Machiavellian Utopia," *Ethics* (1945), Vol. 55.

Morgenthau, Hans J. "The Moral Dilemma of Political Action," in *Politics in the Twentieth Century* (Chicago: University of Chicago Press, 1971, abridged edition).

Morgenthau, Hans J. "The Nature of Contemporary World Politics," in *Principles & Problems of International Politics. Selected Readings*, ed. Hans J. Morgenthau and Kenneth Thompson (Washington: University Press of America, 1982, reprint).

Morgenthau, Hans J. "The Perils of Empiricism," in *Politics in the Twentieth Century*, ed. Morgenthau (Chicago: University of Chicago Press, 1971, abridged edition).

Morgenthau, Hans J. "The Political Science of E.H. Carr," *World Politics* (1948), Vol. 1, No. 1.

Morgenthau, Hans J. "The Problem of Germany," in *Truth and Power. Essays of a Decade, 1960–1970* (New York and London: Praeger, 1970).

Morgenthau, Hans J. "Thought and Action in Politics," *Social Research* (1971), Vol. XXXVII.

Morgenthau, Hans J. "The Political Science of E.H. Carr," *World Politics* (1948), Vol. 1.

Morgenthau, Hans J. *A New Foreign Policy for the United States* (New York and London: Frederick A. Praeger, 1969).

Morgenthau, Hans J. *Human Rights and Foreign Policy* (New York: Council on Religion and International Affairs, 1979).

Morgenthau, Hans J. *Human Rights and Foreign Policy* (New York: Council on Religion and International Affairs, 1979).

Morgenthau, Hans J. *In Defense of the National Interest. A Critical Examination of American Foreign Policy* (Washington: University Press of America, 1982).

Morgenthau, Hans J. Kenneth Thompson, ed. *Politics among Nations*, 6th ed. (New York: Knopf, 1985).

Morgenthau, Hans J. *Politics among Nations. The Struggle for Power and Peace*, 5th ed. (New York: Knopf, 1973).

Morgenthau, Hans J. *Science: Servant or Master?* (New York: New American Library, 1972).

Morgenthau, Hans J. *Scientific Man versus Power Politics* (Chicago: Chicago University Press, 1946).

Morgenthau, Hans J. *The Decline of Democratic Politics* (Chicago and London: University of Chicago Press, 1958).

Mouritzen, Hans. "Kenneth Waltz: A Critical Rationalist between International Politics and Foreign Policy," in *The Future of International Relations. Masters in the Making*, ed. Iver B. Neumann and Ole Waever (London: Routledge, 1997).

Nicholson, Michael. "The Enigma of Wight, Martin," *Review of International Studies* (1981), Vol. 7, No. 1.

Nietzsche, Friedrich. "On the Uses and Disadvantages of History for Life," in *Untimely Meditations*, ed. David Breazeale, trans. R.J. Hollingdale (Cambridge: Cambridge University Press, 1997).

Nietzsche, Friedrich. "On Truth and Falsity in Their Ultramoral Sense," in *The Complete Works of Friedrich Nietzsche*, ed. Oscar Levy, Vol. II (Edinburgh: Darien Press, 1911).

Nietzsche, Friedrich. *Beyond Good and Evil. Prelude to a Philosophy of the Future*, trans. R.J. Hollingdale (London: Penguin, 1990).

Nietzsche, Friedrich. *Daybreak: Thoughts on the Prejudices of Morality*, ed. Maudemarie Clark and Brian Leiter, trans. R.J. Hollingdale (Cambridge: Cambridge University Press, 1997).

Nietzsche, Friedrich. *Ecce Homo* (London: Penguin, 2004).

Nietzsche, Friedrich. *Human, All Too Human. A Book for Free Spirits*, trans. R.J. Hollingdale (Cambridge: Cambridge University Press, 1996).

Nietzsche, Friedrich. *On the Genealogy of Morals: By Way of Clarification of My Last Book Beyond Good and Evil*, trans. Douglas Smith (Oxford: Oxford University Press, 1996).

Nietzsche, Friedrich. *The Gay Science: With a Prelude in German Rhymes and an Appendix of Songs* ed. Bernard Williams, trans. Josefine Nauckhoff and Adrian Del Caro (Cambridge: Cambridge University Press, 2001).

Nietzsche, Friedrich. *The Will to Power*, ed. Walter Kaufmann, trans. Walter Kaufmann and R.J. Hollingdale (New York: Vintage, 1968).

Nietzsche, Friedrich. *Thus Spoke Zarathustra*, trans. R.J. Hollingdale (London: Penguin, 1969).

Nietzsche, Friedrich. *Twilight of the Idols and The Antichrist*, trans. R.J. Hollingdale (London: Penguin, 2003).

Nietzsche, Friedrich. *Untimely Meditations*, ed. Daniel Breazeale, trans. R.J. Hollingdale (Cambridge: Cambridge University Press, 1997).

Nobel, Jaap. "Realism versus Interdependence. The Paradigm Debate in International Relations," *Bulletin of Peace Proposals* (1988), Vol. 19, No. 2.

Oakeshott, Michael. "Rationalism in Politics," in *Rationalism in Politics and Other Essays* (Indianapolis: Liberty, 1991).

Pichler, Hans-Karl. "The Godfathers of 'Truth': Max Weber and Karl Schmitt in Morgenthau's Theory of Power Politics," *Review of International Studies* (1998), Vol. 24, No. 2.

Pin-Fat, Veronique. "The Metaphysics of the National Interest and the 'Mysticism' of the Nation-State: Reading Hans Morgenthau," *Review of International Studies* (2005), Vol. 32, No. 2.

Popper, Karl. *The Logic of Scientific Discovery* (London: Hutchinson & Co., 1977).

Ricouer, Paul. *The Conflict of Interpretations*, ed. Don Ihde (London: Athlone, 1989).

Roberts, Adam. "Foreword," in *International Theory: The Three Traditions*, ed. Gabriele Wight and Brian Porter (Leicester: Leicester University Press, 1991).

Rosecrance, Richard. "Review: Has Realism Become Cost-Benefit Analysis?" *International Security* (2001), Vol. 26, No. 2.

Rouchard, Donald F. "Introduction," in *Language, CounterMemory, Practice. Selected Essays and Interviews*, ed. Michel Foucault (Oxford: Basil Blackwell, 1977).

Sandler, Ted. *Nietzsche: Truth and Redemption. Critique of the Postmodernist Nietzsche* (London: Athlone Press, 1995).

Schmidt, Brian C. "Anarchy, World Politics and the Birth of a Discipline: American International Relations, Pluralist Theory and the Myth of Interwar Idealism," *International Relations* (2000), Vol. 16, No. 1.

Schmidt, Brian C. "Lessons from the Past: Reassessing the Interwar Disciplinary History of International Relations," *International Studies Quarterly* (1998), Vol. 42, No. 3.

Schmidt, Brian C. "The Historiography of Academic International Relations." *Review of International Studies* (1994), Vol. 20, No. 4.

Schmidt, Brian C. *The Political Discourse of Anarchy. A Disciplinary History of International Relations* (Albany: SUNY Press, 1998).

Smith, Michael Joseph. *Realist Thought from Weber to Kissinger* (Baton Rouge: Louisiana State University Press, 1986).

Snyder, Glenn H. "Mearsheimer's World Offensive Realism and the Struggle for Security. A Review Essay," *International Security* (2002), Vol. 27, No. 1.

Spegele, Roger D. *Political Realism in International Theory* (New York: Cambridge University Press, 1996).

Stebbing, L. Susan. *Ideals and Illusions* (London: Watts & Co, 1941).

Taliaferro, Jeffrey W. "Security Seeking Under Anarchy. Defensive Realism Revisited," *International Security* (2000), Vol. 25, No. 3.

Thomas, Scott M. "Faith, History and Martin Wight: The Role of Religion in the Historical Sociology of the English School of International Relations," *International Affairs* (2001), Vol. 77, No. 4.

Thompson, Kenneth. *Masters of International Thought: Major International Theorists and the World Crisis* (Baton Rouge: Louisiana State University Press, 1982).

Vasquez, John A. *The Power of Power Politics* (Cambridge: Cambridge University Press, 1998).

Vasquez, John A. "The Realist Paradigm and Degenerative Vs Progressive Research Programs," *American Political Science Review* (1997), Vol. 91, No. 4.

Vattimo, Gianni. *The Adventure of Difference* (Baltimore: Johns Hopkins University Press, 1993).

Walker, R.B.J. *Inside/Outside: International Relations as Political Theory* (New York: Cambridge University Press, 1993).

Walker, R.B.J. "Realism, Change, and International Political Theory," *International Studies Quarterly* (1987), Vol. 31, No. 1.

Walt, Stephen M. "The Progressive Power of Realism," *American Political Science Review* (1997), Vol. 91, No. 4.

Waltz, Kenneth N. "Evaluating Theories," *American Political Science Review* (1997), Vol. 91, No. 4.

Waltz, Kenneth N. "Realist Thought and Neorealist Theory," *Journal of International Affairs* (1990), Vol. 44, No. 1.

Waltz, Kenneth N. "Reflections on *Theory of International Politics*. A Response to My Critics," in *Neorealism and Its Critics*, ed. Robert O. Keohane (New York: Columbia University Press, 1986).

Waltz, Kenneth N. "Structural Realism after the Cold War," *International Security* (2000), Vol. 25, No. 1.

Waltz, Kenneth N. "The Emerging Structure of International Relations," *International Security* (1993), Vol. 18, No. 2.

Waltz, Kenneth N. "The New World Order," *Millennium: Journal of International Studies* (1993), Vol. 22, No. 2.

Waltz, Kenneth N. "The Origins of War in Neorealist Theory," *Journal of Interdisciplinary History* (1988), Vol. 18, No. 4.

Waltz, Kenneth N. *Theory of International Politics* (New York: McGraw-Hill, 1979).

Wight, Martin. "Christian Pacifism," *Theology* (1936), Vol. 33, No. 1.

Wight, Martin. "An Anatomy of International Thought," *Review of International Studies* (1987), Vol. 13, No. 3.

Wight, Martin. "The Balance of Power and International Order," in *The Bases of International Order. Essays in Order of C.A.W. Manning*, ed. A.M. James (London: Oxford University Press, 1973).

Wight, Martin. "The Balance of Power," in *The World in March 1939,* ed. A.J. Toynbee and F.T. Ashton-Gwatkin (London: Oxford University Press, 1952).

Wight, Martin. "The Balance of Power," in *Diplomatic Investigations: Essays in the Theory of International Politics*, ed. Martin Wight and Herbert Butterfield (London: Allen & Unwin, 1966).

Wight, Martin. "The Church Russia and the West," *Ecumenical Review* (1948), Vol. 1, No. 1.

Wight, Martin. "Western Values in International Relations," in *Diplomatic Investigations: Essays in the Theory of International Politics*, ed. Martin Wight and Herbert Butterfield (London: Allen & Unwin, 1966).

Wight, Martin. "Why Is there No International Theory?" in *Diplomatic Investigations: Essays in the Theory of International Politics*, ed. Martin Wight and Herbert Butterfield (London: Allen & Unwin, 1966).

Wight, Martin. *Christian Commentary*, BBC Radio Broadcast, October 29, 1948.

Wight, Martin. *International Theory. The Three Traditions* (Leicester: Leicester University Press, 1991).

Wight, Martin. *Power Politics*, 2nd ed. (Leicester: Leicester University Press, 1978).

Wight, Martin. *Systems of States* (Leicester: Leicester University Press, 1977).

Williams, Linda L. *Nietzsche's Mirror: The World as Will to Power* (Lanham, Md.: Rowman & Littlefield, 2001).

Williams, Michael C. "Neo-Realism and the Future of Strategy," *Review of International Studies* (1993), Vol. 19, No. 2.

Williams, Michael C. "Why Ideas Matter in International Relations: Hans Morgenthau, Classical Realism, and the Moral Construction of Power Politics," *International Organisation* (2004), Vol. 58, No. 4.

Wilson, Peter. "The Myth of the First Great Debate," *Review of International Studies* (1998), Vol. 24, No. 5.

Wilson, Peter. "Carr and His Early Critics: Responses to *The Twenty Years' Crisis*, 1939–1946," in *E.H. Carr: A Critical Reappraisal*, ed. Michael Cox (London: Macmillan, 2000).

Wilson, Peter. "E.H. Carr: The Revolutionist's Realist," *The Global Site*, http://www.theglobalsite.ac.uk/press/012wilson.htm.

Wilson, Peter. "Radicalism for a Conservative Purpose: The Peculiar Realism of E.H. Carr," *Millennium* (2001), Vol. 30, No. 1.

Wilson, Peter. "The New Europe Debate in Wartime Britain," in *Visions of European Unity*, ed. Philomena Murray and Paul Rich (Boulder: Westview, 1996).

Wilson, Peter. *The International Theory of Leonard Woolf: A Study in Twentieth Century Idealism* (New York: Palgrave, 2003).

Woolf, Leonard. "Utopia and Reality," *The Political Quarterly* (1940), Vol. 11, No. 2.

Young, Oran A. "Aron and the Whale: A Jonah in Theory," in *Contending Approaches to International Politics*, ed. Klaus Knorr and James Rosenau (New Jersey: Princeton University Press, 1969).

Zimmern, Alfred. "A Realist in Search of a Utopia," *The Spectator*, November 24, 1939.

Index

Printed and bound by CPI Group (UK) Ltd, Croydon, CR0 4YY